THE GENESIS OF AN ORIENTALIST

Thomas William Rhys Davids and Buddhism in Sri Lanka

ANANDA WICKREMERATNE

MOTILAL BANARSIDASS
Delhi Varanasi Patna Madras

Head Office : Bungalow Road, Delhi 110 007
Branches : Chowk, Varanasi 221 001
Ashok Rajpath, Patna 800 004
6 Appar Swamy Koil Street, Mylapore,
Madras 600 004

First Edition: Delhi, 1984

ISBN : 978-81-208-2361-7

Printed in India by Shantilal Jain, at Shri Jainendra Press,
A-45, Phase I, Naraina, New Delhi 1100 28 and published by
Narendra Prakash Jain for Motilal Banarsidass, Delhi 110 007.

To Swarna

Channa & Ranmini

. . . and to my Father

in affectionate and loving remembrance

When I read the book, the biography famous,
And is this then (said I) what the author calls
a man's life?
And so will some one when I am dead and gone
write my life?
(As if any man really knew aught of my life,
Why even I myself I often think know little or
nothing of my real life,
Only a few hints, a few diffused faint clews and
indirections
I seek for my own use to trace out here).

Walt Whitman, *Leaves of Grass*, 1871

CONTENTS

PREFACE

Prefaces serve diverse purposes. To begin with they tell the reader why the book which he is invited to read has been written. The explanations are usually revealing. In contrast to the self assuredness and *panache* of the text there is in a preface an apologetic tone, as if the author is sorry for inflicting the book on a reading public already embarrassed by a plethora of learned treatises and monographs. It should also seem that the writer, at the late stage when a preface is presumably put together, suddenly wakes up to the fact that ere long he will confront his reader, who has till now remained an abstraction in his mind. Would the reader see the point of the book as the author saw it? Would he savour something of the enthusiasm which induced the author to write his book?

A book on Thomas William Rhys Davids does not warrant apologies. Rhys Davids was one of the foremost orientalists of the nineteenth century. He stands in close relationship to Max Muller, who was a contemporary and associate. Max Muller's contribution to Sanskrit studies and Hinduism is well known. Pali and Buddhism were Rhys Davids' own claims to greatness and fame. Nobody did as much as he to make Europeans familiar with Pali and Buddhism. As the books on Buddhism multiply, it is edifying to note how skillfully the pioneer mariner maneuvered his craft in what were virtually uncharted waters. And yet today Rhys Davids is much less known than Max Muller. Perhaps historiography has its own peculiar logic. Perhaps the light shines more fully and generously over a man who was concerned with a wider area of Indian studies. In the Imperial connection with Asia it was Hinduism, rather than Buddhism, which held sway as the undisputed *prima donna* of the stage. In a more unconventional sense, Rhys Davids himself would have declared that it was all a matter of *Karma* that subtle intangible force which determined the relative positions of men in the world. Here was the power which made it possible, as the poet remarked, for one man to flutter in brocade and for another to make do with rags. It should of course be a gross exaggeration to suggest that Rhys Davids had ever to make do with rags in a strictly literal economic sense. But throughout his life Rhys Davids was extraordinarily sensitive to economic dimension of a scholar's life and complained about the absence of a just measure of recognition of the scholar by society.

Prefaces also give a veritable last chance to a writer to add a word of explanation or caution about some aspect not dealt with in either the Introduction or the text. It should be rash to forego the privilege. My purposes in writing a book on Rhys Davids have been spelled out at some length in the Introduction. One point, however, must be explained. The title page should give the impression that this book is solely concerned with the Sri Lankan phase in the life of Rhys Davids. The book is much more than that. It deals with the vicissitudes in his life after Rhys Davids returned to England. The emphasis has been more on his ideas and what he stood for rather than on banal biographical trivia which add so much to the weight of conventional biographies without necessarily throwing much light on the subject of the biography. I have throughout tried to bring out the sort of man Rhys Davids probably was. The word *probably* is advisedly italicized, as I believe that no biographer could be so presumptuous as to imagine that he has faithfully brought to life his subject.

A word too about the structure and organisation of the book— it is divided into four clearly identifiable parts. Part I sets the stage for what follows and deals in broad outline with Rhys Davids' life in England prior to his visit to Ceylon. It is the least important part of the book. Part II focuses in depth on his career in Ceylon as a British civil servant. His work as an administrator is critically evaluated. The section concludes with an analysis of the events which led to the dramatic termination of Rhys Davids' stay in Ceylon. Part III is mainly concerned with his struggles to establish himself as a Buddhist and Pali scholar in England following his return from Ceylon. Specifically Part IV has as its theme the interesting relationship of Rhys Davids to Buddhism both as a philosophy and as a living culture.

At first sight, it might seem as if there is a sharp thematic discontinuity between Parts II and III. In an obvious sense it is a discontinuity that arises from the very nature of Rhys Davids' career. At one moment he is an administrator in Ceylon. In the next he is metamorphosed to a struggling scholar more than a trifle overawed by the philistinism of the Victorian world to which he returns. It was possible theoretically to mitigate the sense of discontinuity by resorting to non-conventional and metaphysically inspired explanations. Karma, predestination, the view that the lives of men and events are part of a rationally purposeful design, are obvious examples. Accordingly Rhys Davids *had to* go to Ceylon. His study of Pali and Buddhism there was no fortuitous undertaking, much less a plausible means of intellectual stimulation to while away the tedium of hours which seemed to pass with excruciating slowness. It must seem too that he *had to* return to England when he did to take up the great work of writing about Buddhism. To use the terminology that is appropriate to the genre of reasoning, all this was part of Rhys Davids' *dharma*, his duty, which alone gave time meaning and cohesion to his entire life. The explanations would be totally meaningful or otherwise depending on one's personal perceptions of such matters.

But was there a discontinuity? Rhys Davids' stay in Ceylon is best seen at two levels. In an obvious sense he was preoccupied with administrative tasks—gathering taxes here, dispensing justice there. In a subtler sense, and one not readily apparent, in the course of carrying out these very tasks, he was continually relating to Buddhists and Buddhism. It is for example inconceivable that Rhys Davids was insensitive to the thousand and one ways in which the Sinhalese Buddhist peasants he was ruling differed from his countrymen back in England, or that he somehow did not see that their responses to the very policies he was implementing---the baffling amalgam of stoicism, fatalism and hope---were derived from the conditioning matrix of Buddhist culture and ideology.

Finally there are the acknowledgements. A Commonwealth University Academic Staff Fellowship to the School of Oriental and African Studies in the University of London (1974-75) enabled me to carry out my researches on Rhys Davids in England. I must thank the Association of Commonwealth Universities for its generosity.

With regard to the material used in this book, I must first acknowledge a special debt I owe to the Secretary and Librarian of the Royal Asiatic Society. I had access to valuable unpublished material in the Society's headquarters in Queen Anne Street and was made to feel very much at home during the time I worked there. My thanks are also due to the authorities of the Public Record Office, the British Museum, and the India Office Library for reader facilities which were made available to me in 1974-75.

In Sri Lanka, I researched extensively in the Department of National Archives in Colombo and in the Peradeniya University Library. I must thank Mr. Harischandra de Silva for the assistance and cooperation which was extended to me. I must also place on record my thanks to Mr. H.A.I. Goonetilleke, the librarian of the Peradeniya University Library.

In a rather more personal sense, I owe much to Professor K.A. Ballhatchet of the School of Oriental and African studies in the University of London. From the time when this book was no more than a mass of unorganised ideas and until its energence in the form of the final manuscript, Professor Ballhatchet gave me considerable encouragement. In spite of the heavy demands made on him by numerous South Asian students, Professor Ballhatchet somehow contrived to spare time for me. I gained much from his characteristically penetrating and incisive comments.

In much the same strain, I must acknowledge my debt to Professor K.M. de Silva of the University of Ceylon,Peradeniya, who gave me much encouragement and assistance.

I am grateful too to Professor H.L. Seneviratne of the Department of Anthropology, University of Virginia who, whilst on a short acadmic visit to Sri Lanka, read the manuscript and gently but firmly brought pressure on me to finally prepare the manuscript for publication. I gained much from the long informal conversations I had with him.

I need hardly add that those who kindly read through the manuscript are in no way responsible for its shortcomings.

A visit to the Center for the Study of World Religions in Harvard University during the spring semester and summer of 1979 enabled me (whilst coping with new academic commitments) to put the finishing touches to this book. I must thank Professor John Carman, the Director of the Center, and its administrative staff and members, for having made our stay at Harvard so very pleasant. During the same period, I was also affiliated with the Department of Anthropology in Harvard and had the privilege of working with Professor S.J. Tambiah. It was a stimulating experience. It would be futile, I feel, to try to acknowledge what I owe professor Tambiah, both professionally and socially.

Finally, a word of thanks to my Swarna. In the various libraries and archives where I worked in London and in Sri Lanka, she sat by me and worked as much as I did. This enabled me to cast my nets wider and to come to terms with the comparatively short time we had in which to finish our work in England. Moreover, without a murmur of complaint she typed and re-typed the entire manuscript. I gained much from her observations and comments. Throughout the work she encouraged me as only a wife would. This book is as much the fruit of her effort and struggle as it is of mine. A word of thanks, too, to

Evelyn Rosenthal of the Harvard Divinity school, who attended to the final typescript.

By way of a final caveat, it must be pointed out that in the text the words "Ceylon" and "Sri Lanka" (the official name of the island since 1972) have been used interchangeabley.

Harvard
July 1979

INTRODUCTION

Some years ago a well known British humorist whose lively pieces often appeared in the pages of the *Observer Review* remarked that when centenaries occur, the Great Victorians are dredged up from the ocean bed-sand, seaweed and all-to be reviled and praised by biographer and public alike.

The centenary of Thomas William Rhys Davids (1843-1922) has however long since passed unmarked, unwept and unsung. He has, it is true, been dutifully noticed in the *Dictionary of National Biography*, and more amply and affectionately commended to posterity in the transactions of the Pali Text Society and the British Academy, which he helped to found. In England he has been almost entirely forgotten. It would seem that Rhys Davids, like the ancient Pali canon of the Buddhists, has survived purely by the oral tradition.

In Sri Lanka, he is remembered by anglicised Buddhists whose views about Buddhism and Buddhist culture have been largely influenced by Western writings on the subject. Buddhists see the importance of Rhys Davids in more ways than one. He was the first Western scholar to translate the Pali canon into a European language: significantly, to English. He thus made the Buddhist scriptures, hitherto virtually confined to the somnolent world of Southern Asia, accessible to a vastly wider segment of human society. Moreover, through his writings Rhys Davids kindled in many Westerners an awareness of Buddhism when few knew anything at all about it. In doing so he helped to scale down to some slight extent the noted British penchant for Hinduism and Hindu studies which had begun to thrive vigorously even before British political power had spread into the Indian hinterland. Lastly, his interpretation of Buddhism was clearly in harmony with the sensibilities, prejudices, and one might add, the dogmas of Buddhists in Sri Lanka who were wont to regard themselves as the proper custodians of the faith and of its doctrinal purity.

However, there was much more to Rhys Davids than that. In England and in Sri Lanka little, in fact, is known about Rhys Davids, his work, his life, and about the man himself. Fifty years after his death, known biographical details about him are clearly of a skeletal nature: that at an early age Rhys Davids left for Sri Lanka, where he worked as a Civil Servant, and thai after a few years, when he was still a young man, he returned to England to devote himself to Pali and Buddhist studies.

However, my purpose in writing this book has not been that of filling a void or of carrying out an act of biographical resurrection. The objects, such as I was aware of them, were of an altogether more pedestrian character. I first began researching on Rhys Davids in 1973. The work has frequently to be set aside because of the demands made on my time and resources by more formal academic tasks. During a long period of gestation, although many of the ideas underwent change-the selection of material, areas of emphasis, the arrangement of the text, to take a few examples-the aims did not.

They were both professional and personal. The history of British rule in South Asia has too often been written within the thematic perimeters of politics (usually the confrontation between the *Raj* and clamant nationalists) or administrative and policy studies. The studies have undoubtedly been useful. They do not however provide a reasonably integrated overview of what British rule was all about. Who were the British in Asia? What was the *raison d'etre* of the British presence? What were the aims of the administration or the ideals of the run of the mill administrator in a remote outpost of the empire? How did he relate to his subjects? One viewed with scepticism all-encompassing ideological explanations. They were facile and simplistic. Many histories of the British *Raj* in India, for example, leave the reader with the feeling that British rule was a pitiless unremitting exercise in the collection of land revenues and nought else; or that from the days of Clive and Warren Hastings the rulers and the oppressed ruled were hell bent on a course of collision and confrontation.

It seemed to me that one could gain subtler insights if the angle of vision were changed to view British rule as a continuous process of interaction of two widely differing civilizations, cultures, values, ethics, and above all, two wholly divergent ways of looking at the world. All this was however easier said than done. To study British rule confining ourselves to a single theater of activity—Sri Lanka for example—was too formidable a task, let alone India where clearly the themes of interaction could be studied profitably.

I had perforce to settle for a more pedestrian and manageable alternative. If I selected a single official and made an intensive study of the manner in which he carried out his duties practically to the last scrap of paper he wrote, shared his thoughts, became thoroughly immersed in the strategies of decision making and implementation, it was possible to get some inkling into the process of interaction. I chose Rhys Davids. Like many Sri Lankans I was aware that he had written books on Buddhism—they were not hard to come by in Sri Lankan homes—but I was not aware that Rhys Davids had been a civil servant in Sri Lanka. The notion seemed wildly improbable. But if such was the fact, I was reasonably sure that there had to be something different, something strikingly idiosyncratic in his stewardship as a British official—the very differences on which I hoped to find what I was looking for. Rhys Davids did not disappoint me.

Meanwhile I became interested too in Western attempts in the nineteenth century to understand non-Western religions and cultures. A century later when our knowledge of Hinduism and Buddhism has been immensely enhanced we had gained a vantage point to survey the work of earlier generations of scholars. In the interval had the perspectives of transcultural understanding changed? What sort of men were Max Muller and Rhys Davids who in the face of tremendous odds and stolid public apathy attempted to understand cultures that to the average European of their day seemed so bizarre and alien? What were the psychological, emotional and cultural limitations to their understanding? Was cultural ethnocentrism a thing of the past? In this respect too his long involvement with Theravada Buddhism made Rhys Davids an ideal object of study.

Finally there was a strong personal impulse too. A religious and cultural revival which occurred in Sri Lanka after political independence made many anglicised Sri Lankans aware—often embarrassingly aware—of the gulf which separated them from the indigenous ethos. The awareness was heightened by the interest of the state in the cultural renascence and the writings of social anthropologists. When I began researching on Rhys Davids, I became aware of my own sense of cultural alienation. Rhys Davids had devoted an entire lifetime to the study of what was to him an alien religion. He had not merely studied Buddhism in the narrow sense of unfolding the Pali canon. He rightly insisted that he was interpreting Buddhism as the basis of a civilisation and culture rather than as a conglomeration of distinctive religious tenets. Rhys Davids made one aware of the richness of that culture which had been inextricably woven into lands like Sri Lanka. I saw that in South Asia, at any rate, more than any other factor, religion was the key to a real understanding of society.

In a word, Rhys Davids was the first stage in a long road to my own personal cultural redemption.

The identification was not altogether fortuitous. It is, I believe, part of the biographical process. A biographer becomes totally immersed in his subject although at first the two are clearly entities with an element of distance between them. At this stage the biographer would survey his subject with clinical detachment as if he were examining a chemical in a crucible. Gradually, however, a sense of empathy manifests itself because the biographer is after all not handling a chemical but a human personality. There is a subtle blending or merging of the two entities of the biographer and his subject, especially in ideas. The biographer begins to feel, as I did with Rhys Davids, that he "knows" his subject.

But really, how close can a biographer get to his subject? My prupose in writing this book has been to let Rhys Davids stand forth in terms of his ideas and what he achieved. The book is not strictly a biography of the man Rhys Davids. Ideally it should have been that, too. It is neither possible nor desirable to study the ideas of a man or what he stood for by totally shutting out the consideration of his personality. Ideally, a biographer must study the man in embryo-the impressionable years of childhood and adolescence-when the essential personality is moulded. In their early years, great men as well as the most ordinary of men have invariably had to confront an inexorable trinity of religion, family, and the schoolmaster. It is hardly possible that many could have survived the catalytic-often abrasive-confrontation without carrying into adulthood some vestigial scar or mark. In the Victorian cultural milieu, with which a book on Rhys Davids would be concerned, the influence exercised by religion on individuals has been well documented. Filial relations with a domineering father or mother and the problems thereof have also been an all too familiar biographical backdrop of the period. In one or the other of these areas the biographer has a reasonably good chance of picking up clues about-to use conventional terminology-the "influences" and "compulsions" which would throw light on the shadowy links between childhood and maturity.

In England I was able, however, to trace the whereabouts of a member of Rhys Davids' family, but was not altogether certain that Miss Vivian Rhys Davids who lived in Chipstead, Coulsdon, Surrey, was a daughter of Rhys Davids. I wrote to her with trepidation and uncertainty. I had come to England to continue my researches on

Rhys Davids. Was she his daughter? If so, could I see her? I was interested in his private papers and hoped that she would let me see them. After a week or so Miss Rhys Davids replied. She could well understand my interest in her father but she could not help me because she was in the "process of compiling a biography myself." She was not sure that I would be interested in meeting her "after receiving this letter." It was possible that Miss Rhys Davids had doubts about my *bona fides*. I was after all a perfect stranger to her. I decided to write to her again. Could she review her decision? I pointed out that her father had had a reputation among his contemporaries for being very open about his work. I added that in scholarly research more than one person could work on a given *corpus* of historical material. Perspectives were likely to be dissimilar. I declared that in working on Rhys Davids, it was not my intention at all "to tarnish his memory much less cause you or anyone dear to you the slightest embarrassment. Indeed there is no reason to do so."

Her reply could not have been more discouraging. Miss Rhys Davids was sorry to have to disappoint me. It was better that I consult her father's work from publications and periodicals. Perhaps I had already done so. There was no point in my waiting to see her. The Parthian shaft was revealing. "I am not in the least afraid," she declared, "of an 'embarrassment'-to quote your own word-for anything which occurred during my Father's life-a more honourable man never lived." Clearly there was no basis for continuing the correspondence.

I understood only too well. The crisis in Rhys David's life—the supreme moment which surpasses all other moments in the life of an individual—occurred when he was in Sri Lanka. In 1873 Rhys Davids was relieved of his duties as Assistant Government Agent in Anuradhapura and was soon afterwards dismissed from the Colonial Service. Neither Sir William Gregory, who was Governor of Ceylon at the time, nor the Colonial Office, presided over by Lord Kimberley, had any doubt that Rhys Davids had been guilty of the charges that he had arbitrarily imposed oppressive fines on many defenceless peasants and that he had used this money as well as other public monies in his care for his personal use. There were other charges as well, involving the abuse of public funds. Opinions will vary as to whether Rhys Davids has a fair trial at the hands of his superiors. But the stark fact was that at the time much opprobrium was attached to Rhys Davids, who was compelled to leave Sri Lanka.

In spite of its obvious importance, no mention of the incident has been made in the few biographical sketches of Rhys Davids' life which have been published. In 1912, when Rhys Davids' reputation as an orientalist had spread far and wide, Mabel Bode, a distinguished pupil writing affectionately of the *Guru* remarked that in his early life Rhys Davids had been a Civil Servant in Ceylon, but had "withdrawn." Lord Robert Chalmers-whose own connections with Ceylon were singularly ill starred-a Pali Scholar, and a friend of Rhys Davids, declared in an obituary notice which he wrote for the *Journal of the Pali Text Society* in 1923, that Rhys Davids had resigned from the Civil Service. Chalmers' essay on Rhys Davids in the *Encyclopaedia Britannica* also referred to resignation. Similarly, in another and rather more evocative biographical sketch which appeared shortly after Rhys Davids' death, written by a group of distinguished orientalists, it was said that Rhys Davids had left the Civil Service of his own accord. Perhaps good taste, or the feeling that the Civil Service was a distant irrelevance, or simply genuine ignorance, would explain what appears to have been a conspiracy of silence on the point. It is only in the writings of Caroline Augusta Foley, who became Rhys Davids' wife in 1894, that there is the definite suggestion that Rhys Davids' departure from Sri Lanka was not something that he had willed. According to Mrs. Rhys Davids, her husband was dismissed from the Ceylon Civil Service because he had stood up for the rights of peasants and earned the wrath of his superiors.

My futile transactions with Miss Vivian Rhys Davids illustrated the truth that biography is often an intrusive business. The biographer is a trespasser, especially if he is a stranger and is not the "authorised" biographer. It is not so much that great men too, like lesser mortals, have skeletons in their cupboards. It is the old question whether a biographer "knows" his subject. How intimately, how accurately, can we know another self even if we have the biographical material at our disposal? Often a biographer does not have all the facts. He has necessarily to be speculative and conjectural. In either situation a biographer could well produce a distortion. It was no doubt for these reasons that George Orwell and T. S. Eliot gave directions that no biography be written about them, "at least with any help from their widows."

The approach to biography too had changed, giving heirs and next of kin additional cause to be wary. First, there was Victorian biography which moved on the simple principle that one did not speak ill of the dead. The great men who adorned the biographical motif in the Victorian period exemplified the rags to riches trasformation which the prevailing economic society seemed to make possible. The lives of great men were also a triumphant reflection of those values which the Victorians cherished, such as perseverance, hard work, and self reliance. The shortcoming, the unflattering traits of character-which were in any event irrelevant to the edifying biographical moral-were glossed over. The result was a considerable window dressing of the dead. As Evelyn Waugh brilliantly put it, biography was "the lying in state of our great men."

The pendulum had, however, swung to the other extreme. Adulatory biography was replaced by biographies of an excessively critical type. The biographer was determined to reveal all, if necessary by resorting to psychoanalytical techniques. The age of psychobiography had dawned. The great man's life was sedulously examined from childhood for clues which could throw light on his adult manhood. The implied candour was, however, sometimes embarrassing.

In spite of its excesses-especially where great literary figures have been the subject of biography-modern biography has taught us that there is no impregnable entity called great men defying analysis and scrutiny. Great men have been full of human frailties, paradoxes, and inconsistencies, and one wonders how they could have achieved what they did to earn in their own lifetimes the sobriquet of greatness. It was in this sense rather naive to remark of anyone, as Vivian Rhys Davids did of her father, that "no more honourable man ever lived."

II

By Rhys Davids' time the broad lines of British policies in Sri Lanka were well defined. Economic policy was in line with the dualistic nature of the Island's economy. On the one hand European entrepreneurship, capital and managerial skills were concentrated in the plantation sector. Coffee, which grew principally in the central highlands, was the island's staple export. It was the basis of Sri Lanka's prosperity as a rapidly developing Crown Colony. By legislative enactments which helped the coffee planter to meet specific difficulties and problems, as well as by refraining from measures which would in any way inhibit enterprise, the government brought about an economic climate which favoured the continued expansion of the coffee industry. More tangibly, by providing the facilities for transportation, the recruitment and mobility of labour-later a rudimentary system of medical facilities-the government also gradually built up the infrastructure basis for a genuinely modern plantation sector.

By contrast there was the peasant sector. Other than in those areas in which coffee plantations were situated cheek by jowl with villages where peasants lived—and therefore there was a certain amount of mutual economic interaction—in Sri Lanka as a whole there was little connection between the vigorously active plantations and the traditional peasant sector. The peasant sector had been ignored both by European entrepreneurs as well as by their Ceylonese counterparts. An undeveloped system of transportation also ensured the absence of change by immunising the village to external economic influences. The production of paddy and sundry dry grains which was the principal occupation of the peasant was for subsistence, rather than for the market. Physically, and in terms of economic orientation, the peasant was far removed from the urban markets. The use of money too was by no means universal. In casual economic transactions barter was the order of the day. In these respects the district of Nuwerakalaviya over which Rhys Davids presided as Assistant Government Agent conformed to the norm of a peasant sector in which a traditional economic order had been preserved. Government economic policies were a blend of paternalism-helping the peasant by augmenting the facilities for greater production-and the fostering of the spirit of individual economic enterprise. The relevant chapters in the text will show how the abstract ideas had been transformed into specific economic functions which an Assistant Government Agent performed. Consequently an Assistant Government Agent like Rhys Davids was more a follower of well trodden paths and very much less an innovator.

In two respects, at any rate, Rhys Davids may be justly remembered. The Government oriented policies of restoring irrigation works begun earlier on in the nineteenth century as a principal mode of developing peasant agriculture were clearly predicated on a certain ideal-the very Victorian ideal of self reliance. What the government spent annually on irrigation was considerable. It partly repaid itself by imposing a small tax on the cultivator. Apart from financial considerations the government was anxious to drive home the moral that government aid would only be forthcoming if the peasants were willing to help themselves to some extent. Thus before the government agreed to restore this or that irrigation work, the peasants concerned had to covenant to repay the government in installments. Rhys Davids, however, saw the limitations of this policy. In Nuwerakalaviya the peasants were too poor and indeed too dispirited to avail themselves of the government terms. Rhys Davids' protest rings loud and clear and in a larger sense draws attention to the assumptions underlying British rule in nineteenth-century Ceylon.

All credit too to Rhys Davids for pinpointing the lopsided nature of Sinhalese agriculture. He saw the need to diversify agricultural production over and beyond the cultivation of paddy and a few dry grains. He wanted the government to take the initiative in beginning the cultivation of tobacco and cotton, for which he thought Nuwerakalaviya was eminently suitable. Rhys Davids was aware that peasants with woefully limited capital resources could not immediately take to non-traditional cultures. Instead, implied in his official letters was the hope that private entrepreneurship would follow any initiative shown by the government in this direction.

The Assistant Government Agent of Nuwerakalaviya was no diminutive figure. Rhys Davids ruled a district which he thought was as big as Yorkshire; indeed it was made an independent province because of its size and growing importance at the beginning of the 1870s. An Assistant Government Agent had to moreover perform a multiplicity of functions which were remarkably varied. "I accumulated in my own person," he wryly recalled, "almost as many offices as Pooh Bah in the Mikado. I was Assistant Governement Agent, Acting District Judge, Archaeological Commissioner, and the head of the Police and the Post Office while I also had to look after the roads . . . the fact is that there was not another Englishman within many miles of where I was."

From a strictly administrative viewpoint too, Rhys Davids' career as an Assistant Government Agent was noteworthy. its climax was his dismissal. The episode sheds light on certain aspects involving the relations between the Colonial Office and the colonies. The Colonial Office was the ultimate authority in matters concerning the colonies. But whether it did in every conceivable situation fulfil this role is a moot point. If the matters at hand involved the feasibility or otherwise of taking a certain step-for example the abolition of a long established tax-the Colonial Office could dispassionately weigh the pros and cons. The possibilities of doing so were, however, markedly reduced when controversial issues involving personalities arose in which the governor himself was an interested party. In the Rhys Davids affair, at first sight, if one takes into consideration the extraordinarily lengthy and detailed despatch which Sir William Gregory, the Governor, wrote, together with an overwhelming *corpus* of enclosures and annexures, it would seem that the Colonial Office had all the facts at its disposal to arrive at a decision. But in fact Gregory conducted himself more as a committed partisan than as a disinterested head of the government and presented the facts to the Colonial Office in a manner which wholly prejudiced the case against Rhys Davids. Indeed, in the Colonial Office a certain scepticism was evident concerning crucial areas in the case against Rhys Davids. But the small voice of doubt-which might have made Rhys Davids' ultimate humiliation less-was stilled by the feeling that after all, the men on the spot knew best. Moreover, the sentiment was also expressed that is was embarrassing to undo a decision already arrived at by a governor on matters of this sort.

III

It is as Pali and Buddhist scholar and an orientalist *par excellence* that Rhys Davids is today mostly remembered. The third and fourth parts of the book are concerned with this phase in his life.

The seeds had already been sown in Sri Lanka. Before Rhys Davids took up duties as Assistant Government Agent in Anuradhapura, he was the Police Magistrate in Galle. Whenever he could afford to do so—the leisure hours of a Civil Servant were few and were therefore inordinately valued—Rhys Davids spent his time in Bentota, a slumbering inconspicuous hamlet some distance away from Galle. Assisted by a scholarly Buddhist monk, or *Bhikkhu*, Yatramulle Unnanse, who lived in Bentota, Rhys Davids studied Pali-the language in which the sacred literature of Buddhism had been preserved. It was an affectionate and fruitful relationship. Rhys Davids had great respect for his mentor's erudition. He also admired Yatramulle Unnanse's saintly ways and all too evident piety. The great monk in turn found that Rhys Davids was a willing and able pupil. He taught Rhys Davids "all he knew" notwithstanding the tradition of the *Gurumushtiya* which usually made it possible for a teacher or *guru* to withhold a special area of knowledge from his pupil. A favourite pupil alone qualified for total enlightenment. Indeed by teaching him Pali, Yatramulle Unnanse had put in Rhys Davids' hands the key to the enchanted door beyond which lay a rich storehouse of Buddhist knowledge. For over a century European scholars had long suspected the existence of this literature and speculated upon its usefulness in achieving a clearer understanding of Buddhism.

It was Sri Lanka, too, which kindled in Rhys Davids his love of archeology and numismatics. The interest led him in later years to conduct significant researches in the Buddhist sites of ancient India. His official position at Anuradhapura-the Assistant Government Agent was technically also an Assistant Archeological Commissioner-gave him ample opportunities for archeological work. Some of his early researches became the subject of papers which he contributed to the Ceylon branch of the Royal Asiatic Society. In short, alone among contemporary British civilians serving in Sri Lanka, Rhys Davids, the callow youth, had already carved out a modest niche for himself as a potential scholar.

There was however no smooth transition between the period of apprenticeship in Sri Lanka and what followed. Rhys Davids returned to England an embittered and ruined man. His early hopes had been rudely shattered. In Victorian England a career in the East as a Civil Servant clearly had its attractions, both as exemplifying an ideal of public service as well as from a narrowly pecuniary angle. By the 1860s, visions of amassing great and sudden wealth, or to use a once popular colloquialism, "shaking the pagoda tree," as in the early days of the East India Company, were no longer subscribed to seriously. But what a young man might reasonably expect when he began life as a writer had been well put by the Civil Service Commissioners. "The emoluments of a writership, the steady advancement in the Service of those who devote themselves to it with zeal and perseverance," it was said, ". . . and the liberal and judicious provisions for retirement at a moderate age, all render the Civil Service a career full of interest and pecuniary advantage." But to Rhys Davids all this was part of the might have beens, the great ifs, of his personal life.

A career in law, which Rhys Davids now decided upon, seemed to offer an alternative and possibly a smoother path of material advancement. It seemed to be also the only career left open to him as he had no great personal or family resources to fall back on. Besides, law gave him the means of living down the scandal of his dismissal and regaining, at it were, the lost badge of social respectability. One other reason seems to have weighed in Rhys Davids' mind. During the long investigations which preceded his dismissal, Rhys Davids often felt that he was at a disadvantage because he did not know law. He commanded neither the great principles of law nor knowledge of the proprieties of procedure which would have been the best safeguards of his interests. His superiors had been lawyers either. But in a quasi-judicial inquiry they became easily the terrifying inquisitors, the professionals, cutting up a naive and perplexed young man who literally and metaphorically stood in the dock. It had been a humiliating experience. But the dificiency in his education which had made it all possible had to be put right.

The next move was wholly unexpected. Rhys Davids successfully completed his law studies and was called to the Bar by Middle Temple in 1877. He was however not seriously interested in practising law. Instead, he startled all and sundry by announcing that he would devote himself to Pali studies. To some of those who were aware of the circumstances in which he had left Sri Lanka, this was further proof of a certain instability of mind and fecklessness. His close friends tried to deter him from a course which they too felt was frankly foolhardy. Few knew Pali, and fewer still were aware of its significance. One could hardly think of an intellectual preoccupation in mid-Victorian England which could have apperared more exotic and lacking in any discernible social relevance.

And yet there was an earthy common sense about his choice. The study of Pali clearly meant two things. There were the Pali Buddhist texts which could be systematically published in their original form with English translations and suitable notes. More significantly, the study of Pali was a means to an end-the study and exposition of Buddhism. If there was no evidence of a great demand for the former, other than among a handful of oriental scholars and specialists, there was a fairly widespread and growing interest in Buddhism. Rhys Davids was aware of the tremendous market potentialities of the situation. In later years he recalled that when he returned to England he hardly knew anything about Buddhism. At the same time he saw that there was an increasing curiosity about the subject. He realized that he was singularly equipped to fill the void because he knew Pali and "a little more" about Buddhism than the average Englishman.

It was a gamble that paid rich dividends, Rhys Davids' first book on Buddhism was published in 1877, the very year in which he seems to have firmly relinquished the idea of practising as a barrister. His second book-on Indian Buddhism in the Hibbert Lectures Series-was published in 1881. Both books-especially the first, which was a remarkably concise and handy manual-enjoyed immense popularity, and were published over and over again during Rhys Davids' own lifetime. Rhys Davids answered many questions which the interested Christian layman in the West would have liked to know about Buddhism-the life and times of the founder of the Buddhist faith, Buddhist doctrine, the spread of Buddhism and above all, the curious monastic order which was reputed to be an integral part of Buddhism as it actually existed in the East.

The establishment of the Pali Text Society-the basis on which Rhys Davids is today conventionally remembered-was as venturesome a step. Initial results were, however, much less spectacular. The fact was that unlike general books on Buddhism, the market for Pali texts was really confined to the specialists. Nor was the market likely to expand. But in spite of an upromising start the Pali Text Society flourished. It outlived both Rhys Davids and Caroline Augusta Rhys Davids, his wife, who took over the work of the Pali Text Society some time before Rhys Davids' death.

Between 1877 and the end of the century, formal bread and butter employment took two forms. In 1884, Rhys Davids was selected by the Royal Asiatic Society as its new Secretary. He received a salary which, though not a princely one, ws certainly adequate-he was at the time a bachelor-especially if one took into reckoning the perquisites such as rent-free accommodation which went with it. As a mark of its regard for Rhys Davids' able services as its Secretary, the R.A.S. gave him a special increment to his salary which of course was not paid to his successor. During this time he was also the Professor of Pali in London University. Remuneration, however, was meagre and uncertain. Rhys Davids was paid by the hour on the basis of the number of lectures given. The lectures were necessarily few. Pali did not figure in a big way when students selected their subject.

In 1901 Rhys Davids left London to assume duties as Professor of Comparative Religion in Manchester University. The position was a permanent one and gave Rhys Davids a salary which clearly exceeded the emoluments he had hitherto received both from the R.A.S. and London University. A chair in Comparative Religion was of course very much of an innovation in England. In the U.S.A. where the university structure was frankly much less rigid and more responsive to changing social needs, and in the European continent too, there was at the time no comparable position. The creation of a new chair and the selection of Rhys Davids as its first incumbent was a recognition of Rhys Davids' approach to the study of religion as well as a tribute to a truly polymath mind. For all his lifelong obsession with the great religion of Buddhism, Rhys Davids always insisted that religion, like history, was best understood in the broadest possible context. When one studies a specific or particular segment of the canvas of human experience, one is aware in a comparative sense of the total expanse, aware too of the cohering principles which hold together seemingly disparate and unconnected phenomena. Thus when one studied Buddhism, one was invariably involved in something more than Buddhism. The principle which today would be regarded as a commonplace had in Rhys Davids' time a clear practical relevance. The study of religion with a segmented bias had in the guise of modern revivalism produced excesses of religious sectarianism and parochialism in both India and Ceylon. As the text will show, Rhys Davids was only too familiar with the development. In a wider sense, his approach to the study of religion was an obvious prophylactic against the widespread European attitude of viewing non-Christian religions and cultures in a rigid value judgement relationship to the single norm of European Christian civilization.

So much has happened since Rhys Davids wrote his treatises on Buddhism. The interest in Buddhism has grown in the West. Its magnitude and intensity are surely noteworthy. Would he have been surprised? Rhys Davids prophesied one hundred years ago that Buddhism would exercise a catalytic effect on religious ideas in the West. Today we are witnesses to the process.

The great scholar, *Clarm et Venerabile Nomen*, stayed on in Manchester till 1915 when he retired. He spent his last years in Chipstead, Surrey. But retirement was neither a period of seclusion nor repose. There was a constant stream of visitors—newspaperman, Sri Lanka Buddhists like the pugnacious Anagarika Dharmapala, pupils like Mabel Bode and fellow scholars and collaborators like William Stede—to all of whom he made himself readily available. His active mind ever contemplated both unfinished and fresh projects. The flame flickered brightest before its final demise. He passed away in December 1922, mourned by a wife—a scholar in her own right—and two daughters.

Part I
England

1

THE ENGLISH PRELUDE

"It is a great event to be born a man and his life is an ever-striving..." ***The Dhammapada.***

RHYS Davids was born at Colchester in Essex on 12 May 1843. In a sense his life falls into three seemingly discontinuous phases, with his visit to Sri Lanka being the crucial turning point. We have first what we may conventionally describe as the English phase in his life which closes with his departure to Sri Lanka in 1866 at the age of twenty three. His sojourn in Sri Lanka, the second phase, ended in 1874 when he returned to England. From the mid-seventies, when his first works were published, and until his death at Chipstead, Surrey, in December 1922, Rhys Davids lived in England. During this period he became the foremost exponent of Buddhism and Pali studies in the Anglo-Saxon world.

The above would, however, be a prosaic way of putting matters which had evidently a more elusive meaning. There is a sharp and almost startling break or hiatus between the Sri Lankan phase in Rhys Davids' life and the period that followed. In Sri Lanka, Rhys Davids' ill-starred career as a civil servant came to an abrupt and dramatic end. It surpasses belief that the embittered, broken young man who returned to England was ere long metamorphosed into an eminent scholar.

There have been theories. Some years after Rhys Davids' death, Caroline Augusta Foley, who had become his wife in 1894, pronounced that her husband's life, taken as a whole, was in reality a response to a higher call—specifically that of the *Mahatmas*. Like some other notable figures in the late Victorian period, Rhys Davids was—to use a word that was fashionable at the time—a *chela* of the elusive *Mahatmas*[1].

[1]Rhys Davids, Caroline Augusta Foley, *Wayfarer's Words*, 3 Vols., London, 1941. Vol. III, *pp.* 880 ff.

Rhys Davids could hardly have been flattered. Unlike his wife, who had increasingly come under its spell, Rhys Davids had consistently repudiated Theosophy. And yet in reflecting on the curious vicissitudes in his life, Rhys Davids too veered towards the mystical dimension. The tell-tale *obiter dicta* in a life-time of extensive writings show how often Rhys Davids spoke in a Buddhist idiom, as a conventional Buddhist would, especially about *Karma* and *Anicca.* The contexts in which he did so—allusions to disappointments and personal setbacks, to the harshness of a world which never seemed to forget or forgive mistakes, the world's ingratitude, its all too evident philistinism—were significant. In a less personal way he related *Karma* to the great work he had accomplished in his life. It had fallen on him to play the pioneering role in making the English-speaking world in the West aware of Buddhism and the Pali canon just as much as the life of Horace Hyman Wilson, the great Sanskritist, had been—so Rhys Davids declared—the fulfilment or working out of a *karmically* determined purpose. *Karma* had helped him to understand all that. It was no mere figure of speech resorted to in fashionable London salons. Re-phrased then, the three lives of Rhys Davids held in firm alignment by *Karmic* threads may be designated as the *Karmic* Call, the *Karmic* Search and *Karmic* Fulfilment.

The English phase in Rhys Davids' life began peaceably enough. He was the eldest child of the Rev. Thomas William Davids, a Welshman who had settled in Colchester. The Rev. Davids, who was a well known Congregational minister, had a great flair for preaching and was affectionately referred to as the Bishop of Essex. Curiously, his real forte was religious history. Like most of his ancestors, the Rev. Davids was an ecclesiastical historian. He had as his special field of interest the religious history of Essex, with particular reference to the tribulations of the Nonconformists. In 1862, he was selected to prepare a treatise on the bicentenary of the eviction of the Nonconformist clergy from Essex. Later, as Rhys Davids himself recorded, his father spent the rest of his life researching into the origins of the lesser known aspects of Nonconformist dogma. Rhys Davids was impressed by his father's pains-taking scholarship and prodigious reading.[2]

[2]Rhys Davids, Thomas William, "Davids Thomas William (1816-1884)." *Dictionary of National Biography,* Vol. V. Rhys Davids wrote the article on his father for the *D.N.B.*

Rhys Davids' mother, Louisa Winter, the daughter of a London solicitor, was a devout Christian. She ran the Sunday school attached to her husband's church with such success that the school was regarded as a model. She wrote a short treatise on the management and organisation of Sunday schools which was published and ran into several editions. She died in 1854 when Rhys Davids was barely ten years old.[3]

We know much less about Rhys Davids' education. At an early age he went to Brighton School, not far from where the family lived. The school was run by his uncle, Robert Winter. Here Rhys Davids had his elementary education. Later, after some years of "private education," at the age of seventeen, Rhys Davids went down to London to a school known as New College in Finchley Road. He studied a great deal of Latin. His mentor was the famous Latin scholar, Sir William Smith, who was also the compiler of the *Dictionary of Christian Biography* to which Rhys Davids' father, the Rev. Davids, had contributed a number of articles.

It was when he was at New College that Rhys Davids decided to join the Indian Civil Service. The threadbare autobiographical notes he has left do not tell us what influenced him. To a young middle class Englishman who was educated but who clearly had no private resources to fall back on, a career in India seemed reasonably attractive. Rhys Davids soon realised, however, that New College was not the best place in which to prepare himself for the ordeal of examination and selection. Some sort of university education was indicated. Family resources being what they were, he could not afford a formal university education. His father, for whom he had throughout a very deep affection, was like most nonconformist clergymen, as Rhys Davids put it, "not over-burdened with worldly riches." He realised that he would have to work or pay his way through a university and the best place where he might do so unobtrusively was the continent. So after no more than a year's stay at New College, Rhys Davids left for Germany. Many English students on short rations financed themselves in German universities by giving lessons in English. He was soon to observe at first hand that in German towns there was a great desire to learn English, not only among students but among the established bourgeoisie. He chose Breslau—sufficiently off the beaten track of English students and tourists—so that he could sell

[3] *Ibid.*

his teaching skills without fear of competition. His expectations were more than amply realised. Rhys Davids was much sought after as an English tutor and earned enough not only to keep body and soul together but also sufficient money to pay for his university fees without having to make demands on his family. There was, of course, a certain amount of self-imposed restraint. But then, Rhys Davids was abstemious and simple in his tastes. Besides, he found that all in all, he was no worse off than his fellow students. Indeed, he thought, he was a good deal better off. He remarked on the privations Germans underwent and the "astonishing" sacrifices they made to get a university education.[4]

Rhys Davids lived in Breslau for three years. He confessed that during this time he became almost "Germanised." Life was pleasant. He made friends easily. The fact that he was an outsider, a social neutral, as it were, who carried no differentiating social badge, helped a great deal. Rhys Davids observed that in Breslau and in Silesian Germany in general, society was rigidly stratified. Using rather archaic nomenclature, he describes four categories—the nobility, the bourgeoisie, the students and the working class. There was, he said, so little intercourse among them that they all might have been living on different planets. The nobility looked down on the *nouveau riche* bourgeoisie, although among that class there were "persons of wealth and respectability." The bourgeoisie in turn had contempt for students possibly because they were the least cohesive social element with an ill-defined economic relevance in the social hierarchy. In particular, Rhys Davids noticed that in Germany, bourgeoisie contempt for the student element touched even professors who simply did not enjoy the prestige which their counterparts had elsewhere. Rhys Davids, however, had access to all, visiting the homes of the nobility and bourgeoisie alike as an able teacher of English.

He spent most of his time, however, with his fellow students, enjoying their easy-going informal companionship. He used to accompany them on their outings to the "kneipe" or meeting place, where usually great quantities of beer were had by all. If on such obviously convivial occasions he never smoked or drank, his German friends readily forgave him. They thought it all part of the eccentricity

[4] *Journal of the Maha Bodhi Society*, Vol. XXIII, No 6, June 1914, for reproduction of interview given by Rhys Davids to the *Morning Post*.

of an Englishman. In Breslau, there were no organised outdoor games as in English universities. But there were wonderful opportunities for skating. Rhys Davids used to enjoy skating on the Oder, which was usually possible for two months of the year. He also played a good deal of chess, which was a familiar pastime of German students.[5]

In more tangible ways, the highwater mark of Rhys Davids in Breslau, especially in terms of his philological training, was his study of Sanskrit under A. F. Stenzler. A distinguished scholar, Stenzler was described as the last of the founders of Sanskrit scholarship in Germany. Early in his career, Stenzler was asked by the East India Company to work on the Sanskrit material in its repositories in London. Later, he was closely associated in the compilation of a major Sanskrit dictionary which was published in St. Petersburg. Stenzler held the post of Professor of Sanskrit at Breslau from 1833 until his death in 1886.[6]

Rhys Davids returned to England in 1863 and appeared in the examination of the Civil Service Commissioners. Sanskrit, German, French and English were among the subjects he offered. He did not, however, obtain a Writership in the Indian Civil Service but was appointed to a Writership to Ceylon which brought him directly under the fiat of the Colonial Office.[7]

It was a rather curious turn of affairs. Rhys Davids' mind had all along been habituated to the idea that he would finally go to India as a servant of the Crown. As it turned out, the great journey to the East took the form of a passage to Ceylon rather than the more fancied passage to India. And when he stepped ashore in Ceylon in 1864, Rhys Davids—the *Mahatmas* notwithstanding—could hardly have foreseen how radically his life was to be transformed with Ceylon playing the role of the crucial catalyst.

[5] *Ibid.*

[6] *Ibid.* Also, *Journal of the Royal Asiatic Society* (Great Britain and Ireland), Vol. XIX, Part III. See Notes of the Quarter.

[7] *Op. cit.*, *Journal of the Maha Bodhi Society.*

Part II
Sri Lanka. A Youthful Proconsul in Sri Lanka

2

MOSTLY MAGISTERIAL FUNCTIONS

IF Rhys Davids' official career* in Sri Lanka ended in a welter of partially resolved and controversial issues, nothing could have been more banal or routinely ordinary than its beginning. In February 1866, Rhys Davids was appointed to the Civil Service in Sri Lanka as a Writer. The term Writer had venerable antecedents going back to the early days of East India Company's rule in India.[1] Apart from affinities in nomenclature, the term in Sri Lanka carried a connotation which was, at any rate in the middle of the nineteenth century, not far removed from its Indian usage.

A Civil Service had been set up in 1802 when Sri Lanka became a Crown Colony. During its first fifty years, the Civil Service had undergone notable changes. Its rather chequered history had been influenced by a number of factors. The successive Secretaries of State for the Colonies had brought about changes. They were, to a large extent, influenced by the principles and traditions of the Civil Service in England. Secondly—and rather more to the point—was the normative influence of the Indian Civil Service since there was a broad similarity between the conditions in India and in Sri Lanka. Thirdly, the change was also determined by less theoretical considerations like the needs of pressure groups, economic development, and the exigencies of a strikingly volatile revenue situation. Usually the Governor in Sri Lanka, as the man on the spot, was more sensitive to local factors than the Colonial Office in England. But by the 1860s the era of experimentation and *ad hoc* changes was over. In both London and Colombo, there was greater unanimity about the principles on which the Civil Service should be developed. Moreover, with improvements in the conditions of service, like salaries, pensions, and prospects of

* N.B. The material used in this chapter has been taken from the files of the Department of National Archives, Sri Lanka, under the reference numbers cited in the footnotes.

[1] O'Malley, L.S.S. *The Indian Civil Service 1601-1930.* London, 1931, p. 3 ff.

promotion, the Civil Service at last settled down to a long period of steady development.[2]

A tradition that survived from the earlier period was the bifurcation of the Civil Service. Theoretically, all appointments to the Civil Service were made by the Secretary of State for the Colonies. In fact, however, the Governor could make his own nominations to some of vacancies. It was a sphere of patronage which the successive Governors had jealously guarded. What became a virtual right, which the Governor could insist on, was justified on the ground that a Governor could advance the claims of local talent which would otherwise be overlooked. On the other hand, there were the nominees of the Secretary of State—incumbents of Writerships, like Rhys Davids—who clearly formed the *corps d'elite* of the Civil Service in Sri Lanka. In spite of the implied idea that the nominees of the Secretary of State or Writers were suitable for administration work in the East, they had all to sit in a special examination which was conducted by Haileyberry College, an institution which the East India Company had established to train its young officials going out to serve in India. In 1856, the Colonial Office replaced the Haileyberry examination with a competitive test organised by the Civil Service Commissioners. No special knowledge of Sri Lanka or of the East was called for at this stage. Instead, a prospective Writer's knowledge of subjects like Latin, Greek, Mathematics, History and Law was tested. The idea was to enlist young men of the public school type, usually between eighteen and twenty three years of age, who had had a liberal education.[3]

The Writers from England were clearly a cut above the appointees of the Governor. Usually the Governor's selections were confined to the upper class Ceylonese elite. Moreover, the best that Sri Lanka could offer by way of a liberal education was a far cry from the education and finesse which the Writers from England were wont to acquire. It could, of course, be said that at least the local men were more knowledgeable about conditions in Sri Lanka. The idea was clearly implied in the criticisms made of Writers who were selected to join the Indian Civil Service. They were stigmatised as "unfledged boys" who were ignorant both of the language and the country they

[2] Mills, Lennox A. *Ceylon Under British Rule 1795-1932*. Oxford, 1933, Chapter 4.
[3] Ibid.

were required to serve in.[4] But steps had been taken, early in the history of the Civil Service in Sri Lanka, to remedy the situation. Thus a young Writer from England was expected to pass a preliminary examination in the local languages within eighteen months of his arrival on the island. He was then confirmed in his appointment. Later, he sat for a stiffer language examination on which depended his promotions. Moreover, far from "unfledged boys" walking into magistracies, collectorships or becoming agents in provinces, in Sri Lanka at least, the newly arrived Writer from England was attached to the Colonial Secretary's Office in Colombo to learn his work. This office was the nerve-centre of the island's administration. Sometimes during this period the young Writhers filled temporary stop gap appointments whenever the exigencies of the administration made it necessary. In general, work during this period was restricted to a few hours a day so that the Writer would have the time to prepare himself for the language examination.[5]

Rhys Davids was no exception to the rule. He was attached to the Colonial Secretary's Office in April 1866. In May he worked temporarily at the Customs Office in Colombo and in July he moved to the Kandy *Kachcheri.* Francis Templer, who was the Government Agent in Kandy, was badly short of staff. One of his assistants had become severely ill and had to be removed to Colombo. The other Civil Servants who were with him were relieved of their duties temporarily to enable them to study for the language examination. Templer was pleased with the manner in which Rhys Davids had coped with his new duties and evidently forgot that he had asked the Colonial Secretary to send by way of relief "one of the older and more experienced Writers."[6] When the pressures to which Templer had been subject had somewhat eased, Rhys Davids was recalled to the Colonial Secretary's Office.

II

The preliminary phase in Rhys Davids' career ended in August 1867 when he was appointed the Acting Police Magistrate and

[4] O'Malley, *op. cit.*

[5] Mills, *op. cit.*

[6] See Lot 6 (5) 2991 for the following: F. B. Templer to Colonial Secretary, 14 May 1866; Templer to Colonial Secretary, No. 182 of 22 May 1866 ; Templer to Colonial Secretary, No. 244 of 3 July 1866. Also Rhys Davids to Colonial Secretary, No. 291 of 25 July 1866.

Commissioner of Requests in Avissawella. In Rhys Davids' time the post of Police Magistrate and Commissioner of Requests involved two distinct tiers of the Civil Service. The Civil Servants who were Police Magistrates and Commissioners of Requests in comparatively unimportant towns like Avissawella, Harispattuwa, Kayts, Mullaitivu and a few other places, held a post which carried a salary of £350 and was in the Fourth Class of the Junior Branch in the Civil Service, virtually the bottom rung in the administration. On the other hand, the incumbents of this post who served in certain other towns considered more important in terms of population and commerce such as Galle and Gampola, received higher salaries and came within the Second and Third Class of the Junior Branch in the Civil Service.

Taken as a whole, however, the jurisdiction exercised by these courts which had been established in no less than thirty nine towns on the island was rather circumscribed. The Police Courts, for example, dealt with the cases of petty assaults, thefts, possession of stolen property and minor disturbances of the peace. The more significant powers the courts possessed concerned statutory offences—breaches of ordinances which the government of Ceylon had enacted from time to time. Thus, the Police Courts were the principal means of dealing with infractions of the law concerning a wide variety of matters ranging from neglecting to pay the road tax or the grain tax, to cattle trespass and cruelty to animals. But the maximum punishment which a Police Magistrate could impose was a fine of £5 or imprisonment with hard labour for a period of three months. Correspondingly, the Police Courts had no jurisdiction over serious robberies, deaths, grievous assaults and riots. Nor had it jurisdiction concerning issues of title to land. However, despite their modest powers, the bulk of the judicial work in the island was done by means of these Courts. The Courts of Requests dealt with civil cases involving claims for money which had been lent either on promissory notes or therwise, disputes involving sales of goods, and disputes concerning boundaries, provided the value of all such cases did not exceed £10. Like the Police Magistrate Courts, the Courts of Requests too handled a large number of cases.

But Avissawella itself was of middling importance in comparison to the other districts in the island. Taking both types of courts together, it was evident that statistically the courts, which had been established in twons like Colombo, Kandy, Galle and Negombo, on an average, dealt with over two thousand cases a year. The courts in

Colombo, for example, dealt every year with no less than five thousand cases. At the other end of the spectrum, there were the courts in Nuwera Eliya, Pussellawa, Dambulla, Haldamulla and Nawalapitiya which dealt with less than five hundred cases a year. In some places, the number of cases barely exceeded a hundred. Avissawella, like Balapitiya. Chilaw, Kegalle and Harispattuwa, was in the intermediary range. One may presume, therefore, that in Rhys Davids' time the Police Magistrate and the Commissioner of Requests in Avissawella had comparatively little work.

Rhys Davids, however, did not think so. The existing judicial districts had been determined at an earlier period when the amount of judicial work on the island was much less. Consequently, a Magistrate was able to sit only for short spells at any one place and travelled leisurely to other localities which came under his jurisdiction and where the courts had to be held. Avissawella was a fairly large district. In December 1866, as a result of a re-organisation of judicial districts, Pasyala, which was situated in the Kegalle District and was quite a distance from Avissawella, was brought under the jurisdiction of the Magistrate in Avissawella. Rhys Davids could justifiably feel that the area over which he was now called upon to exercise his duties was a very considerable one. Moreover, as he ruefully observed, much of his extended legal domain was covered with thick jungle.[7]

Moreover, Rhys Davids also felt constrained by certain extraneous difficulties. By January 1867 he was wondering whether he should after all hold Court in Pasyala. "As far as I can ascertain there is no building at that place fit for the purpose", he observed, "and at the adjoining village of Veyangoda there is only a rest-house."[8] The Colonial Secretary replied that steps were being taken to build a court-house in Pasyala and until such time Rhys Davids could use the rest-house in Veyangoda.[9] In a subsequent letter to the Colonial Secretary, Rhys Davids pointed out that the building of the court-house should be expedited. He said that as a result of the re-organisation of judicial divisions, the Pasyala area was "beyond the

[7] Lot 6 (1) 3141 D. N. A.; Rhys Davids to Colonial Secretary, 24 January 1867. It is, for example, noteworthy that in 1869 the Police Magistrate Courts throughout the island handled as many as 69,000 cases. By 1879, the number of cases was 71,403. Indeed, the average for the period 1865-1870 was about 69,000.

[8] *Ibid.*

[9] Lot 7 (1) 3141 D. N. A.; Colonial Secretary to Rhys Davids, 13 February, 1867.

jurisdiction of any Court save that of Pasyala and until a Court is really established there (the inhabitants) are left without justice of any kind."[10] Indeed, in a petition which they submitted to the Governor on the subject, the inhabitants of the area declared that when litigants went by habit to their Courts either in Negombo or in Kegalle, they were invariably directed to Pasyala Courts. "When they go there, they find there is nobody to whom they can submit their grievances."[11] The petitioners added that the "Magistrate at Avissawella who is appointed over these Courts has not come there even once since January last." Rhys Davids himself felt compelled to write to the Colonial Secretary in May 1867. He pointed out that as the court-house in Pasyala had not been built he should be permitted to use the rest-house in Ambepussa "which is now seldom used". Besides Ambepussa was easily accessible to the litigants in Pasyala. Alternatively, Rhys Davids asked permission to rent a three-roomed house in Paysala one room being set aside to hold the Court. "The people," he added, " have now been six months out of the jurisdiction of any existent Court."[12]

By August 1867 Rhys Davids was writing to the Colonial Secretary again ". . . there is no house better than a mud hut to let within a mile of the court-house at Pasyala and I would venture to point out that a temporary bungalow of mud and talipot might be built on the plan of Veyangoda Rest-house for a few months rent."[13] The protracted correspondence ended when a new Court was built in Ambanpitiya for the Pasyala area. Rhys Davids however was not destined to stay in Avissawella for too long. In November 1867, he was appointed to Matale as Police Magistrate and Commissioner of Requests. Rhys Davids had good reason to be pleased with the turn of events. The Matale appointment was a generous promotion. It carried a salary of £600 and came within the Second Class of the Junior Branch in the Civil Service. Till 1865, the Assistant Government Agent in Matale had also been the Police Magistrate and Commissioner of Requests for the Matale area. In that year Matale was combined with Dambulla to form a single judicial area under the authority of a Police Magistrate and Commissioner of Requests.

Rhys Davids, who was always sensitive to his surroundings, took

[10]Lot 6 (1) 3141 D. N. A.; Rhys Davids to Colonial Secretary, 18 February 1867.
[11]Lot 6 (1) 3141 D. N. A.; Rhys Davids to Colonial Secretary, 24 March 1867.
[12]Lot 6 (1) 3141 D. N. A.; Rhys Davids to Colonial Secretary, 11 May 1867.
[13]Lot 6 (1) 3141 D. N. A.; Rhys Davids to Colonial Secretary, n.d. *circa* August 1867.

to Matale, which he described as one of the most pleasant places in the island. Typically, he also showed extraordinary concern about the more pedestrian matters of his accommodation. It seemed that the repairs to the Magistrate's bungalow in Matale had been held back because the plans to construct a stable had not been completed. "I can do without a stable," Rhys Davids wrote. Instead, he found intolerable the condition of the brick floor of the bungalow which collected dust and vermin. There were also the white ants "so numerous that they seldom allowed themselves to be forgotten." It was only by constant sweeping that he had been able to prevent the white ants from "forming their tunnels up the legs of the furniture."[14] Rhys Davids also complained about the court-house which required urgent repairs and wrote feelingly about the thatched houses of some of his subordinates. He thought it a shame that the native officials, all of whom had families with small children, were not permitted to use new quarters which had been built for their use because of official delays of one sort or another.[15]

And yet, although in surroundings so basically agreeable, Rhys Davids willingly adjusted himself to the increased tempo of work which the place demanded. His stay in Matale was not free from the difficulties of the sort which rather tragically marred his official career in Ceylon. Rhys Davids' letters to the Colonial Secretary show clearly how much he was surprised at the unexpected turn of events which destroyed the charm which Matale had held for him.

The *Causus Belli* was Reginald Pole, who was the Acting Assistant Government Agent and Additional Police Magistrate in Matale. Pole's antagonism towards Rhys Davids, which was first made evident in May 1868, possibly had much to do with the fact that both were performing functions of a similar nature. Pole complained to P.W. Braybrooke, who was the Government Agent in the Central Province—Matale was at the time part of the Central Province—that Rhys Davids was indifferent to the interests of the government whenever there were cases before Rhys Davids in which the Crown was involved as a party to the dispute.[16] According to Pole, it was the duty of a Magistrate to inform the Assistant Government Agent when such cases were to come up for trial and to ensure that the Crown was adequately represented. In the absence of a Deputy

[14]Lot 6 (I) 3236 D. N. A.; Rhys Davids to Colonial Secretary, 23 March 1865.
[15]Lot 6 (I) 3232. D. N. A.; Rhys Davids to Colonial Secretary, 12 October 1868.
[16]Lot 7 (I) 1736 D. N. A.; Colonial Secretary, to Rhys Davids. 8 May, 1868.

Queen's Advocate who usually represented the Crown, it was the duty of a Magistrate to postpone a case, thereby "safeguarding the interests of the Crown." Pole contended that Rhys Davids habitually neglected to do so.

An example which Pole discussed in some detail was concerned with twenty three men who had been accused of illegally clearing fifty acres of jungle land belonging to the government for Chena cultivation in October 1867. When the case came up for trial in April 1868, in spite of the absence of a Deputy Queen's Advocate, Rhys Davids had taken up the matter.[17] Rhys Davids, however, pointed out that the case had come up for trial on several occasions before April 1868 but had perforce to be postponed in the absence of the Counsel of the Crown. On the day in question, the Deputy Queen's Advocate, who had been told about it well in advance, was not present. Rather than postpone the case again, he decided to hear evidence as all the witnesses for both sides were present. Rhys Davids assured the Colonial Secretary that he had been prepared to adjourn the trial if the need should have arisen from the point of view of the interests of the Crown. As it turned out, it soon became evident that the defendants could not deny the charges and had to plead guilty. He had been able to vindicate the interests of the Crown "without troubling the law officers of the Crown." Moreover, in drawing attention to the fact that Pole had written a letter "so calculated to injure a fellow civilian on such slight grounds", Rhys Davids asked the Colonial Secretary whether it was ever likely that he as a Magistrate should have been opposed to the idea of postponing a case on behalf of the Crown when he himself was a paid servant of the government[18].

During this time Pole's behaviour seems to have been frankly inconsistent. Indeed, when Rhys Davids made arrangements to present himself for a Civil Service examination which made it necessary for him to travel down to Colombo, Pole had readily consented to act on Rhys Davids' behalf. Rhys Davids, who at first had applied for a month's leave in early March, subsequently had the period of leave amended to begin from mid-March when Pole would be better able to do his work.[19] But in spite of his arrangements with Rhys Davids, Pole went on circuit to remote regions of the Matale District. He did not return to Matale until the Colonial Secretary who had become

[17] Lot 6 (1) 3236 D.N.A.; Rhys Davids to Colonial Secretary, 30 May 1868.
[18] *Ibid.*
[19] Lot 6 (1) 3236 D. N. A.; Rhys Davids to Colonial Secretary, 18 February 1868; also Colonial Secretary to Rhys Davids, 17 July 1868.

aware of Pole's absence almost by chance, summarily ordered Pole to attend to Rhys Davids' work. With the mild reprimand that was addressed to Pole, the matter might have ended had Pole not made serious allegations against Rhys Davids' general conduct as Police Magistrate. Pole declared that Rhys Davids, whose work he said was generally unsatisfactory, had ignored the standing instructions which had been issued to the Police Magistrate in Dambulla that Court should be held for six days of each month beginning with the first Monday of the month. Instead, Rhys Davids had made constant changes which had put Pole into "great personal inconvenience" in arranging his own particular circuits. Pole was aware that the litigants were themselves dissatisfied.

In referring Pole's letter to Rhys Davids, the Colonial Secretary drew particular attention to another allegation that it was Rhys Davids' practice not to sit in Court on Saturdays.[20] This was evidently a sore point with the administration. It had long since been known that Police Magistrates throughout the island did very little work on Saturdays and it was not uncommon that Courts were not held at all on that day. A minute circularised in May 1866 had pointed out that this practice unnecessarily slowed down the work of the Courts and caused "the needless detention of accused parties from Friday till Monday."[21] In a well-reasoned reply, Rhys Davids explained that the Dambulla Courts were open on Saturdays but that as the cases called on Saturdays were first appearance cases, he had not thought it always necessary to sit personally in Court. Rhys Davids pleaded that the Colonial Secretary's letter was really the first intimation he had about the existence of the minute of May 1866. He felt let down that the Chief Clerk in the Court, who had been serving in that capacity for several years, had not put him wise on the matter. Rhys Davids scored a telling point against Pole who after all had all along been aware of the minute but had not cared to draw Rhys Davids' attention to it.

Rhys Davids dismissed with contempt the more general allegation that he had made constant changes in the schedules of the Dambulla Courts. "I will only request you to be kind," he asked the Colonial Secretary, "to consult the returns of the work done, from which you will find that I do more work than any other outstation

[20] Lot 6 (I) 3236 D. N. A.; R. C. Pole to Colonial Secretary, 23 July 1868.
[21] Lot 6 (I) 3236 D. N. A.; Colonial Secretary to Rhys Davids, 25 August 1868.

Magistrate in the island."[22]

He was evidently puzzled by Pole's animosity. "This is the fourth time that these unseemly differences have been brought to your notice and it has not I hope escaped your notice," he pointed out to the Colonial Secretary, "that in every case Mr. Pole has been the aggressor". Pole after all had an irascible temperament and there was a history of unfriendly relations with the other Civil Servants with whom he had worked. As for himself, Rhys Davids pointed out that since his arrival in Ceylon he had been on friendly terms with "all the Civil Servants with whom I have been stationed." He had indeed tried to make up with Pole. But his overtures, which might have been effective with most others, had been rebuffed. In a postscript to this letter, Rhys Davids begged that Pole should not be permitted to attack him "in such haste whenever he can exaggerate some slight act into a disregard of your instructions."[23]

Gradually the idea took hold of Rhys Davids' mind that Pole was bent on ousting him from the post of Magistrate. Indeed the *contretemps* with Pole evidently affected Rhys Davids a great deal. He wrote to the Colonial Secretary that on their account Matale had become "utterly distasteful". He had resolved to work out an exchange of duties and was re-doubling his efforts to secure a release from Matale ere long. So that when the post of Police Magistrate in Gampola fell vacant, Rhys Davids wrote hopefully to Colonial Secretary begging him to consider Rhys Davids' claims[24].

Instead in January 1869 Rhys Davids was transferred to Galle. He had in effect fallen from the frying pan into the fire. Rhys Davids' proneness to be querulous on questions of accommodation, which was soon to elicit official comment, was therefore proportionately more evident. Primarily, he was bitter about the condition of the Police Court which was being held in the verandah of the District Court.

> There is absolutely no way of preventing witnesses being tampered with during trial . . . there is no access for the public . . . it is impossible for the weak person to force his way through the narrow doorway . . . cases are often struck off because the complainants cannot push their way to the door and the host and crowding are almost impossible.[25]

[22] Lot 6 (1) 3236 D. N. A.; Rhys Davids to Colonial Secretary, 3 September 1868.
[23] Lot 6 (1) 3236 D. N. A.; Rhys Davids to Colonial Secretary, 12 August 1868.
[24] Lot 6 (1) 3236 D. N. A.; Rhys Davids to Colonial Secretary, 6 May 1868.
[25] Lot 6 (1) 3230 D. N. A.; Rhys Davids to Colonial Secretary, 22 February 1869.

Consequently, when he was summoned to attend the Supreme Court in Kandy as an important witness in a case, Rhys Davids made it the pretext to take a few days additional leave. "Chiefly owing to the crowded state of the court-house, I have been suffering from fever since my arrival."[26] Predictably, on his return to Galle he wrote with unfeigned fervour on the old problem. The small room in which the Police Court was being held was very unhealthy; ". . . a very large number of people mostly half clothed many of whom have walked long distances in the sun is crowded into so small space that the air is consequently loathsome . . . at times absolutely sickening," he wrote.[27]

The Colonial Secretary made a placatory reply. Rhys Davids himself had proposed that it would not be necessary to put up a new building if certain modifications to the existing building could be effected. Indeed, the Colonial Secretary had thought Rhys Davids' suggestions sufficiently worthwhile to forward them to the Director of Public Works. Nevertheless, in a draft which was not incorporated in the official reply, the Colonial Secretary wondered why some of Rhys Davids' predecessors had not complained about the accommodation provided for the Police Court. This was, he mused, all the more remarkable if one considered that Rhys Davids had after all barely begun his duties in Galle.

Rhys Davids clearly felt the burden of his judicial duties in Galle. For one thing the number of cases to be dealt with in Court was markedly larger in Galle than in Matale or in Avissawella. Indeed, in Avissawella the Colonial Secretary had queried Rhys Davids about the little work done in the Magistrate's Court.[28] Adjustment to an increased tempo of work in Galle had unhappily to be effected in surroundings that Rhys Davids hardly thought tolerable. Moreover, he found that in Galle the amount of judicial work was steadily increasing. Under these pressures, he urged the Colonial Secretary to relieve him of the responsibility of going over and certifying the fines collected by the various government departments in the area. This was a function which devolved on him as Justice of the Peace and entailed tiresome visits to several offices. In this endeavour, however, Rhys Davids was presumably unsuccessful.[29] In spite of these

[26] Lot 6 (I) 3320 D. N. A.; Rhys Davids to Colonial Secretary, 1 March 1869.
[27] Lot 6 (I) 3416 D. N. A.; Rhys Davids to Colonial Secretary, 25 April 1870.
[28] Lot 7 (I) 1566 D. N. A.; Colonial Secretary to Rhys Davids, 6 December 1866.
[29] Lot 6 (I) 3416 D. N. A.; Rhys Davids to Colonial Secretary, 5 January 1870.

irritations, Rhys Davids was compelled to stay on in Galle till August 1871, when the more significant phase in his career in Ceylon began.

III

It was evident that Rhys Davids chafed under certain constraints which were part and parcel of the office of Police Magistrate. There was the irritating surveillance which the Colonial Secretary's Office customarily exercised over the magistracies. For example, the travelling claims submitted by Rhys Davids were gone through with the proverbial fine-tooth comb and a great deal of effort was expended on correspondence involving comparatively small sums. As interminable was the correspondence on questions involving "irrecoverable fines" which had to be disposed of periodically. Authority to strike off such debts was only given after Rhys Davids had been asked for detailed explanations as to why he thought the fines concerned could not be collected.[30]

At times he also encountered a certain small-mindedness which was characteristic of the bureaucratic apparatus. When Rhys Davids wanted a fresh set of ordinances for use in the Matale Courts, he was asked to buy one for himself, "as govt. [sic] should not be called upon to provide another set of ords. [sic] because the set already supplied to the Matale Courts has been allowed to become dirty and torn and imperfect."[31] On another occasion when he made an application for certain printed forms for use in the same courts he was called upon to explain "the large indents for forms and the heavy cost of providing for your courts as compared with courts of greater importance."[32]

With the passage of time, and in spite of himself, Rhys Davids became part of a compulsive preoccupation with trivia. "I have the honour to request," he wrote, "that I may be supplied with a new belt for one of the court messengers here whose present one is become quite worn out by long use."[33] On another occasion, in submitting a

[30] Lot 7 (1) 1808 D. N. A.; Colonial Secretary to Rhys Davids, 25 May 1869; Lot 6 (1) 3232 D. N. A.; Rhys Davids to Colonial Secretary, 13 July 1868.

[31] Lot 7 (1) 1737 D. N. A.; Colonial Secretary to Rhys Davids, 6 November 1868.

[32] Lot 7 (1) 1736 D. N. A.; Colonial Secretary to Rhys Davids, n.d. *circa* 1869.

[33] Lot 6 (1) 3141 D. N. A.; Rhys Davids to Colonial Secretary, 21 July 1867.

statement of the furniture in the Dambulla Courts, Rhys Davids solemnly reported that

> one chair is missing and is said to have been missing for the last year . . . the writing desk in the last return has been broken to pieces. One ruler is also missing. There are three square inkstands not four as mentioned in the last return, but as there is one round pewter inkstand in the return I presume that the number is correct.

On the other hand, some of the difficulties which Rhys Davids had to face were largely of his own making. The fact was that he was extraordinarily sensitive, almost to the point of pugnacity, if any criticisms were made concerning his official work which even remotely threw doubts about his abilities. Rhys Davids, whose business it was to submit figures with regard to crimes committed within the areas that came under his jurisdiction, had asked the Colonial Secretary how certain types of offences should be classified. The Inspector General of Police, who required such information for his annual report, thought that Rhys Davids' query was superfluous. "A little moment's thought will show the appropriate heading in each case," he declared. Rhys Davids, however, retorted that the implied accusation of utter thoughtlessness was "uncalled for and will be found undeserved . . . indeed I can hardly understand how any officer can have made up the returns without further information."[34] On another occasion, in Galle, following a sharp exchange of letters between certain government medical officials and Rhys Davids concerning a boy who had died after he had been discharged from the hospital, Sir Hercules Robinson, the Governor, observed on Rhys Davids' share of the correspondence that "matters of private pique should not be imported into the transaction of public business."[35]

A more significant incident occurred when Rhys Davids assumed duties in Matale. He was asked to explain why he had taken more time than he should have in journeying from Avissawella to Matale. He replied in cantankerous tones. As a result he was sternly told that Sir Hercules Robinson had expressed "disapproval of the concluding paragraphs of your letter than which nothing could well be more

[34] Lot 6 (1) 3232 D. N. A.; Rhys Davids to Colonial Secretary, 20 January 1868 ; Lot 6 (1) 3236 D. N. A.; Rhys Davids to Colonial Secretary, 6 January 1868.

[35] Lot 7 (1) 1659 D. N. A.; Colonial Secretary to Rhys Davids, 15 February 1870.

insubordinate and unbecoming. I am to call upon you," wrote the Colonial Secretary, "to withdraw that letter and to substitute for it another free from such improprieties of style and tenor."[36]

Indeed, at times Rhys Davids rather unnecessarily exposed himself to official pique. In Avissawella he wanted Sir Hercules Robinson to give him permission to spare a boy on whom Rhys Davids himself had imposed the sentence of corporal punishment. In the same breath he explained that really the offence merited a jail sentence.[37] More revealing were his reactions when certain persons, whom he had himself sentenced to imprisonment with hard labour for knowingly buying timber cut in Crown forests, petitioned the Governor to have the sentence reviewed. Rhys Davids took care to reiterate that there was no doubt as to the facts of the case, declared that there was considerable force in the plea of the petitioners that they were after all "respectable men" who would be humiliated by the stigma of imprisonment with hard labour. Rhys Davids—with little regard for the consistency of his actions—expressed himself pained by the spectable of "respectable men" having to work on public roads. He explained that this was what the sentence amounted to. He, therefore, urged the Governor to commute the sentence to a fine of £15. This plea too was summarily turned down.[38]

The other side of the medal, however, revealed fitful glimpses of a young Magistrate in a more flattering light. His judicial functions necessarily brought Rhys Davids in contact with the principal legal officer of the government. Sir Richard Morgan, the Queen's Advocate, had often been impressed by evidence of Rhys Davids' initiative. In a well-reasoned letter which Rhys Davids wrote to the Colonial Secretary in June 1870, he discussed the subject of Coroners and their functions. The letter was passed on to Morgan. Rhys Davids pointed out that there was no uniform practice with regard to the exercise of the Coroner's functions in the various districts in the island. It was, of course, the presumption that this function was performed by Police Magistrates who were also the Justices of the Peace in their areas. According to Rhys Davids, this was actually the prevailing position in the towns of Colombo, Kandy and Jaffna. In Galle, however, the Coroner's work was being done by the District Judge. On the face of things this was a satisfactory arrangement, as the Police Magistrate had "as much work to do as the officers could

[36] Lot 7 (1) 1659 D.N.A.; Colonial Secretary to Rhys Davids, n.d. *circa* 1870.
[37] Lot 6 (1) 3416 D.N.A.; Rhys Davids to Colonial Secretary, 7 December 1870.
[38] Lot 6 (1) 3141 D.N.A.; Rhys Davids to Colonial Secretary, 25 June 1867.

get through." In effect, however, the District Judge himself was so overwhelmed with work that the Coroner's duties were comparatively neglected. In spite of his anxiety to show how burdened the Police Magistrate was with regard to his ordinary duties, Rhys Davids suggested that in Galle the Police Magistrate should be made Additional Coroner. Morgan fell in line with Rhys Davids' ideas. Galle was in many ways an exception to the general position prevailing elsewhere in the island concerning the amount of work which a District Judge had to do. Morgan believed that generally "these judges had ample time" to attend to additional duties imposed on them. Morgan decided to make all District Judges as Additional Coroners. In those areas where the District Judge was already functioning in this capacity, a formal cognizance of the fact was to be taken in Gazette notifications[39].

On another occasion, Rhys Davids pointed out that in the annual returns of the work done by Police Magistrates, no provision was made for mention of their work as Justices of the Peace. It had almost been assumed that these particular functions were a negligible backwater. Rhys Davids, for his part, was convinced of the importance of this sphere of the Magistrate's work. With casualness he let it be known that although when he came to Galle there were over a hundred unsettled Justice of the Peace cases, he had virtually cleared the backlog. Morgan thought that Rhys Davids' proposal was "excellent" and decided to alter the manner in which judical returns should be prepared.

Morgan was particularly impressed when Rhys Davids submitted a scheme for the registration of domestic servants. Rhys Davids was convinced that the majority of petty thefts and burglaries in towns were committed by domestic servants. He pointed out that servants who had served short terms of imprisonment for theft usually succeeded in finding employers who were wholly ignorant about their antecedents. Such employers soon became victims themselves. Rhys Davids' scheme, which according to him had been tried out with success in Germany, involved, to begin with, the issue of certificate books to domestic servants. These books which were issued by the Government Agents were intended to be a record of the details of a servant's service under sucessive employers. Duplicates were to be kept, presumably in the *Kachcheris*, and a Magistrate was

[39]Lot 6 (I) 3416 D. N. A.; Rhys Davids to Colonial Secretary, 1 June 1870.

to record details of convictions. Indeed, there was striking evidence of the influence of Rhys Davids' ideas in an ordinance for registering domestic servants which Morgan introduced in the Legislative Council in the sessions of 1871[40].

Meanwhile, however, the exigencies of the administration caught up Rhys Davids in its complex machinations and placed him in an altogether novel and possibly more challenging theatre.

[40]Lot 6 (1) 3416 D. N. A.; Rhys Davids to Colonial Secretary, 5 July 1870. Also Lot 6 (1) 3320 D. N. A.; Rhys Davids to Colonial Secretary, 14 September 1869.

3

A JOURNEY TO ANURADHAPURA: THE LAND OF TEMPLES AND TANKS

"I received an intimation this morning that I was to act at Galle as District Judge and that Mr. Davids will succeed me here." On 3 August 1871 Louis Leisching, the Assistant Government Agent in Anuradhapura, was making a hurried entry in his diary. "As I must leave tomorrow for the sessions," he continued conscientiously, "I have locked up in the large iron chest £1549, the key of which I shall take with me. In the second iron chest I have lodged £300 . . . I shall probably meet Mr. Davids on the way."[1]

Louis Leisching was glad to turn his back on Anuradhapura, a place for which he had little affection. As virtually the only European official in the place he had been overpowered by a sense of isolation. He had particularly felt the lack of intercourse with others as well as the sheer inability of knowing what was happening elsewhere. Even the extensive travelling which his work called for had been at best a plausible distraction. In a characteristically flat land covered with forests, the roads ran for miles "through sombre foliage . . . most depressing in its influence on the mind." The monotony was barely relieved by the occasional appearance of a hamlet near a tank where the villagers came out to stare at the solitary figure of a European riding by. But before long, one plunged again into the "gloomy solitudes of the jungle." Small wonder, then, that Leisching should have found even the tasks of riding to and from the tanks to the *Kachcheri* tiresome.

Nor had the spectacle of ancient ruins, which had moved others, impressed him. On the contrary, they contributed to the melancholy state of his mind. He spoke of "the indescribably depressing influence of solitary residence among mournful ruins." Anuradhapura seemed to him to be "a city of the dead." Turn where one will and one encountered various mounds which were really the sepulchres of ancient kings. Everywhere there was "a silence as profound as that of

[1]Lot 41.252. D.N.A.: Diary entries. 3 August 1871. Louis Leisching. Also Lot 41. 184. D.N.A. Rhys Davids to W.C. Twynam, G.A. Northern Province, No. 92 of 16 August 1871.

the gave."[2]

Moreover, as he had confided in Rhys Davids, difficulties which Leisching had encountered in working with his native subordinates in the *Kachcheri* in Anuradhapura had strengthened his resolve to leave the place. The native officers as a rule had been incompetent and had irritated him by their attitudes toward work. If the most able native official fell ill, the work in the *Kachcheri* slowed down very considerably. From a more general point of view, there had been a lack of movement—a stagnation in administration. Leisching also complained that one never quite knew when or how to begin taking things in hand, which was not a confession of his own sense of inadequacy—Louis Leisching was regarded as an able officer—as much as a reflection of the difficulties of keeping in touch with the administration centre of the vast province which was situated in Jaffna.[3]

It was no doubt on account of these hardships that Leisching's health broke down after a stay of barely five years, which made his removal to a more congenial locality necessary, preferably near the coast. Hence the exchange of places between Rhys Davids and himself.[4]

Meanwhile, Rhys Davids, who had met Leisching briefly at Matale on his way, arrived in Anuradhapura on 15 August 1871 and assumed duties on the following day. In effecting the exchange, the Colonial Secretary's office in Colombo no doubt had in mind the stern stipulations which the redoubtable Percival Dyke, who had been the Government Agent of the Northern Province for over thirty years, had laid down as the qualifications which an Assistant Agent in Nuwerakakawiya should possess. In Dyke's old world phraseology, the Assistant Agent should among other things, be "without encumberances," that is, without wife and family; possess "active habits of body," be free from "all apprehensions as to climate," and be generally "full of resources to meet and supply the deficiencies of the place." Leisching himself cynically observed that the idea was that even a comparatively junior Civil Servant could be appointed as the Assistant Agent in Nuwerakalawiya provided these requirements

[2] Administration Reports. 1869. pp. 102ff. Report on the Nuwerakalawiya District. L.Leisching.

[3] *Ibid*. Also C.O. 54. 479. Gregory to Kimberley, no. 238 of 16 December 1872.

[4] Lot 20. 311. D.N.A. for details of exchange of duties arranged between Rhys Davids and Leisching. The exchange of duties was periodically extended by the Colonial Secretary. Such exchanges between Civil Servants was not unusual. Lot 6 (5) 2991 D.N.A., Aelian King to Colonial Secretary, 21 July 1866.

were met. In return the government evidently hoped that once appointed, the Civil Servant concerned would remain in Anuradhapura for a reasonably long period of time.[5]

There had been other considerations too. Sir Hercules Robinson, the Governor, had been moved by a single factor in approving the arrangements made between Leisching and Rhys Davids. Aware of Rhys Davids' penchant for such subjects as philology and archeology, the Governor was anxious to make use of his talents for archeological work for which Anuradhapura provided ideal opportunities. In the event Rhys Davids loved the ruins amidst which he spent much of his time. He also conceived a warm affection for the Sinhalese in Nuwerakalawiya, a feeling to which he constantly alluded. The degree of rapport which he established with the simple peasants was in a sense engendered by his ability to speak "the language of the district"—another stipulation in Dyke's compendious list—with a fluency that was rare among contemporary Civil Servants. Indeed, almost as a matter of principle he dispensed with interpreters who figured largely in the conduct of official business involving English Civil Servants and the indigenous inhabitants.[6]

II

Rhys Davids liked Anuradhapura. He was happily immune to the intense melancholia and forebodings which had plagued Leisching. The very mounds and scattered ruins held secrets which aroused his scholarly interests. They were the symbols of a religion and culture the study of which became a lifelong obsession. To his more subtle and refined mind the very absence of change in Anuradhapura was its principal attraction and invested the place with a timeless old world charm.

In a sense, the vagaries of economic change held the clue to the state of Anuradhapura or Nuwerakalawiya. A striking feature of the Nuwerakalawiya district—and indeed of several neighbouring districts—was the absence of any real economic change. In the context of the nineteenth century, the major catalyst of such change was clearly British capital, which had made such significant inroads into the Central and Western Provinces. Geographically it would seem

[5] Administration Reports. 1869, pp. 102ff. Report on the Nuwerakalawiya District.
[6] C.O. 54. 479. Gregory to Kimberley, no. 238 of 16 December 1872.

that the main thrust of British entrepreneurship had spent itself at the peripheries of the Matale district, leaving the vast area further north comparatively undisturbed.

Any economic importance which Nuwerakalawiya enjoyed was derived from the fortuitous circumstance that on account of its midway position, this district lay in the path of several traditional internal trade routes. Of these, the most important was the route which linked the districts of Jaffna to the Central Province. The Central Road, as this was somewhat picturesquely called in contemporary documents, touched Anuradhapura at Mihintale and extended southwards to reach Matale, which was the gateway to the economically important central regions.

A part at least of the trade that took place on this road was stimulated by the presence of coolie laboureres who were brought from India to work on the coffee plantations. The Indians who disembarked at Mannar struck off inland until they joined the Central Road at Madawachchiya, not far north of Anuradhapura, and thence travelled southwards until Matale was reached. Principally, however, it was the larger economic usefulness of this route that was noteworthy. To begin with, it was along the Central Road that the Jaffna tobacco which was not sent overseas was despatched to the interior for internal consumption. The tobacco, for which there was an increasing demand within the island, was also popular among the coolies from India who customarily bought considerably quantities of it in Matale.[7]

Moreover, it was not unusual for the tobacco traders on their journey southwards to collect as much rice as possible in the Nuwerakalawiya district. The rice was sold to the traders at several points of the district which touched on the Central Road, such as Rambewa, Mihintale, Madawachchiya and Maradankadawela. The last named had become a particularly thriving centre of trade. It was not so much that rice was to be plentifully had as much as the lure of low prices that attracted the tobacco traders. In good seasons when cultivation had not been hampered by inclement weather, a measure of rice in the Anuradhapura markets could be purchased for the lowly sum of 1½d per measure and in the more remote parts of the district for ¾d. The rice was sold by the tobacco traders at Matale—terminal point of their

[7]Adinistration Reports, 1873, p. 170. Report on the Northern Province, W.C. Twynam. Also Administration Reports 1874, p. 61.

journey—at prices which brought them a notable margin of profit. It was also the custom of the tobacco traders on their journey back to buy rice as well as dry grains like gingelly in the Nuwerakalawiya bazaars for sale in Jaffna. But this rice did not fetch as high a price as it did in the markets of Matale and beyond.[8]

Cattle were also driven southwards in great numbers along the Central Road to Matale and beyond. Leisching, who conscientiously kept records of the traffic on this road, had found that as many as 35,000 sheep and goats passed Mihintale southwards in 1870 alone, which was incidentally an index to the enormous number of animals which were imported from India during this period.

Apart from the Central Road, the Anuradhapura district was conveniently linked with the North Western Province in which economic resources were incomparably richer and more varied. Indeed, the fact that the Anuradhapura district customarily drew the largest portion of its supplies from the North Western Province was as true at the end of the nineteenth century as it had been in Rhys Davids' time. Principally there were two routes. The first, the Anuradhapura Puttalam road, linked the district of Nuwerakalawiya with Puttalam, which was the principal seaport of the North Western Province. Naturally, therefore, it was from Puttalam that Nuwerakalawiya obtained its supplies of salt and dried fish. Theoretically Puttalam was also an outlet for the district of Anuradhapura in the direction of Colombo. The second route connected Anuradhapura with Kurunegala, which was connected with the railway at Polgahawela. Despite this, as Rhys Davids complained, the road from Anuradhapura to Kurunegala—theoretically a "principal road"—was in a bad condition. Besides, there was no bridge at the point at which this road had to cross the kala Oya before reaching Kurunegala. This virtually made it impossible for the carts—which were the principal means of conveying goods—to use this route during the rainy season.

Finally, in the Eastern direction, Anuradhapura was conveniently connected to Trincomalee. Timber, which was about the sole commercial commodity which Nuwerakalawiya produced, was taken to Trincomalee for shipment to Colombo or Jaffna. Towards the end of the nineteenth century, the extension of the railway from Kurunegala further north was a great boon to Anuradhapura because it made possible the more expeditious despatch of timber which in Rhys Davids' time had to be "laboriously" taken by cart to Trincomalee. To some extent, Nuwerakalawiya dry grains such as gingelley and *Kurakkan* with a little cotton found their way to Trincomalee along this road. These commodities were traded for the salt fish which was produced in such considerable quantities in Trincomalee and for which there seems to have been a steady demand in Nuwerakalawiya.

There was, of course, a great deal of cart traffic along the Central Road and on the roads to the North Western Province. The railway to Polgahawela had the effect, it would seem, of actually increasing this traffic. Rhys Davids observed in 1871 that the numbers of carts which had been licensed in Nuwerakalawiya alone had within the previous six years almost doubled.

As elsewere in the island, the pressures of economic change had done little to alter the traditional modes of transportation. In the main there were the carts drawn by bullocks which were in widespread use. They particularly suited districts like Nuwerakalawiya in which the Government, due to financial considerations, was compelled to adopt a certain broad division of roads. There were firstly the Principal Roads, also known as the carriage roads. The object was to maintain these roads in good condition and spend less on the second category – the minor roads – which were often called cart roads. The third class of roads, really bridle paths, or riding roads, were of even less importance.

A somewhat picturesque mode of transportation which was popularly resorted to in Anuradhapura and elsewhere were the *tavalams* or pack bulls which were particularly adaptable to the more remote parts of the country where there were only bridle paths. In Rhys Davids' time, there were certain famous *tavalam* routes in Uva and in the Laggala area of the Matale district. For example, salt was moved from Hambantota to Uva along the Wellawaya Lemastota *tavalam* route. There were also the *tavalam* men who brought coffee, arecanuts and other goods from Ratnapura to reach journey's end at Ambalantota in the Southern Province, from which place they collected salt to take on their journey back. In the Nuwerakalawiya district, transportation by pack bulls – the *tavalam* – was a common occurrence even along the principal routes of the district. In 1870 alone the number of *tavalam* cattle that passed Mihintale to and from Matale exceeded 3,800 as compared with the figure of 1800 carts.

III

In other ways too, Rhys Davids found the conditions of work in Anuradhapura much to his liking. Although as a rule he was a trifle over-sensitive about the accommodation provided for him, for once he was pleased on this score. His house, which was reasonably large, had more than three bedrooms with ceilings made by nailing mats on a wooden framework. It was situated within fairly large grounds which were enclosed by a fence. There were three separate gates from the compound, one of which conveniently opened towards the *Kachcheri,* close to where Rhys Davids had to spend many of his working hours. With the onset of the rains in November, however, Rhys Davids was complaining to Twynam that his bungalow was hardly habitable. With his customary fervour, he also wrote about the plight of his subordinates whose more modest houses too had leaking roofs. But by December, these irritations had disappeared and Rhys Davids wrote warmly to Twynam, thanking him for the promptness with which the Government Agent had attended to the repairs.[9]

During this early phase, however, the problem of providing formal monetary security for the post he was holding caused Rhys Davids some uneasiness. On assuming duties, Government Agents as well as certain other categories of public servants—specified in a circular of 1862—were required to sign security bonds. An Assistant Government Agent, who also handled fairly large sums of money in the course of his duties, was not exempted from the requirement although in effect his transactions came constantly under the close scrutiny of his superior. Accordingly, Rhys Davids himself had to provide security for a sum of £10,000 which was regarded as the approximate sum of money which an Assistant Agent would have in his keeping in the course of his duties. Rhys Davids, who had written to friends in England urging them to stand surety on his behalf, was disappointed that they had not answered his letters. He was convinced that they would have done so had he sent along with his letters copies of the bond. This Rhys Davids had been unable to do because John Douglas, who was the Auditor General, had refused to give him additional copies. By January 1872, when he had received a reminder

[9]Lot 41. 185. D.N.A. Rhys Davids to Twynam, 7 December 1871. Lot 41. 184. D.N.A. Rhys Davids to Twynam, 24 November 1871. Lot 41. 217. D. N. A. Rhys Davids to Principal Assistant Civil Engineer and Commissioner of Roads, Jaffna, 26 May 1872.

from the Colonial Secretary about the bond, Rhys Davids was more hopefully looking to friends in Ceylon to help him. Significantly, he wrote to his friend Louis Leisching, who consented to stand security on his behalf.[10]

In spite of this problem which hovered in the background, Rhys Davids threw himself with enthusiasm to his new functions, which were quite numerous. Leisching had listed no less than fourteen distinct spheres of duties which an Assistant Agent had to perform, some of which were in one way or another connected with various ordinances which the government had already enacted. Moreover, there was little prospect of relief as the government took no notice of the suggestions made by the Assistant Agents—not always enclosed by the Government Agent—that additional Assistant Agents should be appointed or that at least the *Kachcheri* apparatus should be strengthened.

Among the more traditional and routine duties of Assistant Agent in Nuwerakalawiya were the judicial functions he exercised as the District Judge, Commissioner of Requests, Police Magistrate and Justice of Peace. It would seem that at first Rhys Davids did not feel the burden of these multifarious judicial duties. Instead, he took upon himself additional tasks. In October 1871, he asked for and obtained appointment as Justice of Peace for the Districts of Kurunegala and Puttalam, which were theoretically outside the administrative and judicial purview of the Nuwerakalawiya district. Rhys Davids believed that such jurisdiction was neccessary if he was to combat cattle thefts which were particularly prevalent in those parts of the Nuwerakalawiya region which bordered on these districts.[11]

Gradually, however, Rhys Davids' zest for his judicial duties evaporated. In spite of himself, the affairs of the District Court became disorganised. This situation was brought about by the prolonged absence on leave of the Court Secretary, a man named Don Wijesinghe, who had not returned to Anuradhapura since December 1870. Leisching, who had reprimanded Wijesinghe, had evidently taken a poor view of Wijesinghe's work. Nevertheless, Wijesinghe's absence was keenly felt. His work was being done by the Tamil Interpreter of the court, an arrangement which Rhys Davids thought

[10]Lot 41. 187. D.N.A. Rhys Davids to Twynam, 9 January 1892. Lot 41. 217. D.N.A. Rhys Davids to Colonial Secretary, 20 January 1872.

[11]Lot 6 (1) 3528. D.N.A. Rhys Davids to Colonial Secretary, 27 October 1871.

was both unsatisfactory and unjust.[12]

In part, at any rate, this unsolved irritation accounted for a suggestion which Rhys Davids made to the Government Agent of the Northern Province, that the Assistant Agent should be relieved of his judicial duties at least during certain periods of the year. Rhys Davids had clearly taken a page from Leisching, who had in his time complained that it was impossible to attend to both the collection of the Grain Tax—which was a tax the Government annually imposed on paddy and other sundry grains produced by peasants throughout the island—as well as the judicial duties, at one and the same time. The former involved extensive work including the preparation of Grain Tax registers. The work had to be done with great care under the personal supervision of the Assistant Agent who diligently visited each village for the purpose.

The unorthodoxy of Rhys Davids' proposal was only matched by a kindred idea he urged on William Twynam that at any rate an additional Civil Servant should be attached to the Nuwerakalawiya agency during the time when the Grain Tax work was being taken in hand. Projecting his own predilection for Nuwerakalawiya, Rhys Davids added that there were few districts in Ceylon where a Civil Servant was brought more into contact with the people or had opportunities of getting acquainted with the work of a Civil Servant.[13]

However, it was but natural that Twynam should have ignored Rhys Davids. For one thing, in all other agencies the Assistant Agents were saddled with similar responsibilities. It has also been a long established—and one may add, an almost hallowed tradition for Assistant Agents to exercise the dual functions of administrative and judicial work. In any event, whatever the merit of Rhys Davids' proposals, there was little that Twynam could individually do. Indeed, Twynam laconically wrote back that he saw no need for an additional Civil Servant in Nuwerakalawiya.[14]

Rhys Davids has consequently to abandon his proposals. He was however personally as convinced as ever that additional assistance would make the administration of agricultural affairs more effective.

[12] Lot 6 (1) 3527. D.N.A. Rhys Davids to Colonial Secretary, 26 August 1871. Also Rhys Davids to Colonial Secretary, 10 February 1872.

[13] Lot 41. 187. D.N.A. Rhys Davids to Twynam, 21 May 1872.

[14] Lot 41. 130. D.N.A. Twynam to Rhys Davids, 1 June 1872.

Quite early in his career in Anuradhapura, Rhys Davids had grasped the notion fully that in an essentially undiversified and simple rural economy, agrarian problems were of paramount importance.

4

PEASANTS, TANKS AND GRAIN

BRITISH rule in South Asia, particularly in the nineteenth century, was largely concerned with the problems of rural economies which traditionally existed in the region. Policy was clearly a blend between a prudent desire to refrain from doing violence to existing economic and social systems, and the encouragement of the ethic of individual competition and *laissez faire* capitalism. The specific everyday tasks of official activity in the rural sector, however, seemed to somewhat make obscure the underlying central theme.

In Nuwerakalawiya economic activity primarily centered around the cultivation of paddy. As elsewhere in the island where paddy was predominant, an Assistant Government Agent had to devote much of his time and energies to the provision of irrigational facilities and the collection of the Grain Tax. These were characteristic ruler functions. Leasing of government lands to peasants for paddy cultivation was a third aspect which the peculiar conditions prevailing in Nuwerakalawiya had also made somewhat important in Rhys Davids' time.

II

The dependence of peasant agriculture on irrigation was a recurring commonplace in the writings of British officials in the nineteenth century. The theme remained unaltered, despite the attention drawn from time to time by some Government Agents to more novel modes of increasing the yield of paddy. The use of fertilizers, experiments with new varieties of paddy, and even the introduction of English ploughs on which certain Government Agents placed a somewhat exaggerated reliance, mirrored this tendency.

The dependence was all the more pronounced in those districts of the island—the central highlands broadly excepted—which were characterised by meagre rainfall, but which were otherwise suited for the cultivation of paddy. In consequence, the preservation of water became a matter of vital necessity if cultivation was to take place at all. In order to do so, centuries earlier, the Sinhalese kings had devised an elaborate system of tanks and canals which suggested that they had commanded vast resources of labour and technical skill. With time, however, the ancient irrigation system had fallen into disuse, signifying too the decadence of the peasant economy with which it was symbiotically connected.

At the beginning of the British era, the picture had changed little. As the successors to the Dutch—who had themselves been aware of the ancient system of irrigation—the British had at first tried to restore some of the tanks. However, they soon abandoned the efforts partly because their economic policies were still undefined. Neither did financial conditions warrant such activity. Nonetheless, throughout the first half of the nineteenth century a few British officials saw obvious economic advantages from irrigation development. Conspicuous among them was Anthony Bertolacci who, in evaluating the island's economic potentialities with painstaking thoroughness, in a book on Ceylon, stressed the connection between an adverse balance of trade which Ceylon had to bear, and which was clearly aggravated by large imports of rice, and the development of irrigation.

In the troubled 1840s, the issue ceased to be one of abstract speculation in which the merits of the Corn Laws, the theories of Adam Smith or the lesser known British economist Patrick Colquhoun had sometimes prefigured. During this period the desirability of restoring the ancient tanks was specifically suggested to the Colonial Office by the Government of Ceylon. But the Colonial Office was sceptical. The benefits which might be fairly immediately expected in a colony continually hamstrung by recurring financial difficulties appeared to be doubtful. Besides, with the clear need to define investment priorities, it was a moot point whether the restoration of irrigation works would be of general economic benefit because in the areas in which the tanks existed there were only a few scattered hamlets. After the exchange of lengthy despatches, the question was once again put by but not before Earl Grey, the Secretary of State for the colonies, had laid down in 1849 a general principle which was of considerable usefulness to the Government of Ceylon when the restoration of irrigation works was ultimately taken in hand. Government expenditure of irrigation was to take the form of grants-in-aid. The grants were to be restricted to those irrigation works in which a considerable amount of native labour was employed or to works from which a fair economic return could be expected, at least, in the sense of "increasing the productive powers of the Island."

The question, however, was revived by Sir Henry Ward, who assumed the governorship of the island in 1856. Ward believed that the Government had almost a moral obligation to take in hand the ancient irrigation works. The Government's decision to commit the Colony to an enormous outlay of capital in order to build a railway from Colombo to the interior which was to benefit a small class of European coffee planters, merely served to augment the sense of obligation. Not unmindful of the objection which had been hitherto urged, Ward declared that the restoration of irrigation works would result in an extension of paddy cultivation which in turn would increase the revenue of the Government which customarily took a tenth of the paddy, produced as a tax. Moreover, what little experience there was to go by warranted the belief that irrigation would stimulate the demand for land, thereby increasing the revenue of the Government through land sales.

Ward's hand was considerably strengthened by the efforts of John Bailey, who was the Assistant Government Agent in the Badulla District. Bailey had restored small irrigation works in the Uva District, with a limited outlay of capital—and what was more significant, with the assistance of the peasants themselves. Bailey's able reports, which were well received in the Colonial Office, had demonstrated that the restoration of irrigation works was practicable quite apart from the effect it had in stimulating the economic interest of the peasant.

Moreover, Ward's governorship coincided with a succession of years in which the Government of Ceylon had the benefit of revenue surpluses. By a series of ordinances which enabled Ward to use the surpluses on useful public works, Ward allocated considerable sums for irrigation. The most notable was ordinance 5 of 1858 which set apart 25,000 for a number of irrigation works in the Southern Province.

More significantly, Ward put the administration of irrigation affairs on an institutionalised basis. In the course of his researches into ancient irrigation, Bailey had uncovered the probable theoretical basis on which irrigation affairs had been administered in ancient times. It became evident that traditionally the cultivators themselves had regulated not only irrigation but the affairs relating to the cultivation of paddy as well by means of custom. They had done so primarily using village councils or the ancient *gamsabas* which they themselves elected. In the course of time these institutions too had become virtually extinct. The practical effectiveness of the few that were presumed to exist in isolated areas had been wholly reduced or emasculated by the laws and institutions which the British had established since the British fiat penetrated the remotest hamlets of the land. In 1856 Ward made legal provision both for the restoration of ancient customs for irrigation and paddy cultivation, as well as for the revival of village councils. The councils were empowered to levy fines not exceeding 2 for breaches of the ancient customs.

The modest scope of these laws was considerably enlarged by the Paddy Lands Irrigation ordinance of 1861 which clearly made the more formal government apparatus involved in the administration of irrigation affairs. Its distinctive features were the creation of irrigation districts for the better enforcement of ancient customs, the election of headmen as an alternative to village councils—but with the same power to enforce ancient customs—and thirdly, the power given to a Government Agent or to his assistant to undertake particular irrigation works if he thought that such works would benefit the lands of more than ten cultivators living in the district concerned. The ordinance further prescribed that a Government Agent should, in such a case, summon a meeting of the landowners, and, if two thirds of their number consented to the undertaking, the amount of subscription which each should pay—either in money or in labour—was decided. These decisions were binding on all the landowners whose lands would benefit by the irrigation work undertaken.

Naturally problems of irrigation had been of proverbial importance to successive incumbents in the Anuradhapura agency—an area which stood to gain much from the irrigation laws. Rhys Davids' own efforts were directed towards the adoption of an irrigation policy geared to suit certain local exigencies.

In his time, as elsewhere in the island, in Anuradhapura too, irrigation activities were largely governed by the Paddy Lands Irrigation Ordinance of 1867. The Ordinance retained some of the features of its predecessor, whose object too had been the restoration of irrigation works. Distinctively, however, the Ordinance brought the

Government into closer collaboration with the peasants. To begin with, there were to be informal discussions between a Government Agent or his assistant and the landowning peasants about the restoration of irrigation works in the area. If the peasants decided that a particular irrigation work should be taken in hand with Government assistance, it was the duty of the Government Agent to make a formal application on their behalf to the Governor. The Government Agent could, on an occasion, urge the feasibility of the project and was expected to mention the names as well as the extents of land of those peasant landholders who would benefit. If he thought the proposal worthwhile, the Governor could formally call for plans and estimates for the consideration of a special board which would consist of the Government Agent concerned, the Surveyor General and the Director of Public Works. If the project was approved, the individual landholders were informed. The Ordinance stipulated also that the money spent by the Government should be repaid in ten yearly installments. In this context, it was the duty of the Government Agent to assess the amount which each individual cultivator should contribute towards the annual installment.

It had also been recognised that the Ordinance could become a dead letter without the active participation of the Government Agents of the various districts. It was the Government Agent who convened meetings of cultivators, explained its provisions and fixed the details of a specific undertaking. In general, he exercised his influence to induce the peasants to avail themselves of a measure which, at least at the time of its implementation, was widely regarded in official circles as likely to benefit the peasants immeasurably.

Rhys Davids, who viewed the Ordinance in this light, showed great energy in getting the peasants together even in the more remote parts of the Anuradhapura district.[1] In presiding over meetings with peasants, he noted everywhere the all too evident desire of the peasants to have the old tanks restored to use. There were in the district over two thousand such tanks. The majority of the tanks had been breached by the peasants themselves cutting the tank bunds indiscriminately whenever water was required. This practice, according to Rhys Davids, had gone on unchecked for several years. Sometimes—

[1]Lot 41.252 D.N.A. Diary entry of Rhys Davids, 19 October 1871. Anthony Bertolacci, *A View of the Agricultural, Commercial and Financial Interests of Ceylon*, London, 1817. Lennox A. Mills, *op. cit.* p. 130ff.

especially in those tanks in which the traditional mechanism or services provided for the egress of water had long ceased to function—breaches were the inevitably consequence of an excess of impounded water spilling over at various points in the bund following heavy rains.[2]

Much depended on the energy and tact shown by the Assistant Agent. Rhys Davids reported that there was a fairly large tank in Maha Halmillewe which had been long since breached by floods. The landholders of the adjacent fields who were summoned by Rhys Davids told him that they had made several unsuccessful attempts to repair the breaches. Rhys Davids estimated that about £75 would be required to effect the repair. "The shareholders say they are willing to pay about £6 a year for ten years if the repair could be executed for £60 or £70. All agree to this and express gratitude to the government."[3]

In Loku Moragasdigillia, Rhys Davids discoverd that there was no proper sluice to the tank which served the area. Instead there were four large and three small breaches which had all been caused by floods. The cost of repairing the breaches, as well as that of installing a new sluice, was estimated at £80. Rhys Davids thought that this amount could easily be repaid by the landholders who would be able to irrigate an additional 15 *amunums* of paddy once the tank was properly restored to use. When summoned, the landholders concerned expressed their willingness to have the tank repaired if the cost did not exceed £50. They were all agreed that Rhys Davids should get an engineer to estimate costs.[4]

In the course of his circuits, Rhys Davids' attention had been drawn to a fairly large tank in the Kahatagasdigilia area which had a defective sluice. The peasants who depended on this tank as well as the *Ratemahatmaya* thought that the repair would cost about £48. Rhys Davids, who was aware that his predecessor had obtained a professional estimate of the repair, was sure that the repair could be effected within £30. The response of the landholders was commendable. Instead of paying the Government by small annual installments, they showed a willingness to pay £15. They were only concerned that the government officials themselves should supervise the work if the work was to be done by hired masons, and that if the repair was not finally undertaken, their money should be returned to them.[5]

[2]Lot 41.185 D.N.A. Rhys Davids,to Twynam, 1 March 1872.
[3]Lot 41.252 D.N.A. Diary entry of Rhys Davids,5 October 1871.
[4]*Ibid.*
[5]Lot 41.252 D.N.A. Diary entry of Rhys Davids. 2, October 1871.

Rhys Davids, who was not unaware of the unsuccessful efforts of his predecessors to repair the Divulwewa tank, was hardly hopeful when he summoned the peasants who had lands in the vicinity. The breach in the Divulwewa tank was indeed formidable, being 64 yards long and 84 yards broad at the base. The estimated cost of the repair was £150. On the other hand, Rhys Davids was aware that about 60 acres of virgin land could be *'asweddumised'*, or brought under cultivation for the first time, once the tank was repaired. In the event the peasants were willing to commit themselves to £200. Not only did they undertake to repay this in ten annual installments, but to maintain the tank in good order when the repairs had been completed. They told Rhys Davids that they were willing to work at the breach as paid labourers. They were anxious that the work should be entrusted to an engineer.[6]

However, it was not always that these discussions with peasants were successful. Rhys Davids encountered a great deal of suspicion among them with regard to the Irrigation Ordinance. Convinced that the repairs to the Kalpe tank would require a modest sum of £20 he had proposed that the tank be entrusted to a Government engineer. But the peasants concerned held fast to the belief that the repair could be effected more cheaply by hiring a Tamil mason. A diary entry which Rhys Davids made was self-explanatory.

> After the usual talk and explanation it is resolved by a majority that government help be not required. One old *Gamarala* in particular one of the principal spokesmen on the occasion seems to think that the irrigation scheme was only a trick to make the people's land (*Wesian Santaka*)government property (*Raja Santaka*) and he simply disbelieved any assertions to the contrary given by *Ratemahatmayas* or assistant government agents who are in government employ. It is most surprising to find among those most concerned such ignorance of a beneficial law passed years ago.[7]

Antipathy of this sort was more explicitly manifested when Rhys Davids met the peasants who lived in the neighbourhood of Manankattiyawewa. The urgency of repairing this tank was brought home to Rhys Davids who saw that the adjacent fields were being cultivated during the *Yala* season only and that, too, not always. What water

[6]Lot 41. 252 D.N.A. Diary entry of Rhys Davids,3 October 1871.
[7]*Ibid.*

there had been in this tank had escaped in spite of a sluice causing the failure of an entire crop. Rhys Davids' diary made dismal reading.

> There was the usual talk . . . one spokesman among the shareholders, a sharp faced little man, suggested in a clever speech that as government had at first on the introduction of the road tax promised to make roads for the people if they paid 1/6 a head and then had raised the rate . . . so this might be a scheme for putting a fresh tax on their paddy lands which they could not possibly bear. This argument combined with the opposition of the older and stupider among the *Gamaralas* (the Bulankulame Gamarala especially showed his stupidity by the questions he asked) carried the meeting with it The statement of the asst. Govt. agent was regarded as untrue and unsatisfactory. It was resolved by majority that the aid of govt. not be requested.[8]

The negative response to the Ordinance was to some measure dictated by self-interest. The truth was that the outlay on repairs which the peasant landholders collectively agreed to reimburse to Government pressed unequally on them. Those who were tolerably well off, or who had the bulk of the land surrounding a particular tank and therefore were likely to gain most by its repair, were disposed to fall in line with the Government Agent when he urged its repair. Conversely, all too evident was the antipathy of the small landholders who used their numerical strength at the meetings with the Government Agent to oppose the proposed repair.

Concerning other aspects of this measure, too, Rhys Davids' observations shed considerable light on peasant attitudes. They were extraordinarily sensitive to the question of costs. The feeling was widespread that it was cheaper to effect repairs to tanks by their own efforts than by means of the Ordinance. There was some reason for the prejudice. For one thing, peasant landholders were often discouraged because the broadly tentative estimates for repair agreed to during the initial discussions with the Assistant Government Agent were invariably altered by the technical officers of the Government, compelling the peasants to pay much more for the repair than they had informally covenanted for. The Ordinance obliged the Government Agent to decide at the meetings of the peasants which he summoned, the amount which each should subscribe—either in money

[8]Lot 41. 252 D.N.A. Diary entry of Rhys Davids, 7 October 1871.

or in labour—towards the cost of the proposed project. Cost considerations were also at the bottom of irritation concerning the installation of "Molesworth" sluices. There iron sluices, which were used in several parts of the island, had been found by long experience to be technically satisfactory and were much favoured by Government officials. As against this, however, one had to weigh the cost of transporting a Molesworth sluice, which in Anuradhapura was sold for about £50. There was in addition the cost of installing the sluice, combined invariably with the necessity of repairing a fairly large breach caused by inserting the sluice in the bund of a tank.[9]

Clearly the problems of irrigation in the Anuradhapura area were beset with difficulties. In their face Rhys Davids' initial enthusiasm gradually evaporated. On one occasion he gave vent to a sense of increasing impotence and remarked to Twynam that as far as Anuradhapura was concerned, the Irrigation Ordinance was a dead letter. On the other hand, Rhys Davids was sceptical about the success which the peasants would achieve in irrigation matters if they were left to their own devices. He noted with misgiving a certain partiality which landholders showed for the traditional methods of repairing tanks. Such repairs were usually undertaken by a class of people who were known as the *Kulamkattis*. These professional tank menders were either natives of the Jaffna District or were those who came from South India to the tank districts of the island during the dry season when repairs to tanks were being taken in hand. In fact, as Professional masons—who incidentally were also Tamils—were in short supply, the itinerant bands of *Kulamkattis* were very much sought after by the landholders who were familiar with their mode of operation. To begin with, the principal *Kulamkattiya* inspected the breach in the tank and having consulted with his men, demanded a certain amount. Usually the landholders succeeded by hard bargaining in reducing this amount by a quarter or even as much as by a clear half. Once agreement was reached and the work had begun, the *Kulamkattis* were supplied with rice and provisions whose value was deducted from the amount which the landholders had agreed to pay. Sometimes instead of a rough and ready estimate, the parties agreed that the repair should be made by the cubic foot, "payment being

[9]Lot 41. 185 D.N.A. Rhys Davids to Twynam, 1 March 1872.

made on measurement not of the repaired breach but of the hole or holes from which the earth was taken." According to Rhys Davids, for a hole of 4 cubic yards, a sum between 35 and 50 cents was charged. Rhys Davids had also observed that, unlike the Jaffna *Kulamkattis*, the "Coast" or Indian *Kulamkattis* actually preferred this mode of payment. Whichever system was adopted, the bulk of the payment was only made when the work had been completed. Interestingly enough, Rhys Davids remarks that "the transaction was very often concluded with a quarrel."[10]

Like many of his contemporaries Rhys Davids took a dim view of the *Kulamkattis*. There was considerable evidence to show that they exploited the peasants who were plainly unaware that the *Kulamkattis* lacked any competence for the type of work which they undertook. As Leisching had remarked, although presumably in ancient times stone hewing had been a common art in the Anuradhapura district, the work of the modern mason was inferior and failed to resist the action of water beyond a short period. Hence the disconcerting need to repair the same breach in a tank several times, an expense which the run of the mill landholder with his slender resources could ill afford.[11]

An example—although admittedly an extreme one—was the Kulundewa tank in the Matale District. The cost of repairing a single breach in this tank had added up to about £1000 over a number of years. In spite of this, when R. Massie, the Assistant Government Agent who incidentally favoured the adoption of some kind of *Rajakariya* system to keep the tanks in good order, reported on the tank, the breach had not been satisfactorily repaired.[12] Insofar as the Anuradhapura District was concerned, there was first the testimony of Twynam who remarked to the Colonial Secretary that until he himself had visited the landholders, he had not realised to what extent they were being duped by spurious tank menders.[13] The observations of Louis Leisching had been more poignantly

[10]Lot 41. 217 D.N.A. Rhys Davids to the Director of Public Works, 21 March 1872.

[11]Report on the Nuwerakalawiya District. L. Leisching, Administration Reports, 1870, p. 95.

[12]Report on the Matale District, R. Massie, Administration Reports 1872, p. 63.

[13]Twynam to Colonial Secretary, 21 April 1871. Twynam observed that the peasant in the Nuwerakalawiya District appeared to think that "giants or some other wonderful race who had disappeared from the face of the earth, had originally made the tanks and that all that could now be done was merely to patch them up."

expressed. "It is heartbreaking to see poor fellows who have paid some swindlers to have their tanks repaired and who when it is all washed away with the rains, stand on the bank mournfully contemplating the ruin."

For his own part, Rhys Davids vividly recalled the vicissitudes that had befallen certain landholders who had attempted to repair the Galapitigala tank in the Habarana area. He discovered that their ancestors had taken in hand the repair of this old tank in 1832 when the village had been first colonised. During the course of this repair, which dragged on for the next seven years, a great many Tamil tank menders had been employed. About 1862 a new chapter of troubles began when a major breach in the tank had occurred. The landholders collected about £35 to employ a number of *Kulamkattis*. But in 1869 a more formidable breach occurred at the identical point in the bund. On this occasion too a sum of £50 was subscribed and the work was handed over to professional Tamils. In addition, the landholders had themeselves given freely of their labour for a month in assisting the repair. Moreover, convinced that the recurring breach had been caused by the absence of a proper sluice, they had collected a further £15 in an unsuccessful attempt to blast a rock in order to install a masonry sluice.

Their woes, however, had not ended. Rhys Davids described the sequel in a picturesque entry in his diary.

> . . . a hali man (cinnamon peeler) came and claimed the land. They paid him 70 *ridis* (or *Loku Tuttus* = £2-7-8.). Then another claimed it. They paid him also £2-7-8. and got *talapats* from both.

When a third claimed the land, but the landholders refused to pay him, they were involved in litigation for a period of seven years. Rhys Davids estimated that in all, within the space of a few years, the landholders had spent a sum exceeding 136 in a desperate bid to make the tank function. In spite of it all, the fields surrounding the Galapitigala tank had been left uncultivated for several years.[14]

The inadequacies of the Irrigation Ordinance were made all the more evident when questions pertaining to the repair of the bigger tanks arose. Such repairs necessarily involved a large outlay of money which in terms of the Ordinance increased correspondingly the demands made on the individual landholder. The Hurulu tank,

[14]Lot 41. 252 D.N.A. Diary entry of Rhys Davids, 7 October 1871.

for example, was formed by a bund which ran for over three miles. This tank had several sluices, some of which had to be repaired. In addition, there was an enormous breach in the bund which had in Rhys Davids' belief clearly occurred decades earlier. The breach had steadily increased until a huge pool had been formed below the tank. Rhys Davids estimated that it would cost £750 to repair the breach, quite apart from the additional expenditure which would have to be met by the wholesale replacement of the sluice nearest the breach and in general masonry work.[15]

In these circumstances, even though the lands surrounding large tanks were sometimes occupied by tolerably wealthy landholders, the Government was wary. Nuwerawewa—a particularly large tank in the heart of Anuradhapura—had a very large breach along its bund. There were also two *horouwas* or outlets which were in a state of disrepair. Much of the surrounding land belonged to the two ancient and wealthy families of Nuwerawewa Banda and Bulankulame Vidane. Rhys Davids reported to Twynam that each family was willing to pay either £25 annually towards the repayment of any expenditure which the Government might incur in restoring the tank to complete use, or to hand over to the Government one crop annually. The Government, however, did not respond to these proposals.[16]

Sometimes the cost factor was complicated by an extraneous consideration. In Rhys Davids' time there was a considerable demand for uncultivated lands surrounding the large tanks. The evidence suggests that this demand emanated not from landless peasants but from those who were already landholders and who were possessed of moderate sums of money to buy small parcels of land. They were convinced that the cultivated lands surrounding large tanks would be better suited for cultivation than the lands near small tanks.

But the Assistant Government Agents to whom such requests for land were made first were sceptical because they realised that it was virtually impossible for the peasants to incur the triple expenditure of repairing a large tank, buying the lands surrounding the tank from the Government, and, in addition, necessarily spending a considerable amount of money in *asweddumsing* the land. Initially, in such

[15]Lot 41. 252 D.N.A. Diary entry of Rhys Davids, 7 October 1871.
[16]*Ibid.* 2 September 1871.

circumstances the parleys which an Assistant Government Agent had with landholders usually came to nought. Well over a hundred peasants who lived in certain villages in the Anuradhapura District had applied to Government for the purchase of lands adjoining Sangili Karandawa tank in the Madawachchiya area. Rhys Davids was impressed by the enthusiasm of the applicants who were looking forward to *asweddumising* about 600 acres of land. "They seem to put themselves entirely into the hands of the Government," he recorded, "and only want to be told what they should do." When he had fully inspected the tank, however, Rhys Davids found that certain repairs which would have to be effected before the tank could be of any usefulness would cost £600. When this was pointed out to the peasants, they virtually declared that they were averse to buying the surrounding land until the Government had repaired the tank.[17]

Generally, however, in urging the adoption of these schemes Rhys Davids put forward a number of considerations. Imbued with an essentially paternalistic approach to administration, Rhys Davids thought that the Government should take prudent note of evidence of enterprise among the peasants, especially since a kind of inflexible apathy was more typical. Moreover, he was outraged at the spectacle of the old tanks passing into slow but certain ruin. In each instance there were certain definite advantages to be secured. For example, he believed that Sangili Kanadarawa should be restored partly because of the proximity of this tank of Madawachchiya, a rising centre of commercial importance at the interstices of the Central, Mannar and Trincomalee roads. Similarly, much of the land that could be irrigated if the Hurulu tank were repaired lay close to an area to which Rhys Davids prophesied roads would be made at some future date from Habarana or Maradankadawela. As for the Nuwerawewa tank, its continued neglect would, he warned, make the occurrence of a second breach near the eastern *horouwa* inevitable. Apart from the hazards this would cause to the town of Anuradhapura, Rhys Davids believed that this would disrupt a supply of water "which though not much in use now will be certainly required hereafter."

In terms of economic returns too, Rhys Davids believed that the repair of the larger tanks would be particularly feasible. Firstly, the Government could recoup its expenditure over the years by the annual payments which the cultivators who directly benefited from

[17] *Ibid.* 20 September 1871.

the ordinance had to make. More significantly in the long run there was the gains government would make indirectly by the extension of irrigable lands bringing in their wake larger increments of the Grain Tax.

However, with mounting despondency Rhys Davids realised that if the large tanks could not be repaired under the Ordinance, because of the bigger outlay involved, there was little that could be done, especially in Anuradhapura. From a revenue point of view, Anuradhapura was not remarkable for its prosperity. Its principal source of revenue—paddy cultivation—was ironically dependent on irrigation facilities. Other than the years in which drought would lead to severe diminution of the grain produced, leading to widespread economic distress, even in the "good years," revenue was at best on a par with expenditure according to Rhys Davids. There were no surpluses, much less a special reserve for irrigation.

Twynam was sympathetic. He discussed in detail the larger tanks referred to by Rhys Davids and recalled how he had himself tried to have them repaired on earlier occasions. Part of the difficulty concerned the unhelpful position taken by the Public Works Department on which the government relied to carry out the actual work of restoring irrigation tanks. For years this department had pleaded the exigencies of irrigation work in other districts to account for its failure to send an Irrigation Assistant to take in hand the demands of the Nuwerakalawiya region. In the same breath, however, Twynam urged Rhys Davids to accept the position fully and squarely that the larger tanks in the district could not be repaired under the Ordinance because of the poverty of the peasants. Instead, he laid down as clear policy the rule that Rhys Davids should concentrate on the restoration of the smaller tanks—some of which he specifically mentioned—which the peasants themselves would be able to cope with.

Nonetheless, Twynam took up the matter with the Colonial Secretary, drawing particular attention to Rhys Davids' correspondence. The Colonial Secretary, for his part, preferred to go by the counsels of prudence urged by the Director of Public Works, who made it clear that the government should do no more than attempt to restore the small tanks by means of the Ordinance. Apart from the poverty of the people which made this policy inevitable, the implication clearly was that in remote areas with a limited and scattered population, large scale irrigation ventures would not be economically feasible.[18]

"In other words," summed up Rhys Davids bitterly, "the Public Works Department have only one officer who makes estimates of tank repairs and he is so overworked that after five years waiting the people of this district are told that their wants cannot be attended to and this is treated as a matter of course." He added that some other provision must be made which would bring "joy to hearts of nearly 60,000 people—which though it sounds sentimental is a fact not unworthy of the consideration of a British government."

III

In spite of these gloomy forebodings, as the restoration of an increasingly larger number of tanks was being taken in hand, there was a perceptible increase in the demand for lands surrounding the tanks.

Usually the peasants leased such land from the government partly in the belief that tank lands were necessarily more fertile than lands situated elsewhere. In Rhys Davids' time the increase in the number of applications for leases was also a reaction to the hardening of official attitudes towards chena cultivation, which had compelled the peasants to resort increasingly to paddy cultivation.

Rhys Davids was enthusiastic. Reflected in the demand for tank lands were the stirrings of enterprise on the part of a conventionally apathetic peasantry. Moreover, the leases were probably the sole means of putting under the plough the large areas of cultivated lands which were found near the tanks.

Conversely, Rhys Davids expressed great dissatisfaction concerning certain features in the system of leasing lands which he feared would have the effect of dampening this enthusiasm. He complained, for example, that peasants who leased tank lands did not have any worthwhile security of tenure and were summarily ejected. Moreover, to insist that lessees should be prompt in the payment of their dues was also fairly unjust if one took into consideration the uncertainties of paddy cultivation in the Nuwerakalawiya Destrict. Primarily, however, Rhys Davids drew attention to the tiresome formalities which encumbered the grant of leases. He pointed out to

[18]Lot 41. 129 D.N.A. Twynam to Rhys Daivds, 20 January 1872. Lot 20. 305, Colonial Secretary to Twynam, 22 April 1872.

Twynam that as a rule, nineteen months elapsed between the application for a lease—made in the first instance to the Assistant Government Agent—and the recepit of the lease bond. The application passed through several hands including those of Government Agent whose endorsement of the lease application was necessary. Rhys Davids declared that there were no less than sixteen stages involved. During this time, the harassed applicant had to make frequent visits to the *Kachcheri.* These difficulties were multiplied if there were several applications for different parts of a land adjoining a tank.[19]

In a subsequent letter to Twynam concerning the number of copies of a lease that had to be prepared, Rhys Davids asked Twynam whether after all it was "absolutely necessary to have leases at all." It was invariably the practice of the Government to grant lease applications. Moreover, the peasants clamoured for leases not so much because of the legal rights which they thereby obtained, but because they held tank lands in high esteem. Instead of leases, therefore, Rhys Davids urged that records kept in the *Kachcheri* of the Crown lands should *per se* be sufficient proof of the obligation of the peasants to pay rent.[20]

Twynam, however, was not prepared to make a radical departure from established practices. If there were delays in the issue of leases in the Anuradhapura *Kachcheri,* Rhys Davids had only himself to blame. Rather unreasonably, Twynam remarked that so long as Assistant Government Agent was personally interested in the welfare of the people,

> The work of supervision in the Head Office amounts almost to a mere matter of form . . . But when for want of supervision on the spot, business such as that connected with the leasing of lands had fallen into a state of confusion in which you report it to be . . .

it was necessary for the Government Agent to go into details even though the issue of the leases would be delayed. Rhys Davids was also mistaken in supposing that it was Twynam's habit, as the Government Agent, to grant every lease application "merely on the recommendation of the assistant agents." On the contrary, in the *Kachcheri* in Jaffna, lease applications from the several sub-agencies were gone into with care, and in fact, certain applications had been rejected.

[19]Lot 41. 251 D.N.A. Diary entry of Rhys Davids, 1 January 1872 (sent as letter to Twynam).

[20]Lot 41, 187 D.N.A. Rhys Davids to Twynam, 15 February 1872.

Twynam suggested to Rhys Davids that, as in the *Kachcheris* of Mannar and Muliaitivu, the applications for leases should in the first instance be referred to the *Ratemahatmayas*, and not to a host of inferior officials. Twynam also cautioned Rhys Davids that it was customary for peasants in Anuradhapura to apply for leases merely to forestall others who genuinely wished to lease tank lands. In fact, such spurious applicants were only too glad to postpone the issue of lease bonds as much as possible.[21]

In spite of Twynam's arguments, Rhys Davids did not alter his views on the question. But whenever he had reason to correspond with Twynam on specific problems relating to leases, he prudently refrained from alluding to the larger issues. Instead when the time came to draft the annual administration report for the Nuwerakalawiya District, he made use of the opportunity to criticise the prevailing system with regard to the issue of leases.

Interestingly, neither Rhys Davids nor Twynam referred to land leases as a potential source of revenue. A striking feature in the revenue structure of the Nuwerakalawiya District was the absence of land sales. In other districts—indeed, wherever conditions were congenial to the growth of coffee—there was a considerable demand for Crown lands, which accounted at least a fifth of the total revenue. In Anuradhapura, of course, there was no comparable demand for land which made annual revenue earnings in this district much less elastic than elsewhere. Moreover, some of Rhys Davids' predecessors had complained that because there were no facilities for surveying Crown lands, there was little prospect of bringing to the market even limited amount of land. It may also be presumed that the native Kandyan peasantry lacked the resources with which to buy land. On the other hand, leasing of tank lands was more realistically within their reach. Significantly, the revenue from land leases increased from a modest Rs. 74.87 in 1868 to Rs. 670.81 in 1872.[22]

IV

A Government Agent's energies were, however, somewhat more wholly taken up with the Grain Tax. In several districts the tax,

[21]Lot 41. 253 D.N.A. Twynam to Rhys Davids, 20 February 1872.

[22]Report on the Nuwerakalawiya District, G.W. Patterson, Administration Reports, 1868, p. 164; Report on the Nuwerakalawiya District, L.Leisching, Administration Reports, 1869, p. 104; Report on the Nuwerakalawiya District, Hay Cameron, Administration Reports, 1872, p. 113.

sometimes referred to also as the Paddy Tax, was a particularly important source of revenue. Economic variations which existed between one region and another—such as for example the cultivation of coffee in certain districts and its absence in others—did not reduce its importance. In Anuradhapura in particular, almost the entire revenue was derived from the source. In 1869 out of a total revenue collection of £4,528, the Grain Tax accounted for £2,963. In 1870 when the total revenue was about £3,451, the Grain Tax amounted to £2,571.

In spite of its universal importance, however, there was no rigid uniformity in the collection of the Grain Tax. For one thing, the proportion of the produce which the government taxed varied considerabiy from half the crop—in those areas where conditions were fairly favourable for paddy cultivation and where high yields might be expected—to a twentieth in the less favoured districts. Moreover, with regard to the mode of collection too, in some districts the tax was rented at special sales which the government held for the purpose, and in other districts it was collected by commutation. In short, the Grain Tax had metamorphosed from the fairly straightforward though cumbersome business of taking the government's share of the grain in kind after the crops had been harvested, to the annual payment of a given quantity of grain, usually in money, before the crops were gathered in.

In Anuradhapura where both modes of collecting the tax had existed for several years, Rhys Davids was particularly critical about the renting system. Its most objectionable feature was that it enabled an intermediary class—the renters—to dominate the cultivators.

To begin with, every year a minor government official, usually a *Korala,* would set about estimating the extent sown and the probable yield from the fields within his administrative division. Not only had several fields to be estimated but this had also to be done within a comparatively short time. An estimate could be made only after the grain was sufficiently mature. On the other hand, there was little time between this condition and the time when the crops had to be reaped. In spite of these drawbacks, the broadly tentative estimates helped the government Agent to determine the sum at which the government should auction the right to collect the Paddy Tax at public sales which were held for the purpose. The records of estimates of previous years were also useful.

The stage was thus set for what followed. In Anuradhapura as elsewhere in the island the rents were usually bought by traders. Legally it was possible for the peasants or the cultivators themselves to farm their rents. In practical circumstances, largely the lack of money, made this virtually impossible. In assessments each field was not treated as a distinct unit and rented separately. Instead several different fields were grouped into large units for the purpose. The larger units carried correspondingly large rents which necessarily precluded the individual cultivator from bidding for the rents himself at the government sales. Nor was it possible for the cultivator to advance in money the government's share—as renters were required to—at the conclusion of these sales and before the crop was actually reaped.

By contrast the traders were not hampered by these limitations. On the contrary they were sometimes able to exercise their economic power in a patently perverse manner. Although Rhys Davids himself makes no mention of it, traders would combine and refrain from competitive bidding in order to secure the rent at a lower figure than the government was hoping to obtain. Primarily the absence of competition from other groups—such as the peasants—brought about this situation. A peripherally contributory factor was the foreknowledge which the traders had of the *Korala* estimates which as a matter of course were made available for public inspection in the *Kachcheris* before the sales took place.[23]

Such situations were, however, clearly exceptional. As the evidence suggests, generally the government was able to secure advantageous terms at the sales. Moreover, theoretically if he were confronted with a combination of refractory renters, a government Agent could always cancel a sale and make alternative arrangements to collect the tax. For their own part, the traders were only too aware that they in turn had the edge over the cultivators in collecting the tax.

This was to some extent made possible by the laws which defined the relations between the renters and the cultivators. A cultivator was obliged to give notice to the renter of his intention to reap his crop, in order to ensure that the cultivator did not defraud the renter by concealing part of the crop. If the cultivator failed to give notice, he was liable to pay damages to the renter over and above the percentage of the crop—a tenth in Anuradhapura—to which the renter was in any

[23]Lot 41. 252 D.N.A. Diary entry of Rhys Davids, 12 September 1871.

event entitled. In practice,unscrupulous renters found it profitable to make things difficult for cultivators who wished to comply with this stipulation. Thus a renter would deliberately evade the cultivators on one pretext or another at the time when sowing was imminent. More subtly, a renter would exploit the ignorance of the cultivators of the law which required the cultivator to give written notice to the renter of his intention to undertake reaping. Instead, the renter would appear to be content with a merely verbal intimation but complain later that the cultivator had not informed him.

It was true that to some extent the law protected the cultivator. For example, if the renter was not living in the village, the cultivator would notify the *Ratemahatmaya* of his intention to reap his fields. Moreover, if the renter failed to turn up on a day that had been mutually agreed on, the cultivator could gather in the harvest in the presence of "two respectable persons whose certificates as to the share of the renter was conclusive."

The evidence does not, however, suggest that these provisions were effectively availed of. Instead, Rhys Davids observed that if the renter did not come, "the poor villagers do nothing but give over their ruined crops." Sometimes in a desperate effort to obtain the renter's cooperation, a cultivator would yield to a renter's demand that the cultivator should give the renter's share of the grain in money. More fundamentally, cultivators also had difficulties in finding out who the renter was and tried to do so "as best they can from those who attend the sale." Above all, Rhys Davids observed that there was "the most surprising state of ignorance" among the peasants with regard to the law.

In these circumstances, Rhys Davids proposed that the cultivators should be made more directly aware of both the identity of the renters as well as the provisions of the law. Over and above the *Kachcheri* records, Rhys Davids urged that the notices of assessment which were given by the government to the renters should be sold to the cultivators at ". . . a chally or 1/2 cents a piece." Rhys Davids also suggested that on the back of such notices the entire Ordinance should be explained in Sinhalese. Apart from these general measures Rhys Davids explained to Twynam that he would explain at the rent sales "the law to the people who are so ignorant of it as if it had never been passed."[24]

[24] *Ibid.*

On the whole, however, Rhys Davids remarked that the renting system was conducive to "great injustice and great timidity and therefore diminished cultivation." By contrast, the alternative mode of collecting the Grain Tax—by commutation—was much less objectionable. Reduced to its simplest terms, commutation implied the payment of the Grain Tax in annual cash installments for a specified number of years. The duration of such settlements varied between three and five years.

First the yielding capacity of the fields in a given area was assessed. It was customary to assume that a yield of twelvefold might be expected after the grain had been sown. But in a basically prospective assessment allowance was made for possible crop failures due to weather and the availability of water. In this way the yield for a period of say five years was calculated. A tenth of the gross yield belonged to the government. The crux of the commutation system, however, lay in assigning a specific money value to the taxable ten percent. This was known as the commutation rate. The unit of reckoning was a bushel of paddy. The price of a bushel of paddy in the market of the district concerned was a determining factor. It was customary to fix the value of the bushel of paddy for the purpose of the tax at a lower figure than the market price of a bushel of paddy. In concrete terms, if the price of the bushel of paddy in the Anuradhapura District was 72 cents—at it was in 1872—the commutation rate was fixed at 48 or 50 cents. The purpose was not only to make the cultivator's obligation to pay the tax less burdensome, but also to popularise the idea of commutation.[25]

On the other hand, there were, however, factors which made commutation seem less attractive to the peasant. For example, yields were assessed prospectively for a period of five or three years, irrespective of whether during the period there might well be a reduction of the area under cultivation for one reason or another. In areas where individual holdings were large or scattered, it was, for instance, the policy of the cutivator to take in hand only certain proportions of the field in a given year. There was consequently diminution in the output of grain. As far as the government was concerned, however, there was no corresponding reduction in the assessment of the grain which had already been theoretically fixed. The fear that drought would cause a loss of crops, the want of money, and a belief that the

[25]Lot 41. 252 D.N.A. Diary entry of Rhys Davids, 4 January 1872.

commutation rates fixed by Government were excessive, were equally inhibiting.

In criticising the commutation system, Rhys Davids emphasised the more humanitarian aspects. He thought, for example, that it was unjust to expect a yield of twelvefold because conditions in the Anuradhapura District were not entirely satisfactory for paddy cultivation. He urged that an eightfold yield should be a more satisfactory basis for calculation. In his letters to Twynam, Rhys Davids also pointed out the importance of moderate commutation rates. He explained that the cultivators were reluctant to commute because the commutation rate which had been 33 cents per bushel in Anuradhapura had been increased to 42 cents per bushel in 1868. Above all, like some of his contemporaries in other districts, Rhys Davids dreamed of enforcing an almost mathematically equitable system of assessing the fields belonging to separate owners. The existing practice was to make assessments of broad tracts rather than of individual holdings. Rhys Davids urged that instead, the yield of each field should be estimated separately, particularly because some fields were better served with water facilities than others.[26] But such a reform required—as his successor in Anuradhapura was to explain years later—a trigonometrical survey of each field, assessments of each single holding, as well as a special department of surveyors and assessors.

Meanwhile the commutation settlement, which had been made in 1868, was about to expire and arrangements had to be made for a fresh settlement. Inevitably Rhys Davids' energies were taken up with purely administrative considerations. Usually the administrative work involved with the collection of the Paddy Tax was handled by the *kachcheris*. But Rhys Davids was reluctant to rely on his staff in Anuradhapura *Kachcheri*. He complained that the clerks were not sufficiently intelligent and that therefore he was on the lookout for "a good man" to whom he was prepared to pay a salary of Rs 50 per month to attend to the routine paper work which a paddy tax settlement entailed. He also complained that although the commutation settlement had been made in 1868, even the commutation certificates had not been issued to those cultivators who had paid the Grain Tax under the terms of that settlement. Moreover, the commutation

[26] *Ibid.* Also, Lot 41. 187 D.N.A. Rhys Davids to Twynam, 6 July 1872.

lists which had details of the owners as well as of the extents of their lands were, according to Rhys Davids, "imperfect."[27] Rhys Davids was hopeful that he could in the course of time compile full and accurate commutation registers which would in effect be compendious land registers. Properly handled, the registers would become a veritable "Doomsday book."

The work had to be done with great care under the personal supervision of the Assistant Government Agent who had ideally to visit each village for the purpose.

[27]Lot 41. 252 D.N.A. Diary entry of Rhys Davids, 20 January 1872.

5

NOT BY GRAIN ALONE

THE rigours imposed by the formal tasks of agricultural administration did not discourage Rhys Davids from taking an active interest in wider problems of production.

Lack of diversification was the most characteristic feature of peasant agriculture. Rhys Davids remarked that other than paddy and "a little miserable *kurakkan* and gingelley" there was not much that the peasants grew. The difficulties of transporting peasant products to the more distant urban markets where reasonably remunerative prices prevailed, as well as the frequent incidence of crop failures, highlighted the basic problem of diversification[1]

It was in this context that Rhys Davids expressed optimism about the possibilities of growing cotton in the Anuradhapura district. In going over the old *Kachcheri* papers he had discovered that in 1858 three casks of American cotton seed had been received by the Assistant Government Agent in Anuradhapura who had distributed the seeds among the peasants with assistance of the headmen. But the experiment—Rhys Davids wondered whether it had ever been seriously regarded as such—had failed. Not even the seeds from a few plants that had thrived had been preserved. He thought that the result might well have been different had the cotton seeds been grown under the immediate care of the Assistant Government Agent alone.[2] Rhys Davids declared that in terms of soil and climate—moderate rainfall and a dry season—conditions in Anuradhapura were ideally suited for the cultivation of a plant which had so far not been systematically attempted elsewhere in Ceylon.

He urged Twynam to obtain from India a supply of cotton seeds and plants as well as the technical information regarding the methods of cultivation. Rhys Davids was determined to grow the seeds in a nursery which he hoped to set up and which was to be maintained by prison labour. He assured Twynam that other than the small cost involved in bringing the seeds from India, there would be no initial

[1]Lot 41. 185 D.N.A. Rhys Davids to Twynam, 2 May 1872.
[2]*Ibid.* Rhys Davids to Twynam, 27 May 1872.

expenses. He wanted Twynam to obtain several hundred cotton seeds and plants in order to give his experiment a fair chance of success.[3]

Rhy Davids was also optimistic about the cultivation of tobacco for which he believed the Anuradhapura District was particularly suitable. He did not say in what ways its cultivation might be taken in hand. It was probably as a first step that he wanted Twynam's permission to make a grant to cultivators to introduce tobacco cultivation in the district. If no genuine attempt was made to plant tobacco, the grant could be revoked. Rhys Davids observed that manure was necessary to grow tobacco and added that it could be procured "in almost any quantity for the trouble of collection." He conceded that in Anuradhapura the lack of water would be in itself an obstacle to tobacco cultivation but in the same breath assured Twynam that this "could be easily remedied by irrigation"—a remark which provoked Twynam to insert two exclamation marks in the margin of Rhys Davids' letter. On the whole, Twynam ignored Rhys Davids' proposals.

A more fundamental consideration had also been left unanswered. Rhys Davids' object was that new crops should be taken in hand by the peasants after the Government had taken the initiative in showing that these crops could actually be grown in the Anuradhapura District. But whether the run of the mill peasant had the resources to plant either tobacco or cotton was a moot consideration. It was possibly the unexpressed conviction that after all the peasants would not be able to do so that induced Rhys Davids himself to suggest that a grant of fifty acres should be made to any single individual for the cultivation of tobacco.

The experiences of other and more favoured districts in the island had also shown that diversification of peasant agriculture was in fact an elusive goal.

II

Within the existing framework, a possible alternative was to increase the productive capacity of paddy cultivation, the mainstay of the rural economy. But in this sphere too, despite the hopes of the Government Agents, there were several obstacles to contend with.

[3]Lot 41. 184 D.N.A. Rhys Davids to Twynam, 26 October 1871; Lot 41. 185 D.N.A. Rhys Davids to Twynam, 2 May 1872.

In Rhys Davids' time fairly widespread attempts were made by several Assistant Government Agents to introduce new varieties of paddy. In particular, Carolina paddy—an imported variety—was much sought after because of a belief that it yielded larger crops than the native paddy. Rhys Davids himself urged Twynam to provide him with a few quarts of Carolina Paddy which could be grown in and around Anuradhapura. Characteristically, he added that previous attempt to grow Carolina Paddy had failed because of the "apathy and carelessness of the peasant." Instead, he was determined to maintain

> personal supervision in a general manner over operations here, visit the several plantations periodically, see that cultivators water the plants properly and at stated times and that the fences and the plantations are in good order.

Twynam, who thought Rhys Davids' suggestion worthwhile, wrote to the Colonial Secretary who in turn ordered C.H. Dias Bandaranaike, who was the *Maha Mudaliyar* of the Siyane Korale in the Western Province, to send the paddy to Anuradhapura. Bandaranaike sent an entire bushel of Carolina Paddy to Rhys Davids. In a letter to Rhys Davids, Bandaranaike declared enthusiastically that the peasants in Anuradhapura were sure to erect a statue to Rhys Davids because the introduction of Carolina Paddy would bring about great prosperity. The experiment, however, failed because of the lack of enthusiasm among the peasants.[4]

Like some of his fellow colleagues, Rhys Davids thought that mechanization was the answer. Aware of the extent to which farming had been mechanized in Europe, many European officials in Sri Lanka were frankly critical of the implements which were traditionally used by the Sinhalese cultivator. In particular, they pointed out that the plough universally used in the island did not cut sufficiently deep into the soil. Even after the ground had been ploughed repeatedly, the sub soil was practically left undisturbed. There were also the processes of reaping and threshing on which great labour and time were usually expended. In certain districts the cultivators had to forego as much as a seventh of the crop as the share of those who undertook to reap and thresh the paddy. Winnowing too was done manually and had to be paid for separately.

[4]Lot 41. 184 D.N.A. Rhys Davids to Twynam, 6 September 1871; Lot 6 (5) 3482 D.N.A. Rhys Davids to Twynam, 26 October 1871; C.H. Dias Bandaranaike to Rhys Davids, Lot 41. 213 D.N.A. 11 October 1871.

However, Rhys Davids was aware that the only notable attempt at mechanization had been made by E. Elliott, who was the Asssistant Government Agent in the Matara District. At his own expense, Elliot had imported an Engilsh plough as well as a wooden threshing machine which he had seen in Scotland. In addition he had also sent out to Matara a manually operated threshing machine which was being produced by an English company for rice cultivation in Spain. The import of an American winnowing machine and a hand rice pealer had crowned Elliot's efforts. Meanwhile, the Irrigation Committee in Matara, which usually worked in close association with the Assistant Government Agent in fostering paddy cultivation, bought the machinery from Elliot who had had to incur considerable personal expenditure in getting the machinery.

If anything was to discourage the widespread adoption of mechanization, it was the question of costs. Elliot had been determined that the cost of each item of machinery should not be more than £10. But when the machinery had been received in Matara, the threshing machine alone had cost £17 a sum which was well beyond the resources of the average peasant. The stumbling block might in a sense have been anticipated. There was the *caveat* of the Cattle Commission to go by. The Cattle Commission appointed in 1869 to go into the question of cattle diseases had also urged the use of more sophisticated agricultural implements and had in turn been particularly sceptical about the effectiveness of the traditional plough. But the Commission had taken a page from the experiences of the Madras Presidency where the cost of imported agricultural machinery had been so prohibitive that only the "native chiefs" had been able to use them. Instead of importing machinery from abroad, the Cattle Commission had declared that the village blacksmith and carpenter could be relied on to make useful modifications in the structure of the plough.[5]

Moreover, the machines were not entirely adaptable to local conditions. Elliott found that the English plough—the lightest available—was too heavy for the buffaloes who, after a shift of dragging the plough were too exhausted to work a second day. The English threshing machine, too, had not been particularly successful. The Scotch thresher, on the other hand, did its work "admirably" but required twelve men to carry it from place to place. Experience showed that the winnowing machine too was not easily portable.

[5]Sessional Papers 1869 Cattle Commission Report.

Naturally the peasants in the Matara District—where alone these machines were being experimented with—were unenthusiastic and ignored the native officials who took great pains to popularise the machines. Elliott, however, attributed their lack of success to the innate conservatism of the peasants rather than to questions of costs.[6]

Rather ruefully, Rhys Davids realized that for his own part he was powerless to follow Elliott's intrepid footsteps. Traditionally the yields of paddy in the Matara District were prolific in contrast to the meagre returns in Nuwerakalwiya. The peasants were consequently comparatively prosperous and were therefore willing and able to undertake experiments. Besides, Matara was thickly populated. It was not economically isolated as Nuwerakalawiya clearly was. Above all, Rhys Davids was only too aware that his superior Twynam—a notoriously conservative Civil Servant—would not countenance the Elliott type of experimentation. Twynam was ever on the lookout for evidence of the maverick temperament in his youthful subordinates. Obviously, too, the much talked of conservatism of peasants was likely to be a more formidable obstacle in Nuwerakalawiya than in the more commercially developed Matara area.

Such conservatism was no doubt at the bottom of the general unwillingness to adopt other effective techniques of production which had no bearing on mechanization. The use, or the non-use, of manure, was a striking example. Two sources of manure, derived from vegetable matter and cattle, were reasonably within the reach of the average cultivator. But the evidence does not suggest that either was being used significantly in paddy cultivation. To some extent after the paddy fields had been harvested, the decomposing stubble nourished the soil. So did the cattle—by means of urine and excreta—whenever they were tied in the paddy fields. After harvesting, the cattle were put to graze on the fields because the stubble provided a modicum of fodder.

More deliberate attempts to use manure were probably rare and significantly attracted an exaggerated degree of attention whenever they occurred. Thus it was officially noted in successive annual Blue Books that in the Jaffna district alone the cultivators had begun to use sea weed as manure. The sea weed was dried extensively in the sun, mixed with animal manure and applied to the paddy fields. In

[6]Report of the Matara District. E. Elliott Administration Report 1870, pp. 114ff.

general, the practise of using manures of one sort or another seems to have been confined to the European planters in the coffee districts. Apart from bone manures and guano—imported primarily from India and from England—they made extensive use of the cheaper local manure resources which were at hand.

III

Rhys Davids was more directly concerned with an allied subject which had a direct bearing on the development of the rural economy.

Considering the fairly large number of cattle which peasants were owning in several districts, cattle rearing might presumably have contributed towards peasant income. The inhibiting factors were, however, too formidable. The traditional uses to which cattle were put were in themselves economically remunerative only in a broadly negative sense. In paddy cultivation they were used for tillage as well as for treading on the corn during threshing. Cattle were also used for general draught purposess and were above all the principal mode of transportation. Moreover, a peasant who owned cattle—and such ownership was by no means universal—could add to his income by hiring out his animals.

On the other hand, some European officials noted that the traditional tasks which the cattle carried out were exhausting and in conjunction with other factors, accounted for the premature degeneration of cattle. The Cattle Commission had drawn particular attention to the unnecessarily burdensome work which cattle were made to do in the fields, and urged the feasibility of mechanization. Lack of proper tending, the frequent incidence of disease, premature as well as promiscuous breeding and insufficient grazing lands, reduced the possibilities of income further. There was also the absence of a serious tradition of dairy farming which above all might have made a more worthwhile increment to peasant incomes.

The Government was more immediately concerned with the eradication of cattle diseases. Correspondingly, Rhys Davids' own interest centred around this aspect. In his letters to Twynam on the subject, he complained about the difficulties with which he had to contend whenever cattle disease broke out in the villages of Nuwerakalawiya. The enforcement of quarantine was made difficult because the Sinhalese peasants were not sufficiently responsive. Rhys Davids' remedy was to make greater use of *Arachchis*—minor village headmen—who presumably were to be armed with larger punitive powers. The reluctance of the Sinhalese to look after their cattle when the cattle were smitten with disease, was also an obstacle. Rhys Davids suggested that Indian coolies should be employed to assist the *Arachchis* on such occasions.[7]

The more noteworthy proposais which Rhys Davids made concerned the problem of cattle fodder. Conditions in Anuradhapura left much to be desired. The pastures were not merely poor in quality but were also limited in extent. Lack of rain made things worse. "During the long drought preceding the October rains," Rhys Davids observed, "the grasses are completely dried up and the feeding grounds present the appearance of a close cropped brown sward." He thought that an imported variety of grass called "prairie grass," grown in other parts of the island, was hardier than the local grasses and was therefore better able to withstand drought. As fodder, prairie grass was also popular with the cattle. Rhys Davids urged Twynam to supply him with seeds and plants belonging to this variety. He suggested that a modest sum of £2 which was lying unexpended in the *Kachcheri* for "miscellaneous services" might be used for the purposes.[8]

IV

Above all, Rhys Davids, like many of his predecessors, grappled with a problem which was in a sense at the heart of peasant agriculture in Anuradhapura.

In the nineteenth century chena cultivation—which was wholly different from the traditional paddy cultivation—existed in several districts. Its aims as well as the methods involved made chena cultivation an object of considerable offical concern.

First the peasants cleared a fairly large block of high land. Such lands which were not usually thought to be as suitable for paddy cultivation as low lying land were, moreover, invariably covered with jungle. The clearing process was completed when this land together with the trees that had been felled was set on fire. With hardly any

[7] Lot 41. 187 D.N.A. Rhys Davids to Twynam, 29 July 1872.
[8] Lot 6 (5) 3482 D.N.A. Rhys Davids to Twynam, 25 August 1871.

preparation of the soil of the sort which the more formal modes of cultivation required, the peasants set about sowing broadcast certain dry grains on the burnt clearing. *Kurakkan,* Indian corn, chillies, mustard and gingelley were the more typical of these grains. On land that was virgin and whose natural fertility was enriched by the heavy mixture of wood and vegetable ash, the grains grew both quickly and prolifically. The comparatively little water that was necessary for the grains was another striking characteristic of chena cultivation which made its adoption in the more drought prone districts particularly feasible.

According to Rhys Davids there were also other reasons which accounted for its widespread appeal. From a purely technical point of view, chena cultivation was simpler than paddy cultivation, which required constant attention over a period of several months. Secondly, much less labour was required. In paddy cultivation, from the time when the fields were being made ready for sowing to the gathering in of the harvest, many hands had to be employed. Even more attractive from the point of view of the peasants was the difference in yields. From paddy was usually obtained a yield of tenfold. By contrast *Kurakkan,* which was the most popular of the dry grains, yielded fortyfold. And according to Rhys Davids, if the land which was converted to use as chena was one in which there had been particularly old trees, a yield of as much as three hundredfold could be obtained. As a form of food, too, the richly flavoured *Kurakann*—which once it was prepared could be kept longer than rice and was more conveniently taken about—was popular among the peasant.

From an official point of view, however, the objections to chena cultivation outweighed the advantages. Apart from the enormous waste of valuable timber resources, it was widely believed that chena cultivation exhausted the soil. The peasants themselves realised this. After sowing the dry grains once or twice it was their custom to abandon the land and make fresh preparations for chena cultivation elsewhere. As Rhys Davids pithily summed up, there was therefore a continuous and wasteful *rotation of the soil* instead of a *rotation of crops* which was practised in European countries largely to preserve the fertility of the soil. Moreover, implied in the chena practice was the assumption that there were unlimited expanses of land to be cursorily cultivated and abandoned. In fact this was not so. Rhys Davids observed that even in the low lying Kandyan districts where the demand for land was much less than in the coffee areas, the land available was not unlimited and was likely to become less.

Moreover, with particular reference to Nuwerakalawiya, Rhys Davids feared that as long as the peasants were attracted to chena cultivation, they could not be induced to direct their energies to the cultivation of other crops which would be remunerative both to themselves as well as to the government. In this context he significantly made mention of both tobacco and cotton. There was also the inevitable reference to the neglect of the "permanent" interest of the peasants which was paddy cultivation. In particular, Rhys Davids drew attention to the neglect of irrigation, manure and drainage. According to him the peasants in Nuwerakalawiya took to chena cultivation in the dry months when they might have more usefully taken in hand the repair of the tanks.[9]

On the other hand, there was no easy solution to the problem. Theoretically the government might have prohibited chena cultivation. It was, however, reluctant to do so. Paddy cultivaion was not everywhere in a flourishihg condition. In some districts not only was the incidence of drought very great but the irrigation facilities on which cultivation depended were also inadequate. The cultivation of dry grains in chenas was therefore the principal means on which the livelihood of the peasants depended. The government had relented sufficiently to allow a limited amount of chena cultivation on permits which were issued by the various *Kachcheris*.

Individual Government Agents enforced this policy with notable humaneness. For example, J. Parsons, who was the Government Agent in the Southern Province, remarked in 1868 that but for the relaxation of "the very stringent prohibition" against chena cultivation, "the people would have starved." He thought that the Government Agent should have greater discretionary powers in the grant of licenses.[10] His successor, F.B. Templer, observed that peasants were necessarily driven to chena cultivation. He thought that no harm would be done if permission was given to cultivate chenas within limits.[11] In his report on the Sabaragamuwa District, F.R. Saunders, the Assistant Government Agent, reported that "it would have been positively cruel" not to have permitted chena cultivation in certain

[9]Report on the Nuwerakalawiya District. T.W. Rhys Davids. Administration Reports 1871, pp. 80ff.

[10]Report on the Southern Province, J. Parsons Administration Reports, 1868, p. 196.

[11]Report on the Southern Province, F.B. Templer Administration Reports 1869, p. 61.

areas.[12] Lionel lee, who administered the Kegalle District, had himself encouraged the peasants to cultivate various types of Indian grains in chenas. "Any measure which increased the food supply of the poorer classes," he remarked, "would be necessarily beneficial."[13]

Leniency was most called for in the Nuwerakalawiya District. In a petition to Sir William Gregory, who had succeeded Robinson as the Governor in 1872, on chena cultivation, certain peasants remarked that in the Anuradhapura District there were "no permanent streams or rivers" and that the water conserved in the tanks was not adequate if the fields were cultivated with paddy twice within a year. The peasants were therefore compelled to take to the cultivation of *kurakkan* "which enables them to maintain their family all round the year." In other petitions which pleaded for the less stringent application of chena laws, much the same point was made.[14]

But it was in Anuradhapura more than elsewhere that elaborate rules had been framed with regard to chena cultivation. It was forbidden within specified distances from the public roads—within 400 yards, from the Central Road and 200 yards from most of the lesser roads. No land could be cleared for chena cultivation if there were valuable trees standing on it. Applications for chena cultivation had in the first instance to be made to the *Arachchis*—minor headmen—but could be granted only by the *Ratemahatmayas* after fairly detailed investigations had been made. Licenses were issued in triplicate and copies had to be deposited in the *kachcheri.*

Rhys Davids opposed chena cultivation with a vigour which contrasted with the mildness of his colleagues in other districts. He did not see anything amiss with the rules which were fairly reasonably criticised by some of the peasants in petitions to the government. They pointed out that in effect there was in the Nuwerakalawiya District—rich in timber resources—hardly a stretch of uncultivated land which did not have valuable trees. They also complained that the native officials whose business it was to go into the applications for chena cultivation were both oppressive and corrupt. Finally, that on account of various official delays, licenses were often granted too late

[12]Report on the Sabaragamuwa District, F.R. Saunders Administration Reports 1868, p. 18.

[13]Report on the Kegalle District, L.F. Lee Administration Reports 1869, p. 32.

[14]Lot 41. 187 D.N.A. for details of these petitions and the comments which Sir William Gregory, the Governor of Ceylon, had himself made whereon.

when the season for chena cultivation was over. If the peasants cleared the land in anticipation of licenses, they were prosecuted.

Moreover, despite a scholarly analysis of what could be said for and against chena cultivation, the evidence suggests that Rhys Davids had underestimated its fairly crucial economic importance to the peasant. Much hinged on the question whether it was more profitable to produce dry grains for market purposes as against rice. A mere comparison of prices unrelated to the factors which governed production would be deceptive. Taking 6 shillings as the average price which peasants in Anuradhapura obtained from itinerant traders for a measure of paddy, a bushel could presumably have been sold for 7 shillings. By contrast, a bushel of *kurakkan*, according to a table of prices mentioned by Rhys Davids, sold for only a little above a single shilling. The price of most of the other typical dry grain products such as mustard and *ulundu* was generally about 2 shillings per bushel. Gingelley alone probably on account of its popularity with the Indian immigrant labourers fetched as much as 4 shillings. On the other hand, one had to take into account the comparatively little effort that went into chena cultivation and the very negligible costs of producing the traditional dry grains. The difference in yields too was particularly relevant. As against the tenfold yields of paddy, mustard yielded a hundred fold, dry chillies two hundred fold and gingelly three hundred fold. Above all, to the peasants dry grains were a means of obtaining the much needed resources in cash in a district in which alternative means of doing so—for example, the seasonal demand for labour in the coffee districts—were patently lacking.[15]

At bottom, there was, one suspects, in Rhys Davids an almost idiosyncratic antipathy to peasants who took to chena cultivation. Reflecting on the readiness with which the simple Kandyan peasants in Nuwerakalawiya realised the immediate advantages of chena cultivation, Rhys Davids observed with a tinge of bitterness that they were blind to its disadvantages. Such considerations were the business of posterity "for which the Kandyan like the German materialist has very little regard indeed."

V

Much of the antipathy to chena cultivation was intimately connected with Rhys Davids' campaign to preserve the timber resources

[15]Report on the Nuwerakalawiya District. T.W. Rhys Davids Administration Reports, pp. 80ff.

in the Nuwerakalawiya District. He found that valuable timber was being cut down constantly by Europeans, Moormen, and by Low Country Sinhalese, who all did so for commercial purposes, as well as by the peasants. He complained that some peasants had once felled a forest of young satinwood trees for "a miserable *kurrakan* crop, the very fence and watch-hut being made lavishly of satinwood worth 1000 times the crop reaped."

Rhys Davids declared that it was impossible for the Assistant Government Agent to check the depredations particularly if they occurred in the outlying parts of the Nuwerakalawiya District. Nominally timber could only be felled by licenses which the *Kachcheri* granted. In fact, however, the licenses—which specified the number of trees that might be cut—were abused particularly by moormen and by Low Country Sinhalese with the connivance of the headmen. In theory it was the business of the headmen to report violations of the terms of the licenses. "The present staff of headmen," Rhys Davids complained, "would scarcely be sufficient for supervision unless they are themselves supervised. I believe them to be more lazy than dishonest," he added. Nor was there supervision when timber was being felled for the use of government departments. Although a license from the *Kachcheri* was necessary, in practice various government departments had set about felling timber as a matter of right. Nor had the *Kachcheri* in Anuradhapura for its part been accustomed to keep records of the timber uprooted on such occasions.

Rhys Davids suggested that the headmen should be called upon to submit weekly reports and then an officer from the *Kachcheri* should occasionally supervise the fellers. As it was, after a license had been granted, no further notice of it was taken until an application was received for its renewal.[16]

Over and above the problems of supervision, certain other proposals which Rhys Davids urged were of wider significance. He thought that the issue of licenses for felling timber should as much as possible be confined to Europeans. Better security could be obtained from Europeans than was usually forthcoming from either the Low Country Sinhalese or the Moormen. There was also the likelihood that European applicants would more genuinely comply with government regulations concerning timber. The prospects of government gains were also greater because timber was felled by Europeans

[16]Lot 41. 185 D.N.A. Rhys Davids to Twynam, 28 May 1872.

largely for export. Rhys Davids suggested that the prices prevailing in the ports of Colombo and Trincomalee should be regarded as the current market value of timber and that the royalty which the government imposed should be a fourth of this value. Rhys Davids also proposed that the licenses should also stipulate that for each tree felled three young plants should be planted.

The establishment of a timber nursery was, however, by far his most valuable proposal. He thought that this should be done near the Assistant Government Agent's bungalow as it would make supervision easier. He said that the plants from the nursery could be grown in a timber plantation in the area between the Ruwanwelisaya and the Jetawanaramaya. The timber plantation was to be surrounded by a protective belt of jungle which should be five fathoms in width. Rhys Davids was optimistic that over four thousand valuable plants could be had by these means. He also thought that the central position of both the nursery and the plantation would facilitate the sale of the trees, so that his plan "might reasonably be expected to be a financial success." Moreover, the cost of setting up the nursery would be about £3, and the monthly salaries of the two coolies who would look after the nursery would not, he calculated, exceed an additional £2.

When Twynam referred Rhys Davids' proposal to the Colonial Secretary, the response was enthusiastic. The Colonial Secretary minuted that Rhys Davids should be thanked for a scheme that was "perfectly feasible at a very little cost."[17]

[17]Lot 6 (5) Rhys Davids to Twynam. 29 January 1872.

6

REFLECTIONS IN A DIARY

THE diaries which Rhys Davids kept provide a strikingly perceptive insight into the varied facets of administration which ordinarily concerned an Assistant Government Agent.

The bulk of the diary entries dealt with periodical circuits which Rhys Davids made to various parts of Nuwerakalawiya. Customarily details of the proposed circuit were forwarded to the Government Agent in Jaffna, and indicated the places chosen for visiting, the number of days which would be spent in each place, and the nature of the business which would be dealt with. A circuit usually lasted for over five days and entailed a considerable amount of travelling achieved evidently in leisurely stages. During the circuits, a great variety of administration work was done. There were the sale of paddy rents, the convening of peasant parleys in relation to the Irrigation Ordinance, inspection of tanks, roads, and the sites for public buildings, as well as inquiries into the conduct of petty officials and, above all, the patient hearing of the numerous grievances and complaints which the peasants invaribaly made to the Assistant Government Agent on such occasions.

Circuits were particularly agreeable to Rhys Davids, who felt the restraints of being continually tied down to the *Kachcheri* in Anuradhapura. "I never get away from the office in the evenings soon enough," he once remarked to Edward Fretz, an officer in the Public Works Department, who had suggested that Rhys Davids should accompany him on an inspection of the Nuwerawewa tank. "And I am already engaged every morn," he explained. On another occasion he recorded in his diary: "engaged all day in the office and finished work by candle light."

In contrast to the formal letters which he wrote to his superior, Twynam, the entries which he made in the diaries, which were also submitted to the Government Agent, were characterised by a relaxed, almost intimate tone.

However it is almost with an effort that one becomes aware that the diaries were the fruits of Rhys Davids' penmanship. They are neither delicate nor finely written—literary facets not commonly encountered in official documents. The abrupt and staccato style of the individual entries seems to emphasise the point. Clearly the diaries were written in the field or during brief moments of enforced leisure in the course of circuit. A certain sensitivity, a sense of being finely attuned to the peasant ethos of which he had genuinely become a part, would seem to constitute the principal merit of Rhys Davids' diaries.

A

During the circuits, and in general, much of Rhys Davids' time was taken up with matters relating to the native officials.

2 SEPTEMBER 1871

Harvda *Korala* present under instruction from Govt. Agent in his letter No. 80 of 3 August 1871. (connected papers) The *Korala* presents a petition (filed) the gist of which is

1. That he is not more in arrears with commutation payments than some other *Korala*.
2. That he performs his other duties well.
3. That he is poor.
4. That he has a large family.
5. That dismissal would disgrace him.

The last two pleas cannot be considered. The 3rd. is against the petitioner holding such an office as that of *Korala*. The 1st seems to be in some degree true but the faults of other *Koralas* who are perhaps otherwise good officers will not excuse the petitioner if he is otherwise unsatisfactory. The question turns therefore chiefly on plea 2 on which I am not now able to judge. The *Korala* is allowed till the 30th to pay up all his arrears. . . and I shall then await further instruction from the Govt. Agent.[1]

10 SEPTEMBER 1871

To Ellagamuwa. Sale of Udurawa, Keralowe, Negampahari and Kelagam *Korales* rent.

[1]Lot 41. 252 D.N.A. The individual diary entries have been reproduced *verbatim* to retain their authentic character. For the same reason the abbreviations used by Rhys Davids have been kept in their original form. The indigenous terms used by him have however been italicized.

Heard complaints. Investigated the case of Negampahari *Korala*. A note of my predecessor as follows having been submitted to me. "The *arachchi* of Dunumadalawe Tulana reported to me that the Keralowe *Korala* had underestimated this. The result of the sale wd. seem to bear this out and the *Ratemahatmaya* also says it was underestimated. The *Korala* is an unsatisfactory individual. Bring this to the notice of Mr. Davids."

The *Korala* being able to give no explanation he was told that he would be allowed no commission for the sales held on that estimation.

Inspected *Kooly* Bungalow and all the trees. Ordered plan to be drawn up showing each tree. Fined *Kangani* 5 sh. for 5 dead Coco palms.[2]

18 SEPTEMBER 1871

Finally closed the census accounts. Some enumerators were still absent, but as they had not accounted for their absence, it was decided that they should not be paid. They were 11 in number and the sums due were 7s/3d as enumerator and 13s/9d as batta.

A sum of 8.2 8 3/4 is due to Don Girigoris *Kangani* of . . . Mihintale who was allowed, on the 22nd June last, to go to Matale on sick leave. He was so ill at Nalanda that he was obliged to be left there and Mr. Leisching as he went to Kandy gave him an extension of leave. He ultimately was able to go to Matale about the end of last month but nothing has been heard and the vouchers we sent for his signature to Matale have not been returned. He is either ill or too ill to attend to business and it is not necessary to keep the accounts open for this item. If he recovers he can petition Govt. for the amount due. We cannot hold the money in deposit as he has furnished the office with no receipts. The accounts are therefore to be considered closed and forwarded to Jaffna as soon as possible.[3]

10 JANUARY 1872

The *Kachcheri Mudaliyar* the Court *Mudaliyar* and the Registrar's Clerk are ill from itch and sores, the consequence probably of their filthy mode of life. The post office clerk is ill with fever, cause

[2]Lot 41. 252 D.N.A.
[3]*Ibid.*

uncertain. The Fiscal's clerk has applied for leave of absence but being unable to find a substitute leave has been necessarily refused.[4]

12 JANUARY 1872

From reports lately called for on the subject it seems that there are many villages without *gamaralas* and many of them are non-resident and illiterate. *Gamaralas* who can read and write should be chosen for each village by ballot of the male shareholders over 25 years of age, the ballot to be held in every case by the Assistant himself.[5]

7 MAY 1872

Kende *Korala*. Mr. Leisching recommended that this officer should be dismissed, and the matter being referred to me for report. I made the diary entry dated 2 September 1871 where it is stated that as the question would have to be decided on the question of the *Korala's* general efficiency or inefficiency I was not capable of expressing any opinion then. After 10 months experience of the *Korala's* work, it is my duty now to state that I think him a thoroughly inefficient officer and the very worst *Korala* in the District. He does everything he had to do in a lazy and perfunctory manner, and he is very unpopular with the people with whom he has no influence and to whom he gives no assistance in their cultivation and general communal wants. I have at least been compelled to fine him for neglecting his duty as a shareholder in the village, which is not only one of the best proofs of laziness but is intolerable in a government officer who ought to set the people a good and not a bad example.

I must therefore thoroughly endorse Mr. Leisching's opinion and would recommend that his services be dispensed with.[6]

19 MAY 1872

The Acting *Korala* Punchi Rala overseer seems to me to be with the exception of the *Ratemahatmaya* West, the most enterprising and enlightened Kandian in the District. There is great similarity between the characters of those 2 men, allowing fo the difference in age and experience.[7]

[4] *Ibid.*
[5] *Ibid.*
[6] Lot 41. 251 D.N.A.
[7] Lot 41. 254 D.N.A.

29 MAY 1872

Kunchuttu *Korale Korala* and *Arachchiship* of Kunchuttu Tulana West.

These two offices are vacant: the first by the Government Agent having accepted in his letter no. 91 of the 24th April the resignation of the last *Korala* and the other by the death of late incumbent reported by *Ratemahatmaya* East on the 9th December last. The delay in filling up the latter appointment was owing to the gross and repeated neglect of the *Kachcheri Mudaliyar.*

The following are the candidates; the last 6 being candidates only for the *Arachchship* . . . of these by far the best in every way is the *Ratemahatmaya's* son Nikawewa Banda.

In general he seems to me as far above the others as in social standing and influence with the people. It is very hard that his birth should be an absolute bar to his employment. (Twynam's comment on the margin reads "why should it be?") In Kandy very often several appointments are held in the same family at the same time, it seems to me very questionable whether in so backward a District as Nuwera-kalawiya East it would be advisable to follow this precedent and Nikawewa *Ratemahatmaya* seems to be not anxious to introduce English ideas of industry and liberty among the people, but rather the contrary. The brother of Relapanawewa *Ratemahatmaya* is Division Officer and Registrar of Marriages, his son was and is still acting as shroff and his nephew is --------(At this point the entry has been deleted with the comment by Twynam, "Erased by me.") No. 2 the Korala's son is too young to be a *Korala* but is quite competent to discharge the duties of Division Officer or Registrar. No. 3 was married to the daughter of the retiring *Korala* and though not quite so intelligent is older and more experienced and is fitted, though scarcely fitted for the post of *Korala.*

The family is one of respectability and is rising into power in the District. The *Korala* was a good officer and had at once been appointed *Korala* of Tamkaduwa, where he is now settled.

Candidates 4, 5, 6, 7, 8, are in my opinion unfited for the posts they seek. No. 7 is a Jaffna Tamil. The others are ordinary peasants and can scarcely write.

No. 9 is a Treasury Watcher intelligent and active he writes with great quickness and extremely well, reads not badly & is a better than any of the candidates for the *Arachchiship* & would make a good *Archchi* and probably thereafter a good *Korala.* Treasury Watchers have several times been promoted before and the plan seems a good one. On Mr. Meir's recommendation Ukku Banda was appointed Kiralawa Korala. On Mr. Pattersons Tikiri Appu was appointed *Arachchi* in Udurawa Korale, and the peasant constable of Anuradhapura was a Treasury Watcher. The capabilities of other candidates are sufficiently apparent from the table and which was carefully drawn up. There are frequent complaints from the *Ratemahatmayas* that the *Koralas* have too much to do. They are generally Division Officers and Registrars besides paddy Tax estimators in addition to all their work as *Koralas*, whereas the *Ratemahatmayas* and *Arachchis* have comparatively little to do. This has lately been brought to the Agent's notice. I will recommend that the 4 offices be divided among the 4 candidates No. 1, 2, 3, 9."

(A minute made by Twynam however reads, "It is impossible for me to come to any decision on this diary entry.")[8]

B

Irrigation was a proverbially important subject and gave Rhys Davids many opportunities of coming into direct contact with the peasants.

20 SEPTEMBER 1871

Proceedings of a *Gansabhawa* held at the instance of T.W. Rhys Davids Esquire . . . concerning repairs to a tank called Pahala or Maha Ratmale.

Present. President. Assistant Govt. Agent. Members. Punchirala Gamaya, Appu Naida, Mudaliya, Vela Arachchiya, Tikkira, Sinna, Dingiry, Punchi Naida, Tikkiri Appua.

It appears from the statements of the members-

1. That the fields of the tank (now jungle) have not been cultivated within the memory of man.
2. That the members have often cultivated the tank in Tavalla and would cultivate a larger extent in Tavalla if the breach were repaired.
3. Breach is 36 x 36 (broad, long) x 10 feet high.
4. Would cost 3 or 5.
5. No *horouwa* required for tavalla cultivation.
6. That the members are unwilling to *asweddumize* the land because a devil is on the rock, but really from laziness.

[8]Lot 41. 251 D.N.A.
[9]Lot 41. 252 D.N.A.

Conclusion

Members agree to repair the breach all the work being earth work and to cultivate in Tavalla.

27 SEPTEMBER 1871

Received application from the Mihintale priesthood to have Mihintale tank repaired. The whole of the land is said in the petition to be temple property but not exempt from tithe and to be at present jungle. The priest promises to repay in 10 instalments if the expenditure is less than 1000. But if the land does not pay tithe it is probably Govt. land. I have therefore fixed this tank for inspection on my next circuit. The priest is an intelligent man and very superior to any of those at the *Bo*-tree *pansala.*[10]

1 OCTOBER 1871

Mihintale tank. Meeting of persons interested in Mihintale tank called to consider a position dated 27th September last from the *Nayaka Unnanse* of the two *vihares.*

Priests.

Uttimaduwe *Unnanse (Nayaka)*

Kubukiwewa *Unnanse*

Residents 10 Boutique Keepers.

Kader Saibo, Mammadu Usen, Saiyadu Ibrahim, Saibu, Moheydin Pitche, Sangili, Velanden Pulle.

The *Nayake Unnanse* says the lands belong to the temple but were not given by the Temple Lands Commissioner Mr. Wodeshouse. The boutiques keepers say they would like the tank repaired if their boutiques (on crown land) were not swamped.

All agree that there are 50 acres of *Asweddumizable* forest land beneath the level of the tank. The priests say the water in the tank if repaired would be sufficient for all these, the boutique keepers think that the water would only be sufficient for 25 *Amunums.* The boutique keepers are very willing to buy 1 *asweddumized* . . . and cultivate the land if the tank is repaired.

Kardar Saibu a Govt. contractor thinks the repair of the breaches would require £100 and £200 or £300 to protect the present roads and boutiques.

[10] *Ibid.*

The boutique keepers are also willing to pay about two rupees per acre for 10 years to make up any deficiency between the value of the land sold and amount of money spent in improvements but they are not willing to pay much more.

It would be greatly to the advantage of Govt. if this tank could be repaired as proposed by the people. There would be an unlimited supply of good water close to the Central Road and at a station where a Rest House has been built and where the Tamils like to halt. And it is especially advantageous to interest boutique keepers in a work of this kind so as by selling them the land to ensure their becoming Colonists instead of mere passing traders.[11]

4 OCTOBER 1871

Ratmale . . . Gansabhawa of shareholders

1. Kanduge Tambik Kandu
2. Tambi Lebbe Lekamge Tambi

There are 20 *pangus* of which 1 owns 7 1/2, 2 own 10 and one Saibu (absent) 2 1/2 shares.

The tank lies about 7 miles SE of Dachi Halmullawa. There is an old sluice silted up and broken and there are two breaches and a spill water in bad order.

The Shareholders say they can repair the spill water . . . but want Govt. aid to repair the sluice and 2 breaches. It would be better to make a new sluice in one of the breaches. The repair of the other would take 20 and the pulling up the sluice say 30. Total required 50.

Only 3 *Amunums* are now cultivated. 10 or 12 would be watered if the tank were repaired. Produce at least 60 a year.

Both the shareholders present state that they would gladly pay 1/10 yearly of the cost of any improvements if the cost were about 50.

Resolved therefore that Govt. aid be requested for this work. The other shareholder agree to this but is too ill to appear. He is a cousin of no. 1.

The *Ratemahatmaya* says these people may be trusted and that the land is really theirs.[12]

16 OCTOBER 1871

Received complaint from Kiriyage Maina that Puspage Patti and her husband keep him out of his share of the land. Patti is present and

[11] *Ibid.*
[12] *Ibid.*

says that her mother Rankiri brought a case no. 12 in Dambulla Court and won the land. Maina says that she brought a case against Kappua and he (Maina) intervened and no decision was ever given.

The present shareholders all think that Maina ought to have a share in Patti's share. Referred to a case. Patti produces her grandfather's tooth as a witness. (*Kettu Sakkiya*)[13]

16 OCTOBER 1871

Habarana tank . . . formerly there were cultivated 60 *Amunums* but the present people cultivated only chenas there. This was said by the *Korala* but he now unsays it saying they were not. It is my opinion that any industrious habits these villagers may ever have had have been corrupted by allowing them to cultivate chenas.[14]

19 MAY 1872

I have measured many fields to ascertain the real measure which the expression *Amuna* or *Pela* represents. I have not found any two *pelas* to agree one with the other. The *Pangus* in Tiripanne of 2 *pelas* real sowing extent each contain about 980 square fathoms= 3,200 square yards which is nearly 2/3 of an acre.[15]

C

In view of the backwardness of the Nuwerakalawiya District the Government attached great importance to the construction of roads.

5 SEPTEMBER 1871

Started late and in rain for Andarawewa 10 miles to Moragahawewa. Road in very bad condition almost impassable for carts which with great labor struggle thro' about a mile an hour. This is owing to the Road having been put into thorough repair by the Public Works Department on the system referred to in Diary entry of Wednesday 3rd May 1871 by my predecessor with whose remarks I entirely concur. Sold rents of Walachiya Korale. Heard many complaints.[16]

[13]*Ibid.*
[14]*Ibid.*
[15]Lot 41. 254 D.N.A.
[16]Lot 41 252 D.N.A.

6 SEPTEMBER 1871

To Nalla Ulachchiya 14 miles. Inspected Western minor road. It would have been very difficult for me to decide whether the estimate made before my arrival had been carried out had not my predecessor carefully marked each repair estimated for in each mile. I consider the repairs unfinished and the overseer who had reported on the 30th of May 1871 that they were finished now said they are not. He will not be paid.[17]

7 SEPTEMBER 1871

To Eppawala. I had fixed inspection of Endagala road in the morning but was too unwell to go through exposure to sun this morning.[18]

13 SEPTEMBER 1871

Inspection of new roads to Kunpikulam the trace seem clever though not very straight having been purposely curved at Dampelesgama to avoid people's hut.[19]

6 OCTOBER 1871

Gansabhawa of Shareholders interested in Konwewa called at the instance of Konwewa *Arachchi* of Mahapotana Tulane.

To the tank are 2 *gamaralas* and 26 1/2 shares & about 24 shareholders.

Present.

1 *Gamarala*

12 Shareholders owning 10 3/4 shares.

The *Gamarala* says that the shareholders want to open a new trace and abandon the old road through the paddy field which require 18 small bridges now being repaired at a cost of 18. A new trace has now been cleared . . . the addition in length would be 12 yards the present road being 990 yards long and the new trace 100 yards long. Govt could afford 101 to change the trace and would save greatly in upkeep in future. There are three small drains costing say 6 required. It is decided that the shareholders shall do all the necessary earthwork to make a perfectly level road along the new trace if Govt. will put up the drain and the gravelling.

[17] *Ibid.*
[18] *Ibid.*
[19] *Ibid.*

Kadar Saibu the Contractor thinks it would cost 25 to do the gravelling and the people think 5 would do.[20]

16 OCTOBER 1871

Habarana Tank . . . *Gansabhawa* closed. The peasants say as usual on being asked whether they would like a road, that they do not want one and very much hope that one will not pass through the village.

Reasons.

1. The *Tavalams* will bring cattle disease.
2. The people will bring smallpox.
3. The road will take part of their paddy land.[21]

7 NOVEMBER 1871

Today inspected the Andrewewa Ottapuwa road. This has been repaired in August last by overseer Baddnala who sent in weekly reports to the *Kachcheri,* but whose work has not been inspected either whilst it was being carried on or afterwards. There was not the slightest sign to me today of any work having been done at all and it is impossible now to estimate or to check his accounts in any satisfactory manner.

It is quite possible that he may have put his friends and relations down on the roll allowing them to do very little work for their day's pay and under a good system this ought to be preventable. The present system might be amended in 2 ways. 1st. The estimates made should specify more particularly what is estimated for they should always be sufficiently clear at least to enable any intelligent person other than the framer to decide without doubt *what spot* any particularly estimate refers to . . . and there is nothing to prevent an overseer from pointing out a work that has really been done the year before.

And again the estimate should be so worded as to convey clearly *what amount of work* the estimate included . . . secondly there must be more prompt and strict supervision over works done by overseers. Each road should be miled and half miled. Each overseer should be compelled to work with such a number of *Koolies* as would ensure his doing sufficient work in 2, 3 or 4 weeks to make it worth the Assistant Agent's time to go at once and inspect and pay for the work

[20] *Ibid.*
[21] *Ibid.*

done. And such roads as are beyond the chairman's reach should be either given on contract or inspected immediately after work done by some person whose report can be relied on . . .

And finally a spirit of emulation among the overseers would probably be encouraged by giving different overseers different parts of the same road, or the same road at different times taking care to reward the industrious by more constant employment.

The road should also be kept in a more practical manner. The plan of the road should be filed with it. Estimates of former years should be included . . . a map should be made however roughly for each road showing the nature of the soil through which it passes.[22]

19 MAY 1872

Seven villagers living about 2 miles off Talawa apply for leave to clear a road fit for carts from the village to the Talawa high road at the bazaar. Allowed gladly.[23]

D

There was also the irritant of chena cultivation and the necessity of conserving timber resources.

4 OCTOBER 1871

Sale of confiscated timber at Ratmale. Connected papers . . . 40 logs sold for £67. Nikawewa *Ratemahatmaya* has to pay the difference between this and the last sale which was for £79. 10. 0. The former purchaser however paid £11. 17. 6 . . . copy of the state of sale is annexed.[24]

11 JANUARY 1872

I continue to receive complaints of unlicensed chena clearing and also lists of chena licenses.[25]

22 JANUARY 1872

Received application to cut free of royalty the following large trees for building purposes . . . It has been the custom to grant these applications as a matter of course but this seems to me contrary to the spirit and letter of the Govt. Agent's instructions, according to which royalty ought to be paid.

[22] *Ibid.*
[23] Lot 41. 254 D.N.A.
[24] Lot 41. 252 D.N.A.
[25] *Ibid.*

The royalty wd. amount to very little but the principle wd. be a good one of teaching the people that all timber is more or less valuable.

My answer was that they might cut the trees and I should inform them afterwards whether the Govt. Agent decided that royalty was payable or not.[26]

20 JANUARY 1872

Received complaint against Constable that on a license issued last year by Mr. Leisching to fell 12 trees he has now felled 90. It seems he paid no royalty and has felled many more trees that he received permission to fell. The Constable has always borne a very high character and I do not think it likely that he would risk his post by openly breaking the law. Saw the timber today lying on the high road opposite his new boutique. He says that it was the custom to cut any timber required for house building without a licence if it was of any kind considered "not valuable." That is anything besides the trees of greatest value ebony, satinwood, etc.

The chief clerk says that in Mr. Pole's and Mr. Patterson's time licences used to be issued for any timber felled, but that about 2 1/2 years ago this practice fell into desuetude and parties were allowed to fell the so called "not valuable" timber without licence. I have altered this, and no one in future will be allowed to fell any Government timber without licence.[27]

E

The sundry matters which were brought to the notice of an Assistant Government Agent when he was on circuit showed two things: what the peasants expected from their rulers and the realization in turn of rulers like Rhys Davids that governance in rural South Asia meant a paternalism which transcended the function of tax collection and the dispensation of justice.

14 SEPTEMBER 1871

The Tirappane well is dry. It is I am informed always dry when the tank dries and some time before. This might perhaps be remedied by blasting deeper. The trees planted round the *Kooly* bungalow and hospital were in bad order. The *kangany's* excuse was that he could not carry water 3 miles to water them.

[26] *Ibid.*
[27] *Ibid.*

Granted permission to 2 Tamils one Bengalee and one Moor to build boutique opposite the Galkulam well and pointed out the sites.

The complaint against the renters and by the renters were as numerous as in other places and show the same ignorance of the law.[28]

25 SEPTEMBER 1871

Sold padi rent of Nuwaragam Korale about 800 bushels for 1200 shillings . . .

Heard complaints. One was concerning a rogue elephant alleged to be on the Mihintale road and its vicinity, but at Mihintale Rest House last night (Whither, I had gone with Mr. Hall of the Public Works Department) Elephants had been heard all night trumpetting. The elephant therefore supposed to be a rogue is probably one of the herd and harmless. In the absence of further proof the request to shoot without a licence is therefore refused. If such requests were granted the Ordinance would be likely to become a dead letter.[29]

29 SEPTEMBER 1871

On order on a petition dated 22nd September 1871 from Walli Etana of Ponimankulam in Kanadara Korale stating that she had been ill treated by her husband and had separated from him about 4 months ago and begging that a formal divorce might be granted.

1. Petitioner Walli Etana
2. Her husband. Kadirattoge Appurala

The *Korala* is absent. The man says he did not and does not wish to be separated. He wants to "seize and keep" his wife. She still says "he is most violent" as indeed appears from his demeanour to be probably the truth and she still wishes for a divorce. It appears on further examination that there is a dispute about moveable property. No adultery is charged. The marriage therefore cannot be dissolved. The parties are told to think over the matter for 8 months and settle if they can and if not apply to me.

Bora the alleged murderer appears upon order. There are charges of threat against him and he is a bad character. He occupies rent free a boutique on Govt. ground which he is ordered to quit. This abortive trial cost Govt. from first to last nearly £100.[30]

[28] *Ibid.*
[29] *Ibid.*
[30] *Ibid.*

4 OCTOBER 1871

Ratmale . . . Heard complaint from

1. Balaya Pediya and
2. Puspa Pediya of Halmillewa

that Vidane Pediya had instituted a false charge against them in the District Court Kandy to recover £40 alleged to have been given to them to keep. The complainant never possessed £40 or any other sum. He came from Kandy District and lived with one of the girls in the village without the parents' consent, and after the present applicants appeared . . . he went away and took another woman at Wagallawa close by this place (Ratmale) and lives there. The *Mudaliyar* states that he knows the man to be a litigious bad fellow.

I believe complainant's statement and have brought the matter to the notice of the District Judge of Kandy.

The Arachchi of Magallakada says he is afraid of this man. Complaint from a villager of kudakappugollawa about a hunting dog stolen by a *violent* character in Wagollawa who keeps it tied up in his hut. On asking the headman mentioned in last entry he says the case is a true one but *he is afraid* to go and have the dog given to its owner. Case referred to Police Court.[31]

22 JANUARY 1872

Received application today for the land between the *Bo*-tree enclosure and the Kurunegala road. This piece ought to be kept free and planted with ornamental trees.[32]

18 JANUARY 1872

The only register of temple lands in this *Kachcheri* is the list of temple lands rejected and those to be registered in the District of Nuwerakalawiya signed by Mr. Wodehouse and dated 27 Oct. 1865. . . and in this the entries as regards the land in the station claimed by the high priest are not only vague but also incomplete and in some most particulars altogether wrong.

Firstly, there are no entries made in the list of any lands or buildings at all situate in the town of Anuradhapura.

It is however incredible that Mr. Woodehouse can have purposely omitted to register the temple of the tooth, or the great *dagobas* or above all the enclosure of the sacred *Bo*-tree. There is no doubt that these belong to the priesthood, the gift of them is a matter of record in the *Mahavamsa* and as regards the *Dagobas* and the sacred *Bo*-tree

[31] *Ibid*

[32] *Ibid.*

the priesthood have been in actual possession of them till this day. Their non register is evidently a mistake and can possibly be explained by the entry of the lands granted to the 8 great places and situate at Gallinbindunewewa in Kandara *Korle* a village about 20 miles from Anuradhapura. There are in that village with one exception no such lands as those entered in the list under its name whereas the name would apply to some of the sacred places in the town of Anuradhapura.

Secondly, if then the entries under Gallinbindunawewa in the Kanadara *Korle* may be read as under Anuradhapura in the Nuweragam *Korle*, it is to be remarked generally that the extent registered is not given as regards every one of them and in particular as follows.

1. *Bodin Wahansa.* The sacred Bo tree. There is one at Gallinbindunewewa but Mr. Armiel has not surveyed it. In the survey forwarded with your letter under acknowledgment but which is not the survey which was before Mr. Woodehouse the outer sacred enclosure no. 4 is named Maha Vihara and sacred Bo-tree *Bodinwahanse* is rightly written against only the inner raised enclosure immediately round the tree.

2. Lowa Maha Paya which calls the brazen palace "Lena." The survey calls this Lowa Maha Prasadaya or Brazen Palace.

3. Thuparama. The *dagoba* and terrace round it are both given in the survey. It is not clearly stated whether one or both to be registered.

4. Meda Pansals. Not in the survey. Possible no. 6 if it does the same remark applies as is made regarding no. 9 in this list.

5. Abayagiri

6. Jetawanarama

7. Lankarama

8. Mirisawetiya

The boundaries of all the above are given as "according to Mr. Armiel's survey," an insufficient description for the reasons remarked.

9. The present *pansala* of the *Nayake Unnanse* marked no. 1 in Mr. Armiel's survey. Under the head is said "the boundary" within the inked lines marked by the Commissioner (meaning Mr. Woodehouse) in Mr. Armiel's survey. These lines are not marked in the survey now forwarded. The *Nayake Unnanse* lived in no. 6 when Mr. Woodehouse visited Anuradhapura. No. 10 *pansala* no. 2. There is no such *pansala* given in the plan.

Lastly nothing is said about plots marked A + B in Mr. Armiel's survey nor about the shrine of the tooth therein given. For the plot A I have received numerous applications for the purchase or lease.

The points therefore on which we must obtain the decision of the Temple Land Commissioner are, firstly, whether having regard to the wrong entires under Galinbundunawewa it may be considered that the omission to register the sacred places at Anurdhapura was not by intention but by mistake and if so considering the wording of the Ordinance that mistake can now be rectified.

2ndly, Whether the outer enclosure of the *Bo*-tree not entered even in the list under Galinbindunawewa is now to be considered Govt. or temple property.

3rd. Whether the word Thuparama can be held to include the terrace round the *dagoba.* The expression used by Mr. Armiel is Thuparamaya *dagoba* and does not include the terraces.

4th. What is to be done with regard to the Meda pansala given by the Commission according to Mr. Armiel's survey but not named in the survey. The word is now applied to no. 6 (exclusive of A & B) in which the *Nayake Unnanse* lived when Mr. Woodehouse was in Anuradhapura . . .

5. How much is to be included as temple property under the head *pansala* no. 1.

6. If the Meda Pansala in the Register be taken for no 6 in the survey what place is meant by *Pansala* no 2 which is described as opposite Lowa Maha Paya, a description which might apply to no. 6.

7. Are the shrine of the tooth and the adjoining ruins marked in the plan but not mentioned by the Commissioner Crown or temple property.

8. Are the plots A & B named in the plan not in the Register Crown or temple property. I have initialed the plan referred to in order to prevent future mistakes and would suggest that the plan before Mr. Woodehouse when he made the entries may have been initialled by him then and may still be found or if not that the Surveyor General might be able to certify that the plan now returned is an exact copy of the one referred to.[33]

[33]*Ibid.* Since lands belonging to Buddhist temples were exempt from taxation, in order to decide which lands were really temple lands and validate claims by means of surveys, in 1856, by an ordinance, the government set up the Temple Lands Commision. Its first chairman was W.H. Woodehouse, a Senior Civil Servant. The temple localities referred to in this diary entry were part of the *Atamastane* or the Eight Sacred Places in Anuradhapura.

7

FACETS OF ADMINISTRATION AND RELATIONS WITH AN IRASCIBLE SUPERIOR

IN Rhys Davids' time the District of Nuwerakalawiya of which Anuradhapura was the administrative centre together with the neighbouring districts of Mannar, Mullaitivu and Jaffna comprised the sprawling Northern Province of the island. Nuwerakalawiya, whose peripheries touched Jaffna, Matala, Kurunegala and Trincomali, was in itself an unwieldy administrative unit approximately 54 miles in length and 50 miles in width. For purpose of administration, Nuwerakalawiya had been divided into the Western, Eastern and Southern divisions, each under a *Ratemahatmaya* who was usually a high born Kandyan and one presumed to wield considerable influence. These major divisions were in turn subdivided into smaller units under a hierarchy of native officials. Presiding over the entire structure was an English Assistant Government Agent whose immediate superior was the Government Agent of the province with his headquarters in Jaffna.

Despite its overwhelming size, the District of Nuwerakalawiya was very sparsely populated. The population numbered about 55,000. The ethnic features of the district were noteworthy. Although more than one Government Agent had expressed scepticism about the verisimilitude of population returns—compiled largely by the lesser native officials—the numerical preponderance of the Kandyan Sinhalese in both Nuwerakalawiya and Tamankaduwa was very evident. Both districts had been part and parcel of the old Kandyan Kingdom and had been regarded as such till 1833 when in the course of a major realignment of provincial boundaries the districts were integrated with the Northern and Eastern provinces respectively.

From the beginning of the nineteenth century, Anuradhapura had acquired a reputation among Civil Servants as a desolate administrative outpost. It was, moreover, widely believed that Anuradhapura was unhealthy and that this unhealthiness was the result of the thick jungles which had spread all around. By the second half of the nineteenth century there had been a change. Some of the jungle had been cleared, roads of one sort or another made, and the restoration of the ancient irrigation tanks, with which the district fairly abounded, were taken in hand. Above all a few settlers—largely Moors from the Coast and Tamils from the neighbouring districts—had come in to take in hand the trade of the place and more significantly to lease tank lands which were being gradually made available for paddy cultivation.

Imperceptibly Anuradhapura too, like other isolated districts, had been drawn into the vortex of change, a process which Rhys Davids—like some of his successors in the Anuradhapura agency, notably Sir John Dickson—viewed with misgiving.

But in 1870 backwardness was the essential stamp of the region. Consequently the administration in the Nuwerakalawiya District was deeply paternalistic both in fact and in spirit. Great care was taken not only to maintain a hierarchy of native officials who by the very nature of their functions came into contact with the peasants but also to rejuvenate the tradition of *Gansabawas* or village councils—the principal institutional means by which it was presumed the peasants had been governed for centuries. Rhys Davids who had great sympathy with the paternalistic approach, identified himself with the wellbeing of these institutions.

It was the experience of several Government Agents that the success of the hierarchy of native officials depended on the influence which these officials were able to exercise over the mass of the peasants. Naturally in the selection of native officals—especially as *Ratemahatmayas* and *Koralas*—a Government Agent or his Assistant exercised the utmost caution.

Good birth and the social standing which with it—notions with which Rhys Davids had much sympathy—constituted the overriding criterion in making these appointments. Rhys Davids believed moreover that there was a certain class among the Sinhalese who by virtue of their birth had almost a presumptive claim to rule the people. Because these families had in fact done so traditionally, their influence was likely to be very great.

Thus in considering applications for the *Koraleship* of Talawa, Rhys Davids ignored the claims of a certain applicant in spite of the fact that the man was already serving the Government as an overseer, on the ground that he was "not of good birth, that is, none of his ancestors were headmen under the Kandian Kings." Instead Rhys Davids recommended Nuwerawewa Banda who belonged to an ancient family "from which the chief headmen of this District were always chosen and for which all the people have such great respect." Besides, added Rhys Davids, Nuwerawewa Banda was "intelligent and loyal" and likely to become "a useful officer."[1]

By the same token Rhys Davids was averse to the employment of Tamils—and one might add Low Country Sinhalese—as *Arachchis* and *Koralas*. The documents show that many Tamils who had settled in the Nuwerakalawiya District competed for these posts in spite of the predominantly Kandyan character of the locality. In filling the *Koraleship* of the Talawa area, Rhys Davids rejected a Tamil although the man was already a Police *Vidana* and was in Rhys Davids' view "an intelligent and good officer." The applicant was, besides, a Buddhist. "But all things being equal," decided Rhys Davids, "his being Tamil is against his being appointed *Korala* over Kandians who have a national dislike of Tamils."[2]

Caste too counted. Like many contemporary British Civil Servants, Rhys Davids recognized caste as a crucial facet in the social structure prevailing in Ceylon. In the Nuwerakalawiya District in particular its influence was very evident. According to Rhys Davids, Nuwerakalawiya was in effect a conglomeration of villages which were clearly differentiated in terms of caste. But there were many villages belonging to the castes of *Dhobis,* tom tom beaters and the blacksmiths respectively.[3] In keeping with the concept of a traditionally ruling *elite* Rhys Davids seems to have been somewhat partial towards the Golgama. He observed that many low caste families were emigrating to other districts where they either tried to pass themselves off as *Golgama* people or were imitating the Burghers by cutting their hair short and wearing trousers. In spite of the exodus, Rhys Davids feared that in Nuwerakalawiya the *Golgama* might be numerically overwhelmed by the lower castes, although the *Golgama* were "richer and better fed."[4]

He noted, moreover, that in Nuwerakalawiya, as in other strictly Kandyan districts, there was a tradition of appointing leaders or headmen over each caste and that this tradition was acceptable to the castes concerned. Leading landowning Kandyan families like the Nuwerawewa family customarily appointed headmen over the var-

[1]Lot 41. 251 D.N.A. Diary Entry 19 November 1872.
[2]Ibid.
[3]Administration Reports 1872. Report on the Nuwerakalawiya District, pp. 95ff.
[4]*Ibid.*

ious castes who lived in the villages which these families owned and from whom service tenure was being exacted. It was Rhys Davids' policy to fill posts of this sort which he presumed came within the purview of the Government. For example, Rhys Davids took steps to appoint the headmen of the *Duraya* caste who was customarily designted as the *Maha Durava.* "The appointments are universal in the Kandian Districts," Rhys Davids explained.[5]

> I inform the applicants that I will recommend to the Agent that the appointment be sanctioned and be conferred on Happua who is descended from the old headman who held the office under the Kandian Kings and is the richest *Durava* man in the Tulana.

Happua's ability to read and write also counted in his favour.[6]

There was also the *vidaneship* of the caste of smiths who lived in the Nuweragam *Korale.* Rhys Davids considered several applicants before he wrote to Twynam.

> There are only two, Sondura and Ukkuwa, both descended from the *vidanas* of the Kandian times. Sondura is young and sickly and produces no work. Ukkuwa shows his work which is passable and can read and write. I beg to recommend him for the post.[7]

Twynam however demurred. According to him if there had ever been a tradition of making caste appointments, it had long since fallen into abeyance. Rhys Davids countered that these appointments would be advantageous from the point of view of the administration, but was ultimately compelled to bow to his superior's views.[8]

Controversies of this nature were singularly absent with regard to the role of the *Gansabawas.* Indeed the policy of the Government in the second half of the nineteenth century was to rely increasingly on these institutions in implementing its policies at the grass roots. Rhys Davids in particular saw the usefulness of the *Gansabhawas* as a means of establishing dialogue with the peasants on a variety of matters.

II

Rhys Davids' tenure of office as Assistant Government Agent in Anuradhapura was certainly marred by his infelicitous relations with

[5]Lot 41. 251 D.N.A. Diary Entry 14 March 1872.

[6]*Ibid.*

[7]*Ibid.*

[8]W.C. Twynam to Rhys Davids, 11 May 1872.

Twynam. As Assistant Agent he was perforce very much under Twynam's thumb. Temperamentally Twynam inclined towards exercising the strictest surveillance over his subordinates. Twynam's correspondence with his assistants in Mannar, Mullaitivu and Anuradhapura was fairly full of an entrenched belief that in the business of government officials must keep to the well trodden paths of accepted policies, precedence and procedure. Deviations of the sort which more resilient minds—such as that of Rhys Davids—were capable of were clearly anathema to Twynam, who never tired of driving the point home. And indeed for all the patient expostulation there was not far below the surface the sharp bite of censure in Twynam's correspondence with his subordinates.

Rhys Davids' predecessor, Leisching, had seen this at first hand. When he was reprimanded for failure to follow established practice with regard to the compilation of statements involving the sale of government lands, Leisching had given expression to his exasperation.

> . . . I will carry out your wishes irrespective of my own opinion. . . for instance though it is my own view that all the names of the places in the sale statement should be in Sinhalese . . . I shall have them in future written in English and although I consider it a waste of time . . . that well known renters should sign the sale statement at the little table usually carried on circuit still I shall do as you desire. I shall also enforce payment of the purchased amount within two days though I know the revenue will suffer thereby. I have tried it and so have my predecessors.[9]

Rhys Davids' comparative inexperience certainly told against him. He was plainly embarrassed by his ignorance of the manner in which official reports had to be written.[10] Twynam had occasion to caution him with regard to compiling the Quarterly Season reports. Rhys Davids' sins—nowhere is the compulsive preoccupation with trivia more evident—were twofold. Firstly, he had dealt with a number of matters without delineating heading. Secondly, "the mixing up of matters connected with the people and cattle in one paragraph" had caused "serious inconvenience" to Twynam who relied on the information provided by his assistants in preparing the overall reports of the province. Rhys Davids was urged to compile the

[9]Lot 41. 184 D.N.A. Louis Leisching to Twynam, 17 January 1871.
[10]Lot 41. 184 D.N.A. Rhys Davids to Twynam, 20 September 1871.

Quarterly Report in forms which had been provided for the purpose. He nevertheless felt helpless and begged Twynam for a specimen of an actual Quarterly Report so that he could get "a general idea" of what was required.[11] Twynam was as critical about the Annual Administration report for the Nuwerakalawiya District which Rhys Davids had submitted. "I decline to accept a report," he frostily remarked, "in which there are so many interlineations and corrections . . ." Rhys Davids was ordered to submit the report "in the form which you wish to have it printed."[12] Nor was the manner in which Rhys Davids had made his diary entries altogether above reproach. Rhys Davids was told that each entry should have a heading as well as a number which were to be entered in the margin. Mention had also to be made of the place at which the entry in the diary was together with the date.[13]

The pressure of Twynam's surveillance was felt in other spheres too. Would Rhys Davids in forwarding estimates for work to be undertaken specify the head under which the expense was to be incurred and indicate too whether funds were available for the purpose? "This practice," Twynam was careful to add, "was always followed."[14] Would Rhys Davids in future submit indents for stamps every half year and not more frequently?[15] Would he submit the report made by headmen more regularly?[16]

The impression of ineptitude which despite himself Rhys Davids had created was unfortunately not dispelled by his penchant for seeking Twynam's advice on fairly trivial matters. Rhys Davids wanted to know in what manner the commission or reward usually paid to persons bringing old copper coins and exchanging them for new tokens should be made, or how entries should be made in the cash book kept in the *Kachcheri* when payments had to be made on drafts or court orders which came from other districts.[17] For his part Twynam found such queries tiresome as the numerous *Kachcheri* forms and printed regulations designed to meet diverse contingencies

[11]Lot 41. 129 D.N.A. Twynam to Rhys Davids, 11 September 1871.
[12]Lot 41. 130 D.N.A. Twynam to Rhys Davids, 18 July 1872.
[13]Lot 41. 127 D.N.A. Twynam to Rhys Davids, 10 January 1872.
[14]Lot 41. 126 D.N.A. Twynam to Rhys Davids, 13 September 1871.
[15]Lot 41. 130 D.N.A Twynam to Rhys Davids, 29 July 1872.
[16]Lot 41. 130 D.N.A. F C. Fisher to Rhys Davids, 23 July 1872.
[17]Lot 41. 187 D.N.A. Rays Davids to Twynam, 4 January 1872.

were thought to be self-explanatory. In reply to one such query from Rhys Davids Twynam remarked "I have the honor to state that by 'chena'

> I mean what is usually called a chena, a piece of jungle cleared by setting fire to the jungle... by valuable tree I meant of course full grown timber trees and saplings of valuable timber such as *milla* . . . *sapu* . . .*ebony* . . .[18]

And to Rhys Davids who had remarked that he did not see the purpose of issuing official receipts with stamps, Twynam meticulously explained why this should on the contrary be always done.[19]

Ironically Rhys Davids' discomfiture was as great whenever he launched himself under his own steam. As Police Megistrate Rhys Davids had imposed fines and sentenced to imprisonment certain persons who had cut timber in crown lands. Twynam thought that Rhys Davids had been needlessly harsh. So that when Rhys Davids subsequently took steps to recover from the miscreants the value of the timber, Twynam put his foot down reminding Rhys Davids that the men concerned had already been more than adequately punished. In Twynam's view all that Rhys Davids needs do was to make sure that the jungle in which the trees had been cut was not cultivated as chena land.[20]

Twynam also took a poor view of Rhys Davids' decision to postpone without adequate reason the sale of the government arrack rents in Anuradhapura which Twynam himself had fixed for a specific day in April 1872. The sale in Anuradhapura was to coincide with similar sales in the Jaffna district. Underlying this arrangement was a purpose about which Rhys Davids was ignorant until he had postponed the Anuradhapura sales and embarrassed Twynam. It had been evident for some time that there was a group of arrack renters from Moratuwa who had formed themselves into a combination. They had been active in certain districts in the island in offering low bids at the government auctions of the arrack rents. Not only had government been deprived of revenue as a consequence but the local men too had been elbowed out. If on the one hand, the sale of government arrack rents in the different districts of the province were

[18]Lot 41., 129 D.N.A. Twynam to Rhys Davids, 8 January 1872.
[19]Lot 41. 129 D.N.A. Twynam to Rhys Davids, 18 December 1871.
[20]Lot 41. 130 D.N.A. Twynam to Rhys Davids, 15 July 1872.

held simultaneously, the combination would be hard put to make itself effective. Or, if bids for the Anuradhapura arrack rents were called for at the same time in Anuradhapura as well as in Jaffna or in Mannar, the discomfiture of the combination would be even greater. Such a device had been resorted to with success in the North Western province where Kurunegala arrack rents had been auctioned in Kurunegala as well as in Puttalam. Rhys Davids' postponement of the arrack sales in Anuradhapura defeated the implementation of a similar plan in the North Central province. Twynam was therefore compelled to make fresh arrangments for the disposal of the arrack rents.[21]

In Twynam's eyes Rhys Davids had also acted arbitrarily with regard to the leasing of crown lands to traders as sites for boutiques. The demand for such sites was particularly evident with regard to land in the Anuradhapura town proper and in some of its environs where sheds had been erected for the use of immigrant *coolies* on their journey southward. Ordinarily the grant of leases would not have warranted the exercise of undue caution on the part of the government. As matters stood, however, no proper survey of the town or of the lands surrounding it had been carried out. Care had therefore to be exercised with regard to the rights of the crown as well as the rights of pasturage of the peasants who lived in nearby lands.

Twynam made no bones about telling Rhys Davids' successor, Hay Cameron, how much Rhys Davids had been remiss in these very particulars. He had not merely ignored certain standing instructions which had long been enforced in the Anuradhapura agency but he had permitted traders to put up boutiques indiscriminately on arrangements which Rhys Davids had described as "leases at will." In cautioning Cameron against taking a page from Rhys Davids' book, Twynam remarked in his inimitably ponderous fashion that

> The proceedings adopted by the late assistant agent Mr. Davids has thrown the business connected with the leasing of lands . . . into some confusion and the highly irregular manner in which the leases of certain sites were disposed of at a so called public auction has caused embarrassment.[22]

[21]Lot 41. 129 D.N.A. Twynam to Rhys Davids, 26 April 1872; Lot 20. 445 D.N.A. Twynam to the Colonial Secretary, 4 June 1872.

[22]Lot 41. 130 D.N.A. Twynam to Assistant Government Agent, Anuradhapura, 20 March 1873.

Apart from these sins of commission or omission, Rhys Davids had occasionally to take a rap for the misdemeanours of his subordinates in the Anuradhaprua *Kachcheri*. In an earlier context Twynam had himself reminded Leisching that an Assistant Government Agent must accept full responsibility for such mistakes. So that when an original letter which Twynam had himself sent to Rhys Davids as well as some original diary entries made by Rhys Davids had been inadvertently and quite unnecessarily enclosed in an official letter from the Anuradhapura *Kachcheri* to Jaffna, Twynam's reactions were predictable. Was this an actual mistake he asked Rhys David? If so, Rhys Davids must call upon the subordinate concerned for explanation and "warn him to be more careful for the future."[23]

Indeed few things could escape Twynam's tenacious watchfulness. So that when in going over lease bonds which had been sent for his endorsement from Anuradhapura, Twynam noticed that the name appearing in a particular lease bond did not tally with the name inserted in the corresponding lease application, he was certain that there had been some unauthorised tampering. Indeed Twynam found suggestive evidence that a name originally inserted had been clumsily erased. Was Rhys Davids aware of the change of names? In any event would he explain the discrepancy? When Rhys Davids had forwarded an evidently unconvincing explanation from the *Kachcheri Mudaliyar* to whom the discrepancy was traced, Twynam ordered Rhys Davids to

> inform the *Mudaliyar* and other members of your establishment that I shall consider such tampering with public documents as sufficient ground for recommending the removal from office of any officer guilty of doing so. Rhys Davids was further required "to obtain the signature of every member of your establishment to this letter in token of his having seen it."[25]

Apart from the mistakes committed by his subordinates Rhys Davids himself left the door open for well deserved criticism of his work. He was either generally ignorant or his lapses were simply the result of negligence. On one occasion after he had gone over some of the official books kept by the Anuradhapura *Kachcheri*, Twynam once made a long recital of certain shortcomings and irregularities

[23]Lot 41. 129 D.N.A. Twynam to Rhys Davids, 9 December 1871.
[24]Lot 41. 129 D.N.A. Twynam to Rhys Davids, 17 April 1872.
[25]Lot 41. 127 D.N.A. Twynam to Rhys Davids, 7 May 1872.

which were, of course, quite evident. That the need to do so should have been felt after more than a year had elapsed since Rhys Davids assumed duties in Anuradhapura hardly reflected well on him. Particularly if one bears in mind that the matters about which Twynam drew Rhys Davids' attention were of a fairly routine nature. It had almost become customary that the Anuradhapura *Kachcheri* did not issue receipts for money paid into the *Kachcheri*. Indeed money paid in by headmen as grain revenue as well as the payments made by arrack renters had been accepted without receipts. "All this is highly irregular and in direct opposition to the positive orders of government. A receipt of some sort must be given to everyone paying in money . . ." Twynam then plunged into rather tiresome details of the manner in which receipt books should be kept and the most feasible mode of making entries in counterfoils.

Other lapses were as evident. There was confusion with regard to payments made in relation to drafts. In the case of drafts made in favour of the Assistant Agent "a note should be made of what is to be done with the money, whether it is to be deposited or paid over to a party at once . . ." Twynam had also discovered that in the Anuradhapura *Kachcheri* there was no official treasury record of stamps received and issued for which ordinarily a separate book was kept. "This book should be kept in duplicate and one always kept locked up in the Treasury." In any event all stamps should be kept under lock and key and "issued personally by the assistant agent." With regard to the check book of payments which was customarily maintained in *kachcheris*, Twynam remarked "I find that this is left in the office. The assistant agent should on no account allow it to go out of his possession till the cash book for the month is checked up and closed."[26]

Twynam also drew Rhys Davids' attention to certain problems concerning which questions of principle were involved. Why had Rhys Davids arrogated to himself the right of withholding the payment of commission to Headmen? Rhys Davids was told that on no account must such payment be withheld without the sanction of the Government Agent to whom Rhys Davids must in any event report all the misdemeanours of Headmen for instructions. As a matter of principle Twynam had also objected strongly against the minor employees of the government—jail gaurds, *Kachcheri* peons, the

[26]Lot 41. 187 D.N.A. Twynam to Rhys Davids 20 July 1872.

servants of the Assistant Government Agent—becoming renters of the government paddy rent. It was indeed surprising that Rhys Davids, who had written so movingly about the evils of the renting system, should have himself condoned a practice which was so partial to abuse. "This very objectionable practice," remarked Twynam, "was forbidden on the most positive orders." As it was peasants who had met Twynam in Anuradhapura had complained that they were being victimised by minor government servants who, in the role of renters, were perpetrating the classic evils of the system.[27]

The predictable reaction—an explosive outburst in his defence—did not occur. Instead Rhys Davids, despite an extraordinary sensitivity about criticisms of his work, merely acknowledged Twynam's letter, undertaking to carry out his superior's instructions to the very letter.

On the negative side it must be conceded—as his official correspondence with his provincial lieutenants suggests—that Twynam's proverbial surveillance was sometimes overdone. Once he asked Rhys Davids in a rhetorical vein whether it was not the practice of the Anuradhapura *Kachcheri* "to lock up all money daily in the chest..."[28] On another occasion in correspondence concerning the construction of certain buildings in Madawachchiya, Twynam remarked in characteristic fashion "the correct spelling of the word Mathavachchi according to the Governor's minute of 28 August 1866 should be Mathavachchi and not MATAKACHCHI as in the esti " (Estimate).

Temperamentally, therefore, Twynam was not the sort of man to ignore the shortcomings of his subordinates. Indeed, if issues transcending mere technical niceties of keeping *kachcheri* books in order were involved. Twynam—as Rhys Davids was to discover—could be quite as unforgiving.

[27] *Ibid.*

[28] Lot 41. 129 D.N.A. Twynam to Rhys Davids, 28 August 1871.

[29] Lot 41. 126 D.N.A. Twynam to Rhys Davids, 16 December 1871.

8

OLD AND FORGOTTEN ALPHABETS

HAD circumstances—discussed elsewhere in this book—been different, the story of Rhys Davids' epigraphical researches in Ceylon might have formed a brilliant and vividly contrasting backdrop to his formal administration work. Instead we have a picture which in spite of every evidence of artistic excellence, has been left curiously half-drawn as if the artist had been unaccountably and abruptly called away from the scene of his labour.

And yet the documents show that epigraphy was a deeply gratifying diversion to Rhys Davids, who was not entirely at ease in grappling with the humdrum tasks of provincial administration. It was, moreover, a sphere in which his superiors gave him considerable encouragement and genuine freedom of action. Anuradhapura with its myriad ruins was a splendidly evocative setting for the young Assistant Government Agent, who was clearly willing to devote both his leisure as well as his money for his researches.

In more ways than one Rhys Davids' stay in Ceylon coincided with what may be regarded as the embryonic phase in the history of archaeological research. Hitherto the subject had aroused the passing concern of the dilettante, but had never become a sphere of official interest. In 1868, Governor Sir Hercules Robinson set up an Archaeological Commission. It was at best a modest beginning. The evidence clearly suggests that during this early phase the work of the Commission was confined to clearing the vicinity of the principal ruins, primarily for purposes of photography. The work was undertaken with the assistance of the Government Agents, who were provided with modest sums of money by the Colonial Secretary's office for the purpose. The Commission lacked both the financial resources as well as the personnel to undertake systematic excavations.

Much of the work during this phase was confined to Anuradhapura and had been begun when Louis Lesiching was Assistant Government Agent. In spite of an eloquently expressed aversion to the ruins in Anuradhapura which he described as "sepulchural monuments,"

Leisching had in fact not only assisted the Archaeological Commission but had also been sufficiently inspired to begin excavations of his own in the precincts of Ruwanwelisaya, by far the best known of all the Ancient monuments in Anuradhapura, in the hope of discovering a subterranean passage.[1]

But although a number of notable sites had been cleared like Ruwanwelisaya, Jetavanaramaya, Abhayagiriya and Isurumuniya, all belonging to the Anuradhapura period in the island's history (*circa* 300 B.C. to 400 A.D.), the work of the Archaeological Commission was considerably hampered by the lack of funds and the absence of a permanent labour force. It became abundantly clear that although the ruins might be painstakingly cleared, they gradually became overgrown with weeds, necessitating the repetition of a rather expensive operation. The only permanent gain was the progress being made in the systematic photographing of the ancient sites.

Meanwhile in distant Galle, Rhys Davids had not been altogether idle. In the course of his travels Rhys Davids had discovered a number of inscriptions which were located in such widely separated places as Galle, Matara, Dambulla, Matale, Tamankaduwa, as well as in Anuradhapura and in Padawiya. These discoveries as well as an abiding belief that Ceylon was "exceedingly rich in old inscriptions," convinced Rhys Davids that the inscriptions would throw "a great flood of light on Ceylon history."

The inscriptions were written in "old and forgotten alphabets." But Rhys Davids was confident that they could be effectively deciphered on the basis of existing epigraphical knowledge which was being added to daily.

> As to the forms themselves we are not hopelessly in the dark. We know they are to be read from left to right, we know on what principle the vowels are expressed, we know what are the consonants to which the vowels give life. Serveral of the more modern inscriptions have already been translated, and inscriptions in cognate characters have been deciphered in India.

[1] Lot 41. 251 D.N.A. The diary entries of Louis Leisching, 14 October 1869-19 September 1870. The monuments referred to in the text were really *dagabas* or *thupas.* These were bell shaped mounds made of brick and earth. In the upper part of the dome of a *dagaba* there was usually a chamber containing the relics of the Buddha or some other renowned Buddhist saint. See also Smither, James G., *Architectural Remains of Anuradhapura, Ceylon,* London n.d., for details and excellent pictorial representations of the major monuments in Anuradhapura.

However, a precondition for the successful deciphering of the inscriptions was to collect as many inscriptions as possible. It was only on this basis that fruitful comparisons could be made. Rhys Davids mused on the fact that "even by means of any small collection the oldest forms and many of the intermediate ones have been deciphered."[2]

In an article to the local *Journal of the Royal Asiatic Society* which he wrote when he was Police Magistrate in Galle, Rhys Davids appealed to readers for copies of inscriptions. He suggested that at least eye-copies might be made, although eye-copies of inscriptions had to be made with fastidious care if they were to be of any practical use. Rhys Davids also suggested methods of making facsimiles of inscriptions which "a friend of the good cause in London" had indicated to him. The latter methods involved the damping and dyeing of sheets of paper of a certain thickness and the use of "lamp black."[3]

Despite this, Rhys Davids rightly felt that the task could not be left entirely to individuals. In a letter to the Colonial Secretary Rhys Davids observed that, ". . . It will be impossible for private persons however industrious and energetic they may be to procure anything like a perfect collection . . ." and declared that unless the Government intervened many valuable inscriptions would as a matter of course be lost. He also pointed out that "the expense of commissioning a competent person to take squeezes and eyecopies" of the inscriptions would be negligible.[4]

After his letter to the Colonial Secretary, Rhys Davids was nagged by the feeling that he had committed an "indiscretion." He had written on a subject that ordinarily did not come within the range of official communications. Besides he had done so unasked. On two grounds, however, Rhys Davids soon overcame his misgivings. In rather conspicuous contrast to his predecessors, the Governor had taken a keen interest in oriental researches. Rhys Davids had been particularly impressed by Robinson's decision to collect books and ancient manuscripts which were lying throughout the country, especially in temple libraries, with a view to establishing an Oriental Library in Colombo. Noted Sinhalese scholars of the day including *Mudaliyar* Louis de Zoysa and James de Alwis had been associated in

[2] Lot 6 (1) 3416 D.N.A. Rhys Davids to Colonial Secretary, 27 June 1870.
[3] *Journal of the Royal Asiatic Society* (Ceylon Branch), Volume V, no. 16, 1870-1871.
[4] Lot 6 (1) 3416 D.N.A. Rhys Davids to Colonial Secretary, 27 June 1870.

an operation that had already made considerable headway. Rhys Davids felt that a systematic collection of the island's epigraphical resources would be a logical corollary to this work. Secondly, as far as Rhys Davids was concerned, the epigraphical project was a rescue operation which had to be carried out as soon as possible. Inscriptions were being rapidly destroyed both by the ravages of the weather and the wantonness of man. In his letter to the Colonial Secretary, Rhys Davids particularly referred to the damage done to inscriptions on account of the practice of chena burning.

> I have seen two stones, one very beautiful octagonal one near Dambulla and one at Dondra head, which were formerly covered with letters but have been used as posts by the Natives round which to pile and burn the trees and shrubs cut down for chena cultivation and the inscriptions on which are now totally lost.[5]

Elsewhere Rhys Davids referred to another inscription also in Dondra which had been destroyed by "ignorant" Buddhist priests of a nearby temple who seemed to have considered that the stone was placed there opportunely by Vishnu for them to heap jungle round and burn. Rhys Davids also discovered an inscription in Dondra in a private land which was "fast yielding to the encroachments of the sea." According to the people in the locality, on some rocks in the surf there was another inscription.[6]

Rhys Davids' letter to the Colonial Secretary to which he had appended a list of thirteen inscriptions about which he had conducted researches, attracted the attention of Robinson who decided that Rhys Davids' "valuable" proposal should be forwarded to the Archaeological Commission. Robinson also decided that Rhys Davids, who had "a considerable acquaintance with ancient oriental languages and takes much interest in questions of historical research", should be made a member of the Archaeological Commission.[7]

The appointment was not entirely fortuitous. Among English officials in Ceylon Rhys Davids enjoyed a reputation for oriental scholarship. He was besides an active member of the local Royal Asiatic Society and had contributed a number of articles to its

[5] *Ibid.*

[6] J.R.A.S., *op. cit.*

[7] Lot 7 (1) 1888 D.N.A. Colonial Secretary to the Archaeological Commission.

journal. Two articles on inscriptions in Dondra and Welligama *Vihare* were particularly notable. The reproduction of the original texts of the inscriptions together with scholarly notes showed the extent to which Rhys Davids was conversant with the traditional literature of the island as well as with the philological work of his Ceylonese contemporaries like James de Alwis and Louis de Zoysa.

Robinson was determined to help Rhys Davids in every conceivable way. Subsequent correspondence helped to strengthen the initial rapport that had sprung up between the two.[8] In August 1870, Rhys Davids was formally made a member of the Archaeological Commission. He could now stake strong claims for leave from his formal work for purposes of archaeological researches. On such occasions he was entitled to a travelling allowance of £1 a day. Indeed not long afterwards a rather generous lease of leave came Rhys Davids' way when Robinson arranged for him to conduct researches in Polonnaruwa from the beginning of September till mid-October 1870.[9]

However, soon Robinson realised that Rhys Davids' interests would be best served if he was actually stationed in a locality in which without long spells of absence from formal work, Rhys Davids could continue with his researches. In this way, due largely to Robinson's intervention, Rhys Davids was given the acting appointment of Assistant Government Agent in Anuradhapura.[10]

Rhys Davids' letters show that he grasped these opportunities fully and Robinson continued to befriend him.

> In taking charge of this station I found the ruins had been well cleared in the rough for purposes of photography but that many spots where inscriptions might reasonably be expected were still unexcavated. Some very interesting inscriptions were found buried or half buried at Topari, inscriptions useful even yet to any administration legislating for a people whose political views have not changed since the inscriptions were engraved.
> No such inscriptions have yet been discovered at Anuradhapura and yet it is reasonable to expect that some may be found if search be made, but there are no funds availabe for the purpose.

[8] Lot 7(1) 1888 D.N.A. Colonial Secretary to Rhys Davids, 19 August 1870; Lot 6 (1) 3416 D.N.A. Rhys Davids to Colonial Secretary, 23 August 1870; Lot 7 (1) 1888 D.N.A. Colonial Secretary to Rhys Davids, 29 August 1870.

[9] Lot 7 (1) 1888 D.N.A. Colonial Secretary to Rhys Davids, 1 August 1870; Lot 6 (5) 3482 D.N.A. Rhys Davids to Colonial Secretary, 7 September 1871.

[10] C.O. 54. 479 Gregory to Kimberley, No. 238 of 14 November 1872.

> His Excellency's Government however has always shown very great interest in any researches into the ancient customs and history of the Sinhalese and there is ground for believing that His Excellency would be glad to sanction as a trial a small expenditure (not to exceed £25) for this purpose.
>
> Under these circumstances, I beg for your instructions whether this expenditure can be allowed and if so whether it will be allowed to me as a member of the Archaeological Commission or whether I should apply through my immediate superiors the Government Agent for the province. I beg generally for your further instructions in the matter.[11]

Rhys Davids' proposal was warmly acceded to and a sum of £25 was sent to him through the Director of Public Works with the proviso that he should provide the latter with vouchers concerning the disbursement of the grant.

In May 1872, Rhys Davids felt constrained to apply for a similar grant.

> A sum of £250 was allowed to me last year for the discovery and clearing of inscriptions. As very few uncleared ones were discovered only Rs. 12 and 37 cents were spent the remainder being returned on 30 Dec. to the Director of Public Works through whom the advance had been made.
>
> I have the honour to request that the sum may be reallowed to me now for expenditure in this year; the Legislative Council having passed the original vote.
>
> I have just discovered an important inscription on three lines of smooth monolith 85 yards long by 2 yards broad and it being fortunately buried the letters will probably be clear. They seem to me to be on the alphabet of the third century.[12]

Meanwhile, Sir Hercules Robinson had been succeeded as Governor by Sir William Gregory. Like his predecessor, Gregory was determined to do everything possible for the cause of preserving the island's ancient monuments. Not long after he assumed duties as Governor, Gregory made an extensive tour of the Anuradhapura District—very much in Rhys Davids' company as a contemporary newspaper noted—and became a lifelong admirer of its ancient monuments.[13]

[11] Lot 6 (5) 3482 D.N.A. Rhys Davids to Colonial Secretary, 19 September 1871.
[12] Lot 20. 311 D.N.A. Rhys Davids to Colonial Secretary, 20 May 1872.
[13] *The Ceylon Times*, 2 July 1872.

On this particular occasion Rhys Davids presumably intimated to Gregory the need for money to carry on more extended researches. Gregory encouraged Rhys Davids, who after Gregory's departure wrote to Twynam soliciting a grant of £150 for the purpose of "clearing ruins at Polonnaruwa, Anuradhapura and elsewhere and for expenses in reporting on the various archaeological resources in the Northern, Eastern, and North Western Provinces."[14]

Significantly at about the same time Twynam himself received a letter from the Colonial Secretary urging him to make a formal application for £150 to be devoted for archaeological work. The letter contained specific instruction regarding the manner in which the grant was to be utilized and Twynam was told to convey the instructions to Rhys Davids.

It was clear that although Gregory was disposed to encourage Rhys Davids, he was also determined to have a greater say in a field in which, as his private papers show, his interest was remarkably sustained long after he had left Ceylon. In one sense, a sum of £150 which was to be used exclusively for archaeological researches was an unprecedentedly large sum of money if one considered the niggardly sums which the Government had been willing to spend. Gregory realized that he would have to ultimately persuade the Legislative Council—to whom the idea of making provision for archaeological work was as yet a comparative novelty—to approve of the grant. On the other hand, Gregory also saw that £150 was far too inadequate to carry out the ambitious scheme of archaeological work which Rhys Davids had suggested. Consequently it was made clear to Rhys Davids that for the time being the Government had decided to concentrate on the main theatres of archaeological researches—Anuradhapura and Polonnaruwa—and ignore the peripheral areas.[15]

Gregory's instructions made interesting reading. Having defined the area of investigation, they added:

2nd. Trees and roots likely to bring ruin on the structures should be cut.

3rd. The areas of the *dagabas* to be cleared.

4th. Other edifices may also be cleared and any stones replaced

[14] Lot 41. 127 D.N.A. Colonial Secretary to Government Agent, Jaffna, 30 July 1872; Lot 41. 185 D.N.A. Rhys Davids to Twynam, 1 August 1872; Lot 41. 128, Twynam to Rhys Davids, 12 August 1872.

[15] *Ibid.*

the restoration of which to their original site will not incur too large an expenditure.
5th. Inscriptions and stone carvings of particular interest to be removed to the Government Agent's compound when it is possible to do so.
6th. All instructions to be carefully copied and a report made of such as can be photographed or reproduced by casts.
7th. A report should be furnished of all large objects which might eventually be removed to Colombo, e.g. Lion at Polonnaruwa.
8th. Prison labour may be employed but it must be strictly confined to prisoners not condemned to paid labour, such as offenders against road ordinance.
9th. Plans in detail to be taken of the different edifices of importance. Also a general plan of the relative position of these structures to each other.[16]

In spite of these mild stipulations, it was clear that Rhys Davids would be left with a free hand in using a rather lavish grant. However, when he was thinking how best he could set about his new work, a combination of circumstances brought Rhys Davids' stay in Anuradhapura, and indeed in Ceylon as a Civil Servant in the Eastern Department of Her Majesty's Empire, to an abrupt termination.

[16] *Ibid.*

9

AN UNEXPECTED CLIMAX: THE END OF THE JOURNEY

"My mind was full of other things and my eyes were blinded by the consciousness of the good I was striving for."[1]

THE words which occur in a letter written by Rhys Davids to Sir William Gregory in answer to one delineating charges against him, were much more than a mere plea for clemency. As ruefully Rhys Davids recalled that a certain "carelessness" and "reckless self confidence" had characterised his tenure as an Assistant Government Agent.

From Rhys Davids' own remarks it would seem that a sense of exaggerated confidence had been induced by a belief that he was making fairly rapid progress in the Civil Service. Face to face however with his phlegmatic superior Twynam, Rhys Davids' "elation" was remarkably shortlived. Instead there was every likelihood of strained relations between two personalities who had temperamentally so little in common.

Other facets in Rhys Davids' character—at least in these years—enhanced the possibility. On his own admission, Rhys Davids was often outspoken and seldom tactful. One such occasion was particularly noteworthy. In June of 1872, Sir William Gregory made an official visit to the District of Nuwerakalawiya. As was customary on such occasions, elaborate preparations were made on the Governor's behalf. Particular interest was attached to this tour as the occasions on which a Governor of Ceylon had visited the wild district of Nuwerakalawiya were few and far between. Rhys Davids, who was playing host to both Gregory and Twynam was anxious to make an impression on the Governor, especially as he was seeing Gregory—who unlike Robinson had no

[1] C.O. 54.No. 238; Sir William Gregory to Lord Kimberley, 14 November 1872; C.O. 54 No.259. Gregory to Kimberley, 27 November 1872. Much of the material for this chapter has been based on these despatches.

firsthand knowledge of Rhys Davids' scholarly talents—for the first time. Indeed, before Gregory had reached his destination a leading newspaper of the period commented that in Rhys Davids Gregory could have no better companion should Gregory decide to visit the ruins with which the district abounded.

During this time Rhys Davids was also writing the annual administration report concerning the Nuwerakalawiya District. It was customary for young Civil Servants to write their reports with considerable care, as they were as much a reflection of their stewardship as they were a record of the state of the various districts. Rhys Davids was no exception. He showed Gregory the draft of his report in the course of which he had suggested that the District of Nuwerakalawiya should be separated from the Northern Province—which was essentially non-Sinhalese—and that it should be integrated with another province which would make its particular administration a far easier task. Privately Gregory thought that Rhys Davids was being presumptuous. Nevertheless, he tactfully told Rhys Davids that although the proposal was not without merit, it should and could only emanate from the Government Agent of the province. He also urged Rhys Davids to consult Twynam before completing the final draft. Gregory recalled that Twynam had himself cautioned Rhys Davids on these lines. In any event, however, Rhys Davids did not take the hint and the report when published carried Rhys Davids' proposal.

Despite its intrinsically trivial nature, the incident deserves attention. Subsequently in a memorial to Lord Kimberley, who was the Secretary of State for the Colonies, Rhys Davids contended that the proposal was the basis of a deep seated antagonism which Twynam had shown towards him. It was vaguely suggested that Twynam resented the diminution of his powers which was clearly implied in a reform which ironically Gergory himself urged on the Colonial Office in 1872, and for which he took entire credit.

For his own part, Gregory assured Kimberley that both Rhys Davids and Twynam had been very much together and that he could recall nothing that even remotely suggested the absence of cordiality. Events, however, showed that although this particular episode had burgeoned disproportionately in Rhys Davids' mind, he had not misread the true nature of Twynam's disposition towards him. He could justifiably point to a history of strained relations which were materially heightened by this incident.

According to Rhys Davids, on Twynam's next visit to Anuradhapura which occurred in early July, 1872, Twynam was barely on speaking terms with him. Rhys Davids recalled that their "estrangement" was plain to all. The next and the more significant occasion on which the two met was when Twynam who was travelling to Kandy for a conference of Government Agent which Gregory had convened—towards the end of July—broke journey in Anuradhapura. On this occasion Twynam, who had evidently decided to spend some time in Anuradhapura, made a sharp departure from precedent insofar as his social relations with Rhys Davids were concerned.

Twynam openly ostracised Rhys Davids. He turned down Rhys Davids' invitation that he should stay with Rhys Davids at the Assistant Government Agent's bungalow or at least that he should dine with Rhys Davids. Instead Twynam took up his quarters at the Rest House which was embarrassingly close to Rhys Davids' bungalow. As he was unwilling to speak to Rhys Davids, Twynam attended to official business by formally writing letters to Rhys Davids. After a number of letters had been exchanged over a variety of matters, Rhys Davids felt that he could make his explanations about one particular matter which Twynam had wanted to know, if he could see Twynam personally. Twynam, however, ignored Rhys Davids' offer to walk over to the Rest House to do so. Instead Twynam, in impeccably formal terms, wrote a further letter to Rhys Davids urging him to furnish him with certain information which he had not been able to obtain. Rhys Davids did not reply and instead, accompanied by a friend who was staying with him, asked to see Twynam at the Rest House. Twynam sent a message to say that he was too busy to see Rhys Davids.

Much of the correspondence between Twynam and Rhys Davids on this occasion was triggered by a petition which Twynam had received on his arrival in Anuradhapura. In the petition a large number of peasants who lived in Nuwerakalawiya alleged that Rhys Davids had caused them great hardship by imposing restrictions on cattle grazing and that they had also been subjected to heavy fines on account of cattle trespass. In forwarding the petition to Rhys Davids, Twynam had asked him under what circumstances the fines had been levied and what had been done with the money. In a second letter Twynam asked Rhys Davids whether the fines had at all been imposed in court and if so, what ordinance had been invoked to do so. In a third letter Twynam pressed Rhys Davids to say whether every single fine had been imposed in court and whether it was not true that some of tne fines had been levied without "due process of law."

If Twynam's immediate object was to embarrass Rhys Davids, the petition was singularly well timed. A feature of British rule in Ceylon in the nineteenth century was the extent to which the notion was widespread in the minds of the people that it was possible to remedy grievances by means of petitions. Petitions on a variety of subject ranging from petty village antagonisms to genuine difficulties, such as the inability to pay certain taxes, were sent to the Government Agent and even to the Governor. The emergence in the various towns of the island of a class of professional petition writers who put to lucrative use a modicum of English they had at their command, was a symptom of the phenomenon. In short, petitions of one sort or another had become so commonplace that in the various provinces the Government Agents treated them with a considerable degree of scepticism.[2]

In view of the predilection for petition writing, one may wonder why the petition against Rhys Davids had not been submitted at some earlier date. It is amply clear that the matters complained of had occurred since he assumed duties as the Assistant Government Agent. A logical moment for such a petition would have been when a short time had elapsed after Rhys Davids came to Anuradhapura, because it was the contention of the petitioners that Rhys Davids had made an unprecedented departure from the policies of his predecessors in taking stringent measures with regard to their cattle. An equally plausible occasion for presenting a petition would have been when some of the cattle owners began to realize after a number of months had elapsed that there was to be no change in Rhys Davids' policies and that they had already been mulcted of considerable sums by him.

A third and admittedly more favourable occasion was the time of Sir William Gregory's much publicised visit to Anuradhapura. When these and other issues concerning Rhys Davids were referred to the Colonial Office by Gregory and Rhys Davids asked how it was that the long suffering peasants had not seized this particular opportunity to ventilate their grievances, Gregory's explanations were clearly

[2]Wickremeratne, L.A. "The Rulers and Ruled in British Ceylon: A study of the Function of Petitions in Colonial Government," *Modern Ceylon Studies*, Vol. 1. No. 2, 1970.

designed to mislead the Colonial Office. He claimed that the peasants concerned had probably felt that they should not trouble the Governor, particularly as Gregory was the first Governor they had even seen. Gregory omitted to disclose that during this tour he had received numerous petitions from the people of Anuradhapura and that he had earmarked for special attention the more important petitions which had dealt with the subject of irrigation and the absence of water for cultivation.

In spite of his reservations about the genuineness of the petition, there was little Rhys Davids could do but to answer Twynam's questions. He had to do so as expeditiously as possible, because Twynam was insisting on prompt replies. Moreover, as Rhys Davids was in effect denied access to official documents in the *Kachcheri*—where Twynam was installed—his answers were undoubtedly ill considered and meagre.

Rhys Davids explained that he had begun to levy fines on the peasants who owned cattle only after his efforts to secure their cooperation had failed. Soon after his arrival in Anuradhapura he had summoned a meeting of the cattle owners with a view to setting up a cattle pound which was to be maintained by small contributions which Rhys Davids had urged the owners to pay. After a time, however, the scheme had failed because the cattle owners had neglected to pay their subscriptions. Rhys Davids added that straying cattle did great harm to cultivation, especially in Anuradhapura where the practice had been long since tolerated without any let or hinderance. He had been particularly distressed because the menace had brought to nought his efforts to plant shade trees, establish gardens, and generally add to the attractiveness of the locality.

Meanwhile Twynam, who was going through the *kachcheri* documents with an unwonted interest, stumbled upon further discoveries which increased Rhys Davids' embarrassment. There were certain "Fine Books" which Rhys Davids had maintained and which contained details of fines which Rhys Davids had at various times imposed on the subordinate native officials who had worked in the *kachcheri*. Twynam observed that fines had been imposed on account of offences of a very trivial nature which were in the main unrelated to the duties normally assigned to subordinate officials. Twynam with his extensive experience in administrative matters also realised that the fines were illegal because the power of fining subordinates which the Government exercised was in fact singularly circumscribed. Fin ing was only possible if a subordinate absented himself from his work without prior permission. Other offences, however trivial in nature, had to be reported to the Colonial Secretary who was the administrative head of all the government departments.

On the third day following his arrival, Twynam resumed his journey to Kandy to attend the conference of the Government Agents, but not before he had addressed a lengthy letter to Rhys Davids. The need to do so had been made all the more evident when Twynam had discovered that in imposing fines on the petty native officials, Rhys Davids had not even spared the class of unpaid headmen who were an important element in provincial administration. Particularly in backward areas such as Nuwerakalawiya the unpaid headmen constituted the real link between the government and the peasants. The greater part of Twynam's letter was concerned with the imprudence of alienating a class which Twynam described as "the gentry of the country." He also ordered Rhys Davids to desist from fining the *Kachcheri* officials who received salaries from the government and also took Rhys Davids to task for exacting levies from the cattle owners.

It was but natural for Rhys Davids to assume—as he evidently did—both from the substance as well as from the commendably restrained tone of Twynam's letter, that Twynam, having admonished Rhys Davids, was content to drop the matter. Indeed, looking to the future Twynam explained that he was anxious to "check a course of proceedings" which might cause embarrassment to the government. For his own part, Rhys Davids promised to carry out Twynam's wishes to the letter "in each of these matters" and expressed regret for having "erred in my judgment regarding them." Somewhat inconsistently he had added

> It is very bitter to me to find that my endeavours which were made with the best of intentions do not meet with your approval.

The affair might well have ended at this point. Twynam, however, seems to have been in two minds when he arrived in Kandy. Ultimately he decided to speak about the matter to Henry Irving, the Colonial Secretary. According to Gregory it was Irving, rather than Twynam, who had decided that Rhys Davids' misdemeanours should be brought to the notice of the Governor. Gregory emphasised the distinction in a second despatch to Lord Kimberley in an attempt to rebut Rhys Davids' contention that from the start Twynam had been antagonistic toward Rhys Davids.

Gregory, who did not view the matter lightly, had decided that further investigations should be made into Rhys Davids' activities. He therefore made arrangements for John Douglas, the Auditor General, to leave for Anuradhapura immediately. He was to be accompanied by Twynam. They were also instructed to furnish Gregory with a report when their investigations had been completed. Gregory explained to Kimberley that he had brought in Douglas to ensure that there would be a fair and full inquiry. That the interests of such an inquiry would have been better served had Twynam had no hand in it, was ignored by Gregory. Granted there was little substance in Rhys Davids' theory that Twynam harboured a certain animus against him, there was no denying that it was the most natural thing in the world for Twynam to look for evidence which substantiated rather than contradicted the preliminary conclusions which he had intimated to Gregory.

II

In retrospect, Rhys Davids was convinced that Twynam had been the principal architect of his ruin. Elsewhere he also claimed that his own subordinates in the Anuradhapura *Kachcheri* were themselves not too well disposed towards him. Rhys Davids' insensitivity, on the other hand, to the possibility that Gregory himself shared Twynam's antipathy towards him was remarkable.

Gregory, who had arrived in Ceylon in March 1872, did not meet Rhys Davids until June when the Governor's tour of the Anuradhapura District began. Rhys Davids, who went southwards to Dambulla to meet the Governor, was very much with Gregory on the first leg of his tour, which took Gregory from Dambulla to Maradankadawela where the Governor's party broke journey. On the following day, accompanied by Rhys Davids, Gregory continued his journey till Mihintale was reached. After he had spent the greater part of the day there, Gregory finally arrived in Anuradhapura where he was received by Twynam as well as by the Assistant Government Agent of the neighbouring district of Mannar. During the first part of this tour, as well as during the stay of three days in Anuradhapura, Gregory spent much of his time in seeing the ruins in Rhys Davids' company. Indeed the setting was particularly conducive to the birth of a lasting friendship between the two, especially as Gregory, albeit an untrained laymen, had a deep interest in archaeology.

Instead, however, the foundations were laid for a bitter enmity—on Gregory's side—on account of an incident which occurred practically on the eve of his departure from Anuradhapura. Its background was an unresolved question concerning the custodianship of the sacred place of the Buddhists in Anuradhapura. Traditionally the position was held by a Buddhist priest who consequently was known as the chief monk of the *Atamastana* or the Eight Sacred Places. The sacred places from time immemorial had been endowed with extensive lands. Consequently the custodian exercised great influence in the management of the lands and properties. There was also the value of the offerings—in both money and in kind—which were made by numerous pilgrims who held the ancient places of worship in great veneration.[3]

At the beginning of the 1860s the chief priest who was the custodian of the sacred places had died. He had held the post so long that there was genuine uncertainty as to the precise mode to be adopted in finding a successor. The chiefs or the *Ratemahatmayas* had put forward the view that according to tradition they had the right of nomination as the representatives of the people. A more widely held belief was that this right had from time immemorial been exercised by the ancient and prestigious Nuwerawewa family. Confusion was, however, worse confounded because two rival branches of this family claimed the right of making the nomination.

Although the British Government had long since determined—in deference to the protests of the Protestant missionaries in the first half of the nineteenth century—that it would not, as a matter of policy, interfere in the affairs of Buddhism, much less play the role traditionally ascribed to the state as the temporal guardian of Buddhist interests, it was clearly the assumption not only of the protagonists in this dispute but of the chiefs as well, that the government should resolve the issue. Indeed, successive Assistant Agents in receiving voluminous petitions and memoranda from one or the other of the parties and in not unequivocally explaining the position of the government had virtually countenanced this view. In any event the fact that the unresolved conflict erupted into violence every now and then emphasised the need to settle the problem as soon as possible.[4]

A way out of the *impasse* had become evident and had been eagerly grasped by the administration as this did not theoretically

[3] Jones-Bateman, R. *An illustrated Guide to the Buried Cities*, London, 1932, pp. 20ff.

[4] De Silva, K.M. de. *Social Policy and Missionary Organizations in Ceylon 1840-1855* London, 1965. See chapters II and III of part I.

conflict with the principle of non-interference with Buddhist affairs. G.N. Paterson, a predecessor of Rhys Davids in Anuradhapura, in his capacity as District Judge—the Assistant Government Agent was also the District Judge—had given judgment in a case which had arisen between the two factions of the Nuwerawewa family. He had ruled that the faction whose head was Owille Kumarihamy had the right of making the nomination to the chief priestship of the Sacred Places. To the Government it was sufficient that a court of law had decided the question, although legally the judgment did not preclude the other faction whose head was Galagoda Banda from appealing to the Supreme Court. Instead of doing so, however, Galagoda Banda was trying to take forcible possession of the Sacred Places, a course of action which led to constant friction between the two factions.

It was in these circumstances that Gregory decided in Anuradhapura that he should summon an assembly of the priests, chiefs, and people, to announce that the Government would abide by the decision of the District Court and recognise the claims of Owille Kumarihamy, thereby putting an end to the question for all time. Gregory also hoped that the occasion could be used to give answers to certain petitions which had been submitted to him.

Considerable preparations were made for this meeting which, but for an unexpected event, might well have been forgotten. Significantly in his long despatch Gregory recounted the incident with a fastidious attention to detail. On the platform which had been put up for the occasion, Gregory took his place at its centre. Twynam and Arthur Templer, who was the Assistant Government Agent in Mannar, sat on one side of the Governor. On the other side Rhys Davids as well as John Young—who was the principal officer dealing with the public works in the district—were accommodated. The *kachcheri* Mudaliyar, whose task it was to translate Gregory's speech into Sinhalese, was standing close by. When Gregory was explaining that with regard to the dispute of the custodianship of the Sacred Places the Government was bound to abide by the decision of the District Court, a woman who was followed by an impressive retinue of servants detached herself from the mass of the crowd, walked slowly towards the platform and handed in a petition which Rhys Davids got up to receive on Gregory's behalf. Under the impression that the person before him was Owille Kumarihamy, Gregory began to address her. It took some time for the officials present to realise that it was not Owille Kumarihamy but Nuwerawewa Kumarihamy—

another member of the old Nuwerawewa family—who was standing before Gregory. Gregory immediately explained to the gathering that a mistake had been made but left no doubt in the minds of the hearers that the Government had categorically recognised the claims of Owille Kumarihamy. Outwardly unruffled by the incident, he next dealt with a number of petitions on other matters which had been submitted to him.

Subsequent developments leave little doubt that Gregory took this incident—trifling as it might seem—very much to heart. He had been needlessly embarrassed and blamed Rhys Davids entirely. Rhys Davids was no stranger to Anurdhapura. It was inconceivable that he should have been confused with regard to Owille Kumarihamy's identity. Indeed, Twynam had assured Gregory that in appearance the two were quite dissimilar. Owille Kumarihamy was young and had a very fair complexion, unlike Nuwerawewa Kumarihamy who was not merely dark but was also very much older. Gregory also felt bitter that at the time Rhys Davids had done nothing to speedily remedy a blunder which might not have been discovered but for the fortuitous intervention of the District Court *Mudaliyar*. Above all, as Gregory explained to Kimberley, Rhys Davids had appeared to be "amused" at the Governor's embarrassment.

Gregory disbelieved Rhys Davids who had hastened to explain at the end of the meeting that he himself had been genuinely misled by the appearance of Nuwerawewa Kumarihamy. Indeed, as Twynam himself later remarked to Gregory, both ladies dressed in the traditional manner of aristocratic Kandyan women and went about with retinues of servants. Besides the fact that Nuwerawewa Kumarihamy led a life of seclusion following the death of her father and was therefore rarely seen in public, added to the possibilities of confusion. Rhys Davids had also explained that seated as he was, he did not get a clear view of who stood before the Governor and that his attention was wholly directed to ensuring that the *Kachcheri* Mudaliyar was translating Gregory's speech accurately. Gregory had given Rhys Davids the impression that he accepted these explanations and that he had forgotten the matter.

Instead, when Twynam in the course of the Government Agents conference in Kandy drew Gregory's attention to Rhys Davids' activities, Gregory resolved that the Anuradhapura incident should also be made a subject of investigation. This resolve evidently hardened when Gregory learned from Twynam that Rhys Davids had on more than one occasion spoken to Owille Kumarihamy and could not therefore reasonably claim that he had been unable to identify her.

Some of the other guidelines for the proposed investigation were clearly inspired by Gregory's conversations with Twynam at this stage. As matters stood it was but natural that Twynam's views on Rhys Davids should have weighed heavily in Gregory's mind. It could hardly have been an impression independently arrived at by Gregory on the strength of his brief sojourn in Anuradhapura that Rhys Davids was making illegal personal gains in collecting the Grain Tax. Much less the assumption—another suggested field of investigation—that Rhys Davids was sufficiently wealthy to be able to loan money on stiff rates of interest.

One may regard with scepticism Gregory's general contention that he had kept an open mind with regard to the allegations made against Rhys Davids. He said that he had expressed the hope to both Twynam and Douglas, who were about to leave to Anuradhapura, that Rhys Davids whould be vindicated as a result of their investigations. Gregory vouchsafed this remark to Kimberley in an attempt to rebut Rhys Davids' claim that he had not been dealt with fairly. This statement was, however, hardly consistent with the fact that Gregory "armed" Douglas and Twynam with the power to interdict Rhys Davids from his duties at the end of the investigation. This left little doubt that before the conference of the Government Agents broke up, Rhys Daivds' culpability was regarded as a foregone conclusion.

The sense of great urgency in the travelling arrangements devised by Gregory for Douglas and Twynam was also significant. As Douglas recorded, ". . . the unusual step was taken of placing relays along the road both of horses and bullocks by which means we were enabled to journey to reach Anuradhapura in thirty five and to return in thirty seven hours remaining in the spot not quite three days."

III

If Gregory had prejudged the case against Rhys Davids, he was partly vindicated by the findings of Douglas and Twynam.

In general, however, opinion in Ceylon was more varied especially within the body of the small though highly articulate European community. The English missionaries living in Ceylon were sympathetic towards Rhys Davids and supported memorials which were hastily got up on his behalf. This was in a sense remarkable in view of Rhys Davids' interests and his close association with Sinhalese Buddhists. On the other hand, the officials were more divided, and as a body their outlook was not governed by narrow considerations of *esprit de corps.*

To the Ceylonese in general, the spectacle of a European in the dock, as it were, was sufficiently rare to warrant the crystallization of firm opinion. It was noteworthy, however, that Sinhalese Buddhists in the Galle District as well as the leading *Ratemahatmayas* in the Southern Province, rallied in Rhys Davids' defence. On the other hand, the *Ceylon Patriot* probably reflected the views of the more critical minded among the Western educated Ceylonese when it mused on the possibility that leniency would be shown Rhys Davids as he was a European.

For his part, Gregory was determined to demonstrate the contrary to the Ceylonese. He persuaded himself that the issues implied in the Rhys Davids affair involved the very attitudes of Oriental people to British rule. In his despatches to the Colonial Office, therefore, Gregory stated the case against Rhys Davids with an exaggerated intensity hardly warranted by the essentially pedestrian considerations involved.

The gravemen of the charges against Rhys Davids concerned the cattle question. Gregory told Kimberley that Rhys Davids had carried out certain policies regarding cattle which the peasants in the Nuwerakalawiya District customarily maintained in large numbers. In an area that was not particularly noted for high yields of paddy, cattle rearing constituted a major means of livelihood. Rhys Davids had frowned on the trespassing of cattle which according to Gregory he had mistakenly regarded as a public menace of the first magnitude. The restrictions which Rhys Davids had accordingly imposed on the movements of cattle to prevent the nuisance of trespassing had caused great hardship to the peasants. They were virtually denied grazing rights which they had enjoyed from time immemorial. Moreover, in enforcing his policies Rhys Davids had begun to impose fines on cattle owners disregarding the legal basis on which alone in certain broadly specific circumstances it was possible to impose moderate fines for cattle trespass. Above all Rhys Davids had enforced his policies without consulting his superior, the Government Agent of Jaffna.

The unflattering portrait of a callous administrator inflicting hardship on an unresisting peasantry was only partially redeemed by Rhys Davids' own account of the reasons which prompted him to decide on the very policies which Gregory considered so repugnant. Rhys Davids had thought that it was not necessary for cattle owners to keep their cattle within the town of Anuradhapura. He constantly urged them to send their cattle, other than the milk cows, to the outlying villages to be taken care of by friends and relations. Such a practice Rhys Davids argued was in harmony with the customs prevailing among the Sinhalese. The cattle owners who allowed their cattle to graze all over the town during the day had the cattle penned at night in the backyard of their dwellings. Because the town itself was small—consisting of almost three streets—the tiny backyards which were hardly suited for the purpose had become receptacles of filth and disease. Rhys Davids declared that if anything was the cause of the reputed unhealthiness of Anuradhapura, it was this.

Indeed, Rhys Davids had lost no opportunity to urge the cattle owners that they must send their cattle away or continue to pay the fines which he would inflict on them for cattle trespass. At least one desperate cattle owner took his advice. Two or three others had sold their cattle. The great majority, however, continued to pay the fines which Rhys Davids imposed.

Other motives, however, gave Rhys Davids' campaign against the cattle owners almost the stamp of sweet reasonableness. In the second of two detailed answers to the charges made against him, Rhys Davids explained that he had grasped the possibilities of developing cattle rearing in Nuwerakalawiya as an industry which could benefit the peasants. Surrounding the large tanks and not far removed from the town were pasture lands of a quality probably not found elsewhere in the island. Secondly, a regular business in despatching cattle to Colombo, where there was a growing demand for meat, was a practical possibility. Rhys Davids claimed that as a practical step he had sent specimens of Nuwerakalawiya cattle to the Alfred Model Farm in Colombo. As things stood, however, no headway could be made because the cattle were ill cared for and emaciated. Above all there had to be a change of heart among the cattle owners who would have to realize the importance of rearing healthy stock for commercial purposes. Instead cattle were allowed to graze in the open spaces of the town which in any event were poor in fodder. Moreover, because the cattle were neither watched over nor tethered, they invariably caused damage to cultivation, especially the buffaloes against whom no fence was adequate protection. Consequently, Rhys Davids had been unable to take in hand the establishment of plantations for cotton and tobacco for which the Nuwerakalawiya area was particularly suited.

For his own part Gregory minimised the problem. He assured Kimberley that there could possibly have been no objection to the practice of untethered cattle grazing in the open spaces of the town which he described as "a hamlet surround by park like ground." Because it was not in his interests to do so, Gregory did not tell the Colonial Office that Louis Leisching had himself attempted to deal with the problem. Leisching, for example, had formally urged cattle owners that they should not allow cattle to stray over the town. He had appointed a man, paid by subscriptions levied from the cattle owners, to look after cattle. Leisching, it would appear, had grown apathetic after four months because the measures were in themselves inadequate to deal with the problem.

There was on the whole much less uncertainty concerning the manner in which Rhys Davids had enforced his cattle policies. When his efforts to maintain a cattle pound had failed, Rhys Davids decided to impose fines on the cattle owners principally by means of his domestic servants and the petty employees in the *Kachcheri.* He commanded his servants to seize cattle which strayed into the premises of his bungalow. The *Kachcheri peons* and watchers could seize cattle within the grounds of the *Kachcheri* and the courthouse. More significantly, the constable—who figured a great deal in the subsequent inquiries—was given power to seize untethered cattle grazing on lands belonging to the government. As the open spaces on which hitherto the cattle had been accustomed to graze were invariably public land, the consequences may well be imagined.

Abuse which was almost inherent in a system of this nature was made all the more certain by Rhys Davids himself, who announced that his servants as well as the *Kachcheri* employees who caught cattle could help themselves to a share of the fines. The large number of cattle owners from whom fines were exacted and the amounts paid left little doubt that they had set about their task with considerable exuberance.

The predicament in which Kaluhami—a woman who, it would seem, had a fair number of cattle—had found herself, was revealing. The aggregate fines paid by her amounted to £22. When in addition four of her cattle died after they had been seized, and she received no compensation, she was in sore straits. In order to pay her fines Kaluhami had not only been compelled to sell the rest of her cattle but she had also borrowed money from the District Court *Mudaliyar*. Although allowance must necessarily be made for Gregory's proneness to dramatize the Kaluhami affair, Rhys Davids, when given the opportunity, did not significantly dispute Kaluhami's averments in relation either to fact or detail. He also let go unchallenged the statement made to Douglas and Twynam in his presence by a peasant named Mary that Rhys Davids' servants had refused to release three of her cattle although she had pleaded that she was unable to pay the fine. She declared that she had got back her cattle by pawning her jewelry to pay the fine of 15 shillings.

Rhys Davids' claim that he had been unaware of the excesses of his subordinates was viewed with a mixture of scepticism and contempt. During the inquiry it would appear that he listened in shocked disbelief to the numerous witnesses whose evidence Douglas and Twynam recorded. Rhys Davids was sure that the witnesses were exaggerating and were part of a conspiracy to discredit him. He argued that the peasants had not complained to him against cattle seizures because they were themselves aware of the offence they committed and did not feel that the fines were oppressive. If in some instance the fines had been oppressive, he would have set matters right, had he only been told.

The evidence, however, clearly showed that the peasants realised the futility of doing so. For one thing, Rhys Davids had firmly announced his intention to impose fines. It seemed, therefore, that Rhys Davids' servants as well as the *peons* were carrying out his orders. If the peasants, on the other hand, refused to pay the fines they had to face formal prosecution in a court of law over which Rhys Davids himself presided.The fact too that Rhys Davids was himself often in his bungalow or in the *Kachcheri* when cattle were being seized, suggested in the eyes of the peasants that he was fully aware of and condoned the activities of his subordinates. A certain Tamil man whose cattle had been seized and who went to the extent of prostrating himself before Rhys Davids' servants in a vain bit to retrieve his cattle, did not think it worth his while to appeal to Rhys Davids, who at the time of the incident was in his bungalow.

Moreover, on numerous occasions Rhys Davids' subordinates had forcibly prevented aggrieved cattle owners from seeing him and concealed from Rhys Davids the evidence of growing dissatisfaction and frustration. Kaluhami alone had succeeded in seeing Rhys Davids whenever she was called upon to pay fines. He had however turned her out summarily, warning her that she must pay the particular fine if she wanted to have her cattle back. His harsh treatment of her was only matched by the lack of any sense of remorse when in the course of investigations he recalled his transactions with her. Having virtually admitted the substantial accuracy of what kaluhami had told Douglas and Twynam—although he thought that Kaluhami had wildly exaggerated the amount—Rhys Davids declared that she could well afford the fines, as she was a wealthy woman who, apart from owning a large number of cattle, had lands as well as jewelry. Indeed, in contrast to Gregory's picture of Kaluhami, the luckless peasant who was reduced to destitution, Rhys Davids painted a picture of an artful woman who simulated distress to revenge herself on him as well as to make the best of Twynam's decision to repay the fines.

Clearly in some instances at any rate Rhys Davids had been aware of what was happening. Henry Martin Williams, who was a clerk in the Post Office in Anuradhapura, supplemented his modest earnings by occasionally giving out on hire a cart and a pair of bullocks which he owned. In April 1872, Rhys Davids who had been summoned to the Supreme Court in Kandy had hired Williams's cart in order to transport his baggage. During his absence Williams had been compelled in turn to hire a cart from a Moorman for the purpose of transporting timber. It happened that just after the timber had been unloaded, the bullocks, who had been untied, had strayed into Rhys Davids' garden where they were promptly seized by his servants. At first, Williams had offered to pay a nominal fine of about a shilling for each bullock. When this offer was rejected, Williams had forcibly removed the bullocks, telling Rhys Davids' servants that they could prosecute him. When Rhys Davids returned from Kandy, his principal servant brought Williams the cart hired for the trip to Kandy which amounted to £1 and 10 shillings. But from this was deducted a sum of 10 shillings being the fine which Williams had to pay for the Moorman's bullocks which had strayed into Rhys Davids' garden. When Williams had remonstrated, Rhys Davids had warned him that if he "talked anymore he would fine the 10 shillings for each."

It was evident that Rhys Davids had at no time serious misgivings concerning the strict legality of his actions. When he was challenged his defence was so much a revelation of the inadequacies of the laws concerning cattle trespass as it was a skillful attempt to vindicate himself.

The law concerning this question was almost wholly derived from an ordinance which had been made in 1835 when it was first realized, particularly in the plantation areas, that some sort of restriction should be imposed on Ceylonese who as a matter of habit allowed their cattle to graze indiscriminately on public roads and stray into cultivated lands and canals. In the heat of the controversy concerning Rhys Davids' actions, the extent to which this ordinance was weighted heavily against cattle owners was overlooked. For example, it was possible for an occupant or owner of land to detain cattle which strayed into his land until damages were assessed, provided he took steps to inform the owner of the cattle of the fact of the seizure within two days. It was also possible for an occupant of land to claim fines even though the offending cattle may not have been caught. Indeed he could—if the nuisance continued unabated—shoot the cattle on sight. Moreover, stray cattle which had been seized but were not claimed within 14 days could be sold by the occupant or the owner of the land concerned.

If a strictly narrow view of the ordinance was taken, only an occupant or owner of the land could seize cattle. When cattle had been seized it was the duty of the occupant of the land to inform the nearest headman who would assess the damage done. The headman's report would then be submitted to the District Court which had power of imposing fines if necessary over and above the headman's assessment. If no damage was proved, the court could nevertheless impose a fine of 10 shillings for every head of cattle on the ground of trespass.

The ordinance was not—as Gregory imagined—the last word in law with regard to this question. Precisely because the ordinance was not sufficiently flexible to cope with various contingencies which had in the normal course of events arisen following its enactment, the courts had relied on common law to deal with cattle trespass. Accordingly not only was it possible for the occupants of land to detain cattle but to stipulate compensation as well for trespass without the intermediary of third parties. Disputes were taken to court only if the parties had failed to agree on the amount of compensation. Alternatively, the courts had dealt with cases in which the owner of cattle had denied liability and instead claimed relief from an occupant of land for illegal detention of cattle.

Rhys Davids who with characteristic thoroughness had studied cases of cattle trespass which had been dealt with by some of the provincial courts in the island, was able to show that in the Central Province—the home of the plantation industry—it was customary for planters to levy a fine of as much as £1 per head of cattle for trespass. And that, although the provincial courts had often shown a certain sympathy to cattle owners—especially when their cattle died after they had been seized—the Supreme Court significantly frowned on cattle trespassing. In the Court of Requests in Kandy a cattle owner sued a planter for the value of a bullock which had died after it had been seized for trespass. The Supreme Court set aside the judgment of the same Court in a case in which a planter had sued the owner of a buffalo for damage done to a grass field. The judge had dismissed the action on the ground that the plaintiff's witnesses had been unable to prove the exact amount of damage done. The Supreme Court, however, had decided that the Plaintiff had proved that the injury had been done to him although "he cannot prove that the injury had cost him a farthing." Moreover, interestingly enough—and this was so germane to the Rhys Davids affair—in more than one instance the Supreme Court had, in assessing damages, taken into consideration that a cattle owner had been already warned by the plaintiff on previous occasions.

On ground that was much less tenable, Rhys Davids had argued that the Thoroughfares Ordinance of 1870, which *inter alia* imposed further restraints on cattle trespass, had enabled him in any case to inflict fines on refractory cattle owners. Gregory however countered that the ordinance was applicable to public roads. Indeed, with regard to a cognate consideration, Gregory had assured Kimberly that Anuradhapura was really a hamlet "surrounded by park like ground." Whether a valid distinction could have been made between the formal thoroughfares of the sort which the framers of this ordinance had in mind, and the tracks which by usage were in Anuradhapura to all purposes roads, was a moot point. Several witnesses had remarked that they had to pass the *Kachcheri* as well as Rhys Davids' bungalow in going from the town to the area in which some of the tanks were situated.

Other aspects of Rhys Davids' actions throw further light on the problem. Gregory, in stating the case against Rhys Davids, placed particular emphasis on the testimony of certain government officials—both European and Ceylonese—who owned cattle. The implied assumption was that as witnesses they were far more reliable than the run of the mill peasant. Ironically, their evidence showed that Rhys

Davids had applied the law to all without fear or favour. Three cows belonging to Edward Fretz, who worked in the public Works Department, had on one occasion been seized by Rhys Davids' servants. As it was too late to pay a fine and recover the cattle—Fretz had only been told about the seizure towards evening—Fretz bitterly complained that his children had had to forego their milk for the night. When his servant met Rhys Davids on the following day, he was told that he must pay a fine before the cattle could be released. Moreover, on several occasions Joseph Town, who was Government Medical Officer in Anuradhapura, had been fined on account of his cattle.

Like Fretz, Town had paid these fines through his servants without himself confronting Rhys Davids. Neither Fretz nor Town, who evidently had reason to speak to Rhys Davids in the ordinary course of their work, had broached the subject with Rhys Davids, despite the misgivings they entertained about the legality of his fines. On one occasion alone when no less than twelve of his cattle had been seized by Rhys Davids' servants, Town had remonstrated with Rhys Davids, who had agreed to waive the fine but much to Town's chagrin had added that he did not strictly see the need to do so as "poor people had to suffer the fine."

The plausibly retrieved image of an impartial though hard administrator which emerged was marred by the fact which Rhys Davids himself freely admitted, that part of the money recovered by these fines had been put to his personal use, the remainder being shared by his servants whose enthusiasm in seizing cattle did not thus go unrewarded. To Rhys Davids it had seemed that this practice was countenanced by the ordinance of 1835 which stipulated that no less than 10 shillings for every head of cattle could be paid to the owner or occupant of a land even though no damage could be proved. Gregory on the other hand contended that as Rhys Davids was a Government Servant he could not consider the bungalow and gardens which he was occupying as private property to benefit personally from the ordinance.

IV

The issues were much less complex concerning a kindred question which weighed heavily in the scales against Rhys Davids.

As Assistant Government Agent, Rhys Davids had at various times inflicted fines on his subordinates in the Anuradhapura *Kachcheri* for alleged shortcomings of duty. Such fines were plainly illegal. Gregory assured Kimberley that a Government Agent had power only to deprive a subordinate official of a day's pay for absence from work without leave. If a Government Agent had reason for dissatisfaction with a subordinate on other grounds, he could do no more than make a formal report to the government for action. A government minute circularised in 1863 among the Government Agents had reiterated the rules. In actual fact, however, over the years Government Agents had customarily fined their subordinates crediting the monies to the revenue. It was inconceivable that on every occasion in which a lapse was discovered, a Government Agent should have had to await instructions from Colombo before an offender could be taken to task.

Evidently Rhys Davids had been genuinely unaware of the strict legal position. In any event, he pointed out that at the time he assumed duties in Anuradhapura, there was already a Book of Fines which contained details of fines which Leisching had imposed on various *Kachcheri* officials and the entries had been initialed by Twynam himself. In spite of this, Twynam stoutly maintained that a fine book which Rhys Davids had maintained was a complete innovation.

Rhys Davids maintained that he had been provoked to fine his subordinates on account of their negligence of one sort or another. The bare entries in the fine book would in themselves make no sense unless certain details—which he had not thought necessary to record therein—were kept in mind. He had certainly fined the Fiscal's Clerk whose habitual lethargy caused needless inconvenience to litigants. An occasion which Rhys Davids particularly remembered was the Clerk's failure to issue a writ in time thereby denying the litigants concerned from practically benefiting from payments which Rhys Davids had entered in their favour. Rhys Davids had also taken to task Williams, who was the clerk who managed the post office. It was Williams's habit to close the post office as and when he pleased because he was anxious to get home early. Moreover, letters which should have been despatched from Anuradhapura on the day they were received were needlessly held over for an extra day. Rhys Davids had also fined the Registrar's Clerk for undue delay in preparing the seasonal returns which were forwarded to Jaffna.

Indeed the complaint had often been made that the returns for the entire Province had been needlessly delayed on account of delays concerning the Nuwerakalawiya district.

However, other fines which Rhys Davids had imposed were mainfestly much less justifiable. He had fined a *peon* ten shillings for breaking a valuable carved stone pillar in the course of clearing some ruins. There had been twelve such pillers. Rhys Davids had decided that a tree which grew in close proximity to one of the pillars should be cut down. He had urged the *peon* to exercise the greatest caution in doing so. "I had a long consultation with him," recalled Rhys Davids, "as to the best way of cutting it down so as to save the piller... I particularly warned him to tie a rope to the tree so as to make it fall properly." The *peon*, however, had neglected to do so and the tree had shattered the pillar.

Other examples were as revealing. The town gaoler had been entrusted with the responsibility of looking after a nursery of *Na* plants which Rhys Davids had set up. In order to maintain the nursery effectively, Rhys Davids had instructed the gaoler to use the labour of the prisoners. Rhys Davids, it appeared, had lavished much care and expense in this connection. Consequently, Rhys Davids was considerably distressed when he discovered on his return to Anuradhapura after an absence of a few days that all the *Na* plants had died. He immediately fined the gaoler. On another occasion Rhys Davids had fined two headmen 10 shillings each for not providing him with suitable accommodation when he was on circuit. He thought that the headmen should have put up "a temporary shed hung with cotton clothes." Such facilities were necessary to carry out the business of government and were in any case consistent with "the old customs of the people."

The cxcessive fines which were imposed on these occasions merely served to emphasise the unorthodoxy implied in Rhys Davids' actions. The Fiscal's clerk who had been fined by Rhys Davids earned a salary of £2.1.6 per month. The fines he had paid in October alone amounted to 15 shillings and aggregated £2-12-0 for the period from August 1871 to February 1872. The fines paid by the Registrar's clerk whose monthly salary was £1-13-4 amounted to 19 shillings during the same period. The fine of 10 shillings which Rhys Davids had imposed on the *peon* for "gross carelessness in destroying a valuable work of art"—the episode of the broken pillar—amounted to a fortnight of the *peon's* pay. Ironically in another context Rhys

Davids himself had drawn Twynam's attention to the small salaries which this type of minor official was being paid.

To make matters worse, Gregory told Kimberley that Rhys Davids had appropriated the fines for his own use. For his part, Rhys Davids did not deny that he had bought certain official publications—Administration Reports and Blue books—for general use. But because Rhys Davids had bought—also with the fine monies—some of these documents in duplicate, Douglas and Twynam accused Rhys Davids of misappropriation. The documents were of such practical usefulness that the purchase of duplicates was in itself not objectionable. Moreover, for purposes of handy reference Rhys Davids had kept some of the duplicates in his bungalow. Rhys Davids, in the course of a meticulously detailed rebuttal, sarcastically asked whether the purchase of a travelling inkstand, an item only made necessary by the exigencies of official travel, a prismatic compass and the purchase of memoranda books—to replace a collection of sundry paper used for the purpose—had been necessitated by his personal needs. The only items which Rhys Davids could not justify on this basis were some human skulls and the carcasses of certain animals, particularly pangolins, which Rhys Davids had sent to the Natural History Museum in Oxford.

V

On other grounds, too, Gregory was determined to run his quarry down to earth. He formally accused Rhys Davids of prevarication. Elsewhere in his long despatch Gregory also made passing references to Rhys Davids' credibility.

There was indeed a kind of farcical incongruity between the ponderous gravity which Gregory resorted to in spelling out the charge of prevarication and the utter triviality of the incidents complained of. For example, fault was found with Rhys Davids for not having disclosed that he had bought certain government publications in duplicate for his "personal use." Secondly, according to Gregory, there was also evidence of prevarication in the initial correspondence between Twynam and Rhys Davids on the cattle question. In reply to a specific question which Twynam had asked, Rhys Davids had denied that there was any truth in the petition which the cattle owners had submitted. Moreover, Rhys Davids had at first maintained that the fines for trespass had been imposed in court, but when pressed, had admitted that some of the fines had been informally levied.

Rhys Davids, however, denied that he had been deliberately untruthful. He declared that in the face of Twynam's hostile behaviour he had been on his guard in his replies. He had realised that some of his answers were inadequate but had hoped to take up the matter with the Colonial Secretary in due course. But the sudden reappearance of Twynam who was accompanied by Douglas had confused him.

"Unhappily this is not the first instnce of Mr. Davids' untruthfulness." With this remark Gregory plunged into certain details concerning Bastian, who was Rhys Davids' principal servant. According to Gregory, Bastian had handled the fine money and generally decided what amounts should be paid to the other servants who helped in seizing cattle. On the second day of the investigations, when Douglas and Twynam wanted to record his evidence, they found that Bastian as well as the rest of Rhys Davids' servants had disappeared. Asked when Bastian had left his service Rhys Davids had vaguely surmised that Bastian had left him about a week before the time of the investigations.

Subsequently when Bastian appeared in Kandy, and made himself available for examination, it was believed in official circles that Rhys Davids had summoned him thither. All the more so because the evidence of Rhys Davids' other servants—who had been traced to Galle—had meanwhile been independently recorded. According to their testimony, Bastian, who was also a native of Galle, had left Galle on receiving a letter from Rhys Davids. Hence Rhys Davids was not believed when he tried to assure the Colonial Secretary that he had no hand in Bastian's sudden reappearance.

The inferences as far as the government was concerned were plain. Had Rhys Davids, for example, calculated that if the evidence of his servants was not made available, the inquiry would have to be abandoned? Or, had he feared that in their testimony his servants would give away too much? And yet on the other hand their evidence—especially that of Bastian who stood up well at cross examination—favoured Rhys Davids a great deal. Moreover in the course of the investigations when Rhys Davids had been asked whether he had any questions to put to Town, whose testimony had been particularly damaging, Rhys Davids had remarked in despair that had his servants been at hand, he could have given a true picture of what had happened. It was just possible that Rhys Davids' servants who had carried out his orders and had no fears regarding the legality of such orders had taken fright at the very first sign of trouble when the discomfiture of their own master was so evident. Hence they left Rhys Davids not at the time of the investigations of Douglas and Twynam but earlier when Twynam first began to look into Rhys Davids' activities.

Moreover, Rhys Davids' explanation about the reappearance of Bastian which might easily have been verified, had been rejected. During the time of the investigations of Douglas and Twynam, a Sinhalese living in Anuradhapura called Goonewardene had pointed out to Rhys Davids that his defence would be materially helped if Bastian could be summoned to Anuradhapura. When Rhys Davids demurred, Goonewardene had asked for permission to write to Bastian. Rhys Davids had agreed, cautioning Goonewardene however that it must be understood that Goonewardene was doing so entirely on his own responsibility. Although the government was determined to make a painstakingly thorough investigation it did not think it necessary to check Rhys Davids' statement by examining Goonewardene.

VI

Indeed, despite Gregory's assurances that Rhys Davids had been dealt with fairly during the investigations, there was ample evidence to illustrate the reverse.

Gregory had issued a letter of interdiction even before the formal investigations had begun. In a narrow sense it could be argued that the intention was to resort to it only if the necessity arose. On the other hand the step also suggested that the case against Rhys Davids had already been decided in spirit and in fact.

Moreover, when the letter of interdiction had been formally handed over, Rhys Davids was compelled to leave Anuradhapura. He began to live in Kandy where he addressed himself to the formidable task of preparing his defence to the various charges which were at this stage formally communicated to him. In effect, therefore, Rhys Davids was debarred from access to official papers. Nor had he the means of consulting with important witnesses in order to refresh his own mind with regard to details and if possible gather evidence in his favour. These difficulties were materially increased because the Colonial Secretary in formally communicating the charges did not send Rhys Davids a copy of the Douglas-Twynam report much less the evidence on which this report was based. The Colonial Secretary contented himself with enclosing an extract from the report. It was only after Rhys Davids had protested that the papers in their entirety were sent to him.

Moreover, after Rhys Davids had left Anuradhapura his successor, Hay Cameron, on instructions from Colombo, recorded further evidence largely concerning the cattle question. The necessity to do so was not evident. It is possible that Gregory wanted to strengthen the volume of the evidence against Rhys Davids. When Rhys Davids heard about these developments quite by chance, he pointed out to the Colonial Secretary that it would be unjust to admit this evidence as he had no opportunity of cross examining the witnesses. He was at the time unaware that Hay Cameron himself had neglected to do so. The Colonial Secretary, whose reply indicated that the government had had every intention of using this evidence, grudgingly conceded the point. Nonetheless, this evidence in its entirety formed a crucially significant part of Gregory's despatch to Kimberley. In fact, from the point of view of the government, it was the evidence collected by Cameron that was more impressive. This evidence was fuller in detail and less vitiated by contradictions than the material which Douglas and Twynam had collected.

By the same token, the evidence which had also been recorded in Galle in Rhys Davids' absence was susceptible to objection. Nonetheless, this evidence too prefigured a great deal in weighing the scales against Rhys Davids.

The only opportunity which Rhys Davids had had of cross examining witnesses was in the course of the Twynam-Douglas investigations. It is remarkable that he should not have availed himself of the privilege to a greater extent than he actually did. Indeed, he sat through the proceedings not as one involved but as a vaguely interested spectator, and only very occasionally interfered to ask a question. When he did so he was able either to cause the witness to contradict himself or to demonstrate that the witness was more anxious to settle old scores than to complain about the injustices of Rhys Davids' cattle policies.

Tragically, however, in view of Rhys Davids' spasmodic cross examination and the predisposition of Douglas and Twynam to believe the native witnesses, Rhys Davids' interests were very much in jeopardy. No allowance was made, for example, for the possibility that the witnesses may have been exaggerating. Indeed, they had every reason to do so. Twynam had ordered Rhys Davids, as well as the petty *Kachcheri* officials, to return the fines that had been levied from various cattle owners. Many exaggerated the amounts due to them. Others who had not been involved pretended that they had been heavily fined. Significantly, when Douglas and Twynam began their investigations, more than one person who had not signed the petition came forward to claim that they have been mulcted of large sums for cattle trespass. According to Rhys Davids, the town bazaar was full of rumours of how people were taking advantage of the situation. In particular it was being said that Kaluhami had been able to get more than she was entitled to.

Moreover, it was not always that the conclusions which were arrived at had sufficient supporting evidence. The facts which clearly emerged from the welter of confusing evidence, were that on Rhys Davids' instructions it had become a common occurrence that cattle were seized and fines were imposed on the owners. The evidence was most suspect however regarding the amounts of the fines as well as the modes resorted to in apprehending cattle. It was stated more as a factual conclusion rather than a plausible surmise that Rhys Davids' servants had deliberately kept the gates leading to his bungalow opened so that straying cattle would come into the garden. The conclusion was based on the testimony of a single witness—Town—whose evidence on the whole was treated with a measure of scepticism in the Colonial Office. Corroboration of a questionable and extremely ambiguous sort was only forthcoming from Rodrigo who was tne *Kachcheri* Mudaliyar. He told Douglas and Twynam that sometimes the gates were opened and at other times closed, but more often they were kept open. In giving evidence before Cameron, however, in reply to a specific inquiry on the point, Rodrigo said:

> It may have been the object of the servants to drive the cattle into the compound that they may get half the share of the fine. It would have been no object of Mr. Davids to have the cattle driven inside the compound as the fine was the same as that imposed upon cattle outside.

It was also significant that when they were asked, Rhys Davids' servants in Galle, who could not have known the drift of the evidence which was being recorded in Anuradhapura, denied categorically that the gates were kept open as a matter of practice. Their evidence on other matters—which incidentally roughly corroborated what the cattle owners had said in Anuradhapura—showed that they were not being untruthful out of a sense of loyalty to their former master. When evidence was basically in an undetermined state on the point, Gregory significantly weighed in to say that when he visited Anuradhapura he had observed that the gates were kept open and that he had casually remarked about it to Rhys Davids without realising its significance.

In other respects too Rhys Davids had reason for bitterness. For example there was the rather questionable resurrection of the "Ismail affair" which placed Rhys Davids in an unfavourable light. When Rhys Davids had been Magistrate in Galle he had on several occasions complained to the Colonial Secretary about M. Ismail, who was the chief clerk in the Magistrate's Court. Rhys Davids was able to prove that Ismail had not only neglected the duties assigned to the chief clerk but that Ismail had also repeatedly ignored certain routine orders which Rhys Davids had made with regard to the work of the Court. After Ismail had been reprimanded and Rhys Davids had reported that in spite of this there had been no improvement, the government had dismissed Ismail without further ado.

Ismail, who was described by Rhys Davids as an "astute Moorman" was however not to be undone. He began to claim that Rhys Davids had imposed excessive fines on him for negligence of duty and that Rhys Davids had used the money for his personal use. Consequently Ismail brought a civil action against Rhys Davids for the recovery of these sums, but was unsuccessful. Not long afterwards Ismail petitioned the government with the same end in view. This petition as a matter of course was referred to Rhys Davids for answer. Rhys Davids evidently thought that this step was superfluous as he had already been exonerated in court. Hence his answers to the Colonial Secretary were short and almost terse. This was remedied by Rhys Davids in subsequent answers which were considered sufficiently adequate to absolve Rhys Davids from all blame. Thus the Ismail affair, which incidentally at the time aroused much interest, passed into oblivion, but not before Rhys Davids had been cautioned against imposing fines on subordinates, however well deserved the step might seem. And yet Gregory, who recalled the incident, took upon himself to remark to Kimberley that his own predecessor in office, Sir Hercules Robinson, should have investigated the Ismail affair more thoroughly, implying clearly that Rhys Davids should not have been exonerated at all.

In a sense it was but natural that the minds of Henry Irving, the Colonial Secretary, and John Douglas should have gone back to the Ismail affair, when it was reported that Rhys Davids had fined his subordinates in Anuradhapura. The Ismail affair was woven into the very texture of the case built against Rhys Davids. In his despatch to Kimberley, Gregory discussed it in fair detail. There was more than the reference to it in the Douglas-Twynam report. Above all, a formal charge against Rhys Davids was that he had fined his subordinates in the Anuradhapura Kachcheri disregarding the previous *caveat* given him when he was Police Magistrate in Galle.

Resurrected from the limbo of things forgotten, the Ismail affair prejudiced Rhys Davids' cause. It was one thing to decide when *in fact* Rhys Davids had fined his subordinates as irresponsibly as it was alleged. It was entirely another thing to say—as Gregory so tenaciously did—that in any event Rhys Davids was the sort of man who was capable of doing so.

VII

Neither had the Colonial Office been sufficiently responsive to these considerations. Charles Cox, who was the Principal Clerk in the Colonial Office, was convinced instead that the charges against Rhys Davids had been proved to the hilt. He minuted that the decision taken by the Government of Ceylon to suspend Rhys Davids from his duties should be confirmed "without entering into details." Indeed Cox expressed regret that Gregory had dropped the charge concerning Rhys Davids' role in the affair of the mistaken identity and the custodianship of the Sacred Places.

Cox had expressed these views after he had seen a minute by R.S.J. Macdonald, who was a comparatively junior clerk in the Colonial Office. Certain strikingly mordant marginal comments which Macdonald had made in reading the papers, especially in relation to Rhys Davids' defence, showed that he had plainly disbelieved Rhys Davids' protestations of innocence. Nonetheless, Macdonald had been willing to concede certain points in Rhys Davids' favour. He thought it improbable that Rhys Davids had deliberately tried to deceive Gregory on the occasion when Goregory had convened the chiefs and people of Nuwerakalwiya to uphold the claims of Owille Kumarihamy. Nor did he seriously think that Rhys Davids had been untruthful regarding the purchase of duplicates of government publications. With wry humour Macdonald observed that Administration Reports and Sessional papers were not "light reading" and could even in duplicate be considered official. On the whole, however, Macdonald believed that the charges against Rhys Davids had been fully established and that Rhys Davids should be dismissed from office.

Knatchbull Huggysen, who was Kimberley's Parliamentary Under Secretary, echoed Macdonald's sentiments and declared that Rhys Davids had been dealt with fairly by the Government of Ceylon in spite of Rhys Davids' prostestations to the contrary.

Kimberley's own reactions were somewhat more complex. He agreed that Davids must "quit the service" but suggested that Rhys Davids should be allowed to resign. Outright dismissal with the "ignominy" attached to it, he thought, would be too severe a punishment. Kimberley believed that Rhys Davids' motives had been honest and that this "alleviated the character of his offences." Kimberley also expressed the view that the Colonial Secretary's letter to Rhys Davids written on the 21st of October 1871 had not been "as judicial and calm in tone as might be desired." He minuted that he would like Sir H.T.Holland to see the papers and was anxious to talk the matter over with R.G.W. Herbert.

Indeed Herbert, who had enjoyed in equal measure the confidence of Kimberley's predecessor in office, Lord Carnarvon, was one of the great Permanent Under Secretaries of the Colonial Office in the nineteenth century. His familiarity with Ceylon affairs was only matched by the vast experience of Robert Meade who was the Assistant Permanent Under Secretary. Whether either saw the papers concerning the Rhys Davids affair is uncertain. One looks in vain for the characteristically lucid and succinct minutes which on many issues decided the policies of the Colonial Office regarding Ceylon.

The Lacuna, however, was, it would seem, partly filled by Sir T. Holland, whose analysis of the Rhys Davids affair was a significant departure from the views of his colleagues. Holland rejected the assumption—on which in the final analysis the case against Rhys Davids had been built—that Rhys Davids had been deliberately dishonest. What the evidence and Rhys Davids' own confessions had established was his ineptitude as a Government Agent. It was this consideration alone that warranted Rhys Davids' removal from office.

Significantly Holland did not think that Rhys Davids' defence had been given the weight that it deserved. This was particularly true of the cattle question on which it had been presumed the real strength of the case against Rhys Davids rested. Implied in Rhys Davids' defence was a distinction between cattle which had been caught within his compound and the seizure of cattle elsewhere. On grounds of Common Law—a consideration which Holland pointed out had been ignored by Gregory as well as by Douglas and Twynam—Rhys Davids was within his rights in seizing cattle that strayed into his compound. Whether the fines he had imposed on such occasions were excessive or otherwise was entirely another consideration. The fines were excessive because Rhys Davids had misapprehended his position in thinking it right "from analogy to the cases of actions in tort where damages are given in respect of continued and aggravated trespass" to impose such fines.

By way of a corollary, if it could be assumed—as Gregory and the Government of Ceylon did—that cattle had been wilfully driven into Rhys davids' compound, there was no doubt that Rhys Davids'suspension from office should be confirmed. But Holland categorically declared that he disbelieved Town, whose evidence alone had been the basis on which this assumption rested.

As regards cattle found outside Rhys Davids' compound too it could in a sense be argued that the ordinances had given Rhys Davids a certain right to have them seized. But there was no gainsaying, on the other hand, that Rhys Davids had erred in not imposing fines by means of the courts and in giving his servants and the *peons* a veritable free hand in seizing cattle. Morally Rhys Davids was responsible for the actions of his servants. But it would, Holland pointed out, be extravagant to maintain that Rhys Davids had been necessarily aware of every single act of cattle seizure committed by his servants.

Holland who on the whole was determined to take a "charitable view of the case" went a step further and drafted the despatch which Kimberley should write to Gregory. To begin with the decision arrived at by the Government of Ceylon that Rhys Davids should be struck off the list of Civil Servants was to be confirmed. The Government of Ceylon, however, was to be cautioned that outright dismissal was too severe a punishment. This view of Lord Kimberley's, it was to be pointed out, did not necessarily imply a lack of faith in the decisions of the Government of Ceylon. In any event—so ran Holland's draft despatch—Lord Kimberley did not think that Rhys Davids had been guilty of oppression in imposing fines on cattle within his compound. Nor did evidence support the contention that cattle had been deliberately driven into Rhys Davids' compound. Moreover, it was also Lord Kimberley's view that in imposing excessive fines "Mr. Davids acted under a *bona fide* misapprehension of his position." In short, Lord Kimberley was disposed to give Rhys Davids"the benefit of this doubt and to acquit him from the grave charge of dishonesty and extortion for the sake of personal gain."

"I am disposed to agree with Mr. Holland," minuted Kimberley. Nonetheless Kimberley was anxious that Knatchbull Huggysen should see Holland's minute. It was unlikely that Kimberley had reservations about the extenuating circumstances which Holland had discussed. Kimberley in fact had suggested the formula of "informal resignation" instead of dismissal. On the other hand Kimberley was really reluctant to override his deputy who had strongly called for Rhys Davids' dismissal.

Predictably Knatchbull Huggysen began "It is invidious and unpleasant task to argue against mercy . . ." However, according tc him, there were two reasons why Rhys Davids should not be permitted to resign. First, the Colonial Office had to take into account the impact of its decision on both the people as well as the Government of Ceylon. "The Charcter of Ceylon officials for probity and fair dealing should be above suspicion." On the other hand, it was also necessary to convince the native population "of the determination of the British authorities" that no leniency would be shown an officer whose conduct was a slur on the administration. Second, although Knatchbull Huggysen admitted that the charges against Rhys Davids had not been entirely proved, there was no getting around the fact that Rhys Davids' dismissal had been advised by "those on the spot," words which were significantly underlined.

Kimberley capitulated. He minuted that he had been aware of "the character of Mr. Daivds for industry and ability." But he was unwilling to override the decisions of the government of Ceylon. "As a rule they are far more likely to err on the side of laxity than severity to European officers . . ." Kimberley consoled himself.

Part III

The Embattled Scholar

10

THE PATH OF AN ORIENTALIST

THE end of Rhys Davids' career in Sri Lanka was the prelude to a strikingly different phase in his life.

In after years Rhys Davids himself made no reference to the circumstances of his leaving Sri Lanka. Here and there one encounters a cryptic allusion. Within the remarkably austere framework of his academic writings, however, there was little room for rambling asides, much less for tortuous self-vindication, especially if prudence dictated that it was best to let the dust settle on the issue.

Caroline Augusta Foley, whom he married in 1894, was, however, less reticent. In references which she made to the episode after his death in 1922, one gets a glimpse of what must have passed through his mind on his return to England. There emerges the picture of a broken man ". . . still young in years but thrown back saddened and ill." We are also told that in contrast to ". . . the bright hopes of his early career in Ceylon," Rhys Davids had become ". . . a man without means . . . with blighted prospects." Moreover Caroline Rhys Davids viewed his dismissal in a way that clearly put Rhys Davids in the light of a heroic martyr. The cause of it all was, according to her, Rhys Davids' attempts to protect the grazing rights of peasants which brought on his head "rebuke and insidious attack" and wrath of the powers that be. We are also told that Rhys Davids was not dismissed but that his services were dispensed with temporarily. Caroline Rhys Davids implied strongly that the way was always open to him to return to Sri Lanka to his career as a Civil Servant. But Rhys Davids "refused to return to Ceylon."[1]

Instead he "pulled himself together" and decided on a career in law.[2] To one who returned from the colonies in the circumstances he did—empty handed and under a cloud—there were indeed few choices left. In a more positive sense law would give considerable independ-

[1] Rhys Davids, Caroline Augusta Foley, *Wayfare's Words* (London, 1941), Vol. III, pp. 880ff.

[2] *Ibid.*

ence and—hopefully—a lucrative income. The decision may well have been also a reflex, of the nagging feeling Rhys Davids had in the course of the quasi-judicial inquiries which had led to his dismissal, that he had not been dealt with fairly.

And yet Rhys Davids did not practice, although he was called to the Bar by Middle Temple in 1877.[3] The truth was that his heart lay elsewhere—in the more rarefied and cloistered sphere of scholarship. In particular his interests centred on Buddhism, and in the immense field of Pali canonical literature, without a knowledge of which neither the origins nor the growth of early Buddhism could be understood. Significantly, Caroline Rhys Davids has left on record that during this phase of his life Rhys Davids was "haunted and pursued by the spiritual legacy bequeathed him from Ceylon." In much the same strain writing in a journal which had come under the influence of the Theosophists—Rhys Davids had himself little to do with Theosophy, which he rejected with contempt—Caroline Rhys Davids remarked that if her husbend abandoned law in pursuit of oriental studies it was because he had responded to "the voice of the greater messengers." At a more credible level, we learn that Rhys Davids on his return to England set about the task of making a systematic study of Pali Buddhism, which he had begun to pursue in Ceylon "without system."[4]

In spite of it all, it was evident that Rhys Davids had made what was in many ways clearly a hazardous choice. Pali studies were a highly specialised field. Few were interested. Fewer still knew anything about it. Nor was Pali taught in English Universities. Prospects of reasonably adequate monetary remuneration were therefore poor. Consequently, one is hardly surprised to read Caroline Rhys Davids' ramark that her husband launched himself on his self-willed career "in the teeth of warnings and prophecies of failure and insolvency, of head shakings and shoulder shrugging."[5]

However, the work Rhys Davids had already begun in Sri Lanka augured well for his task. In later years his writings showed how much Rhys Davids had pursued his researches—especially of an epigraphical and philological nature—during his sojourn in Sri Lanka. His contributions to the Journal of the Ceylon Branch of the Royal Asiatic

[3] *Journal of the Royal Asiatic Society*, 1923, pp. 323ff. Obituary Notice on T.W. Rhys Davids. Robert Chalmers.

[4] Rhys Davids, Caroline Augusta Foley, *op. cit.*

[5] *Ibid.*

Society of which he was an enthusiastic member had demonstrated clearly that Rhys Davids was no mere dilettante hopelessly out of his depth in spheres in which he had no real competence. Rhys Davids' most unrelenting critics could scarce refrain from acknowledging his special talents. Gregory, who described Rhys Davids as "a young man of great ability and high promise" also referred to his "scholarship in the Pali and Sinhalese languages" as well as to the inborn qualifications which Rhys Davids seemed endowed with for research therein. The sentiments had been echoed in the Colonial office, albeit with less conviction.[6]

In England, 1875 saw the beginnings of what was to become a veritable cascade of scholarly writings. Rhys Davids published in the *Journal of the Royal Asiatic Society* three essays on some ancient Sinhalese inscriptions which he had painstakingly researched on in Sri Lanka. The essays were reprinted soon afterwards by Trubner—the well known London publishers of oriental books. In 1877, as if it were a symbolic expression of faith in the choice he was ere long to make between a career in law and his researches, Rhys Davids published in the *International Numismata Orientalia* an essay on "the ancient coins and measures of Ceylon" which was in scope more comprehensive than its modest title suggested. The piece reflected Rhys Davids' familiarity with Ceylonese epigraphical researches. It showed too that he was maintaining close contact with kindred spirits like John Dickson (later Sir John Dickson) who had ultimately succeeded Rhys Davids in Anuradhapura, and was himself a collector of coins and a Palist.

More noteworthy than the essays he had so far written was the publication in 1878 of his first work on Buddhism which Rhys Davids wrote for the Society for Promoting Christian Knowledge in its series on non-Christian religious systems. The unpretentious title of the book—*Buddhism*—concealed the skill with which Rhys had woven into a single well integrated web the life of Gautama Buddha, the essence of his teachings, the unique order of mendicants which the Buddha founded and the manner in which Buddhism had spread to neighbouring Asian lands after the demise of its founder. The "little manual," as Rhys Davids liked to call his book, caught the public imagination to an extent which surpassed the most sanguinary hopes

[6] C.O. 54. 238, Gregory to Kimberley, 14 November 1872; C.O. 54. 259, Gregory to Kimberley, 27 November 1872.

of its author. The lectures which Rhys Davids gave in 1881 on the *History of Indian Buddhism*—lectures which the Hibbert trustees published—dealt with much the same themes but within the wider context of general religious history. It was his second major publication.

The contributions are best understood in the context of the time. The published literature on Buddhism in English was in many ways a microcosm of the larger British confrontation with Hinduism in India. The literature fell into certain broad categories. There were the accounts of Buddhism which had been published as tracts and pamphlets by various missionary societies working in Sri Lanka. The Wesleyans and the C.M.S. were particularly fecund pamphleteers. The publications were intended to enlist the goodwill of an apathetic Victorian public for the missionary cause. The accounts of Buddhism were as a rule made up of extracts from letters and reports sent to London by missionaries in the field in various parts of the island.[7] Their innate polemical character was often exaggerated because of the belief of Protestant missionaries that the British government in Sri Lanka was supporting Buddhism for political reasons.[8] However, a serious student anxious to know what Buddhism was all about would have found little to guide him.

Missionary in origin, but standing apart as a category, were a handful of books written on Buddhism by some of the more creative and gifted missionaries. The best known was the Rev. Spence Hardy, a Wesleyan missionary who had lived in Sri Lanka in the middle of the nineteenth century.

In 1850 Spence Hardy published *Eastern Monachism*. Much of the book, as its title would imply, was concerned with the Buddhist mendicant order or priesthood. There were, however, a few chapters which dealt with Buddhism as a religious system. As a book, however, it was less known than *A Manual of Buddhism In Its Modern Development* which Spence Hardy wrote in 1852, wherein the writer

[7] The archival resources of the Church Missionary Society and the Wesleyan Methodist Missionary Society which I was able to research on consist of letters from individual missionaries to the London secretaries of the societies, copies of replies, annual reports of missionaries in the field and minutes of local and district meetings.

[8] Wichremeratne, L.A., *Policies of the Government of Ceylon Concerning Religion and Education, 1865-1885* (Unpublished Oxford D. Phil. thesis, 1966); also De Silva, K.M., *Social Policy and Missionary Organisations in Ceylon, 1840-1855* (London, 1965), Part I, chapters I, II and III.

tried to come to grips with the recondite metaphysical aspects of Buddhist doctrine.

In writing both, Spence Hardy relied heavily on traditional Sinhalese sources—manuscripts written during and after the twelfth century. According to Rhys Davids the use of the comparatively recent Sinhalese manuscripts in contradistinction to the older Pali authorities weakened the claims of Spence Hardy's *Manual of Buddhism* as a reliable exposition of Buddhism. Bishop Bigandet's *Life and Legend of Gautama the Buddha of the Burmese,* published in Rangoon in 1858, also came within the limited genre of missionary works on Buddhism. Bigandet's account, too, was based on traditional Burmese sources—Pali works which had been translated into Burmese.

There were also accounts of Buddhism written by some of the abler British officials who had served in Sri Lanka. The books were usually general descriptions of the island—its history, customs, religion, physical features, and vegetation. Buddhism was dealt with both from a theoretical standpoint—the delineation of its salient doctrines—as well as a religion which influenced the daily life of the Sinhalese, among whom the writers had lived. The latter aspects—pregnant with perceptive sociological insights into contemporary Buddhism—compensated for the rather superficial and sometimes manifestly inaccurate treatment of Buddhist teaching. The best known among such works were the two volumes on Ceylon which Sir Emmerson Tennet published in 1860.

Finally—to complete our survey of Buddhist literature—there were the books on Buddhism written strictly by scholars like Rhys Davids. They were free from theological prejudices which, for example, had crept into Spence Hardy's writings. It was a genre of literature which was inspired by a desire to understand Eastern religions as part of the wider European understanding of Eastern culture and civilizations. Many of the books which by definition come into this category were, however, published in the last two decades of the century, rather than before 1878, when Rhys Davids first wrote on the subject. It was clear that books which dwelt exclusively on the subject of Buddhism in the English language were few and far between. Spence Hardy's *Manual of Buddhism*—in spite of all its imperfections—held pride of place as a pioneering work until it was superseded by Rhys Davds' two works. In any event, by 1878, Spence Hardy's book had long been out of print, copies being sold at extraordinary prices by means of public auction.

In another sense, too, Rhys Davids had filled a void. In the English speaking world he was the first to interpret Buddhism in close relation to the Pali texts—the oldest and most reliable of the various sources germane to the study of Buddhism. As a noted Palist aptly described it, Rhys Davids had, by his works on Buddhism, "laid sure foundations for the early interpretation of Buddhism without the stratigraphical confusion hitherto prevalent."[9]

II

The success of his early publications induced Rhys Davids to undertake the more significant work in his career as an orientalist. In the course of the Hibbert Lectures, Rhys Davids announced that he had been in touch with Pali scholars in Europe so that a new association, known as the Pali Text Society, could be formed.[10] Its object was to collect the Buddhist scriptures, or the *Piṭakas*, as they were called, which had been written in the Pali language. The *Piṭakas* consisted of a number of separate texts. The idea was to systematically publish the texts in the Roman script with translations into English. The texts were comparatively unknown. A few had found their way to Europe. Many, however, were widely scattered in temple repositories in Buddhist lands, especially in Sri Lanka.

As a source of historical material, the Pali texts were of undoubted importance. Gautama Buddha had lived in the sixth century before Christ. The Pali *Piṭakas*, in the form in which they existed, had been written between the fifth and fourth centuries. In point of time and in relation to other evidence which has a bearing on the problem, the Pali texts were the most authoritative and reliabe source for the study of early Buddhism. Moreover—a point which Rhys Davids understood more readily than many of his contemporaries—the Pali *Pitakas* were the means of understanding the social milieu from which Buddhism rose and flourished. Perceptively interpreted they threw considerable light on social and economic conditions of the time. From a linguistic point of view, too, in the words of Rhys Davids, the *Pitakas* contained "unimpeachable

[9] *Dictionary of National Biography*, 1922-1930. Sketch on T.W. Rhys Davids. Robert Chalmers.

[10] Rhys Davids, T.W., *Lectures on the Origins and Growth of Religion as Illustrated by Some Points in the History of Indian Buddhism* (Hibbert Lectures: London, 1881), pp. 70ff.

evidence of a stage in language midway between Vedic Sanskrit and the various modern forms of speech in India."[11]

Rhys Davids was partly inspired by similar ventures which had been undertaken in Europe. Attempts had been made by fellow orientalists, like Julius Eggeling, the Sanskritist, in the University of Edinburgh, and E.B. Cowell, to induce the Royal Asiatic Society to revive the defunct Sanskrit Text Society which had earlier begun to do much the same thing as Rhys Davids had in mind, for Sanskrit works of acknowledged value.[12] There was also the altogether more successful example of Max Muller's *Sacred Books of the East*, which had been begun in 1875. Rhvs Davids had been associated with Max Müller in planning the project—which, when it was completed, ran into fifty-one volumes—and had himself been a contributor to the series.

But notwithstanding the solitary beacons of inspiration, the task Rhys Davids had undertaken was fraught with considerable uncertainties. There were the difficulties in making the actual translations in an idiom which had somehow to convey the subtle nuances of the original and at the same time be intelligible to the modern reader. The problem of gathering together the scattered manuscripts, too, would have daunted a less venturesome spirit. Moreover Pali could not usurp the prestigious position which Sanskrit enjoyed in Europe ever since William Jones, the first of the great British orientalists, had made Europeans aware of its richness and philological implications. The study of Sanskrit had surged forward being in no small way encouraged by the government in India for reasons of administration, especially during the time of the East India Company. In the administration of justice, for example, British judges had to know what the traditional law was. It was elucidated in ancient Sanskrit tomes which they were themselves unable to read, rendering the judges a little too dependent on Hindu learned men or *pundits*. William Jones, who had first hand knowledge of the problem in Bengal, planned to compile a digest of Indian laws once the Sanskrit law books had been translated.[13] In a wider sense, as the heirs to the Mughuls, the East India Company had to maintain the tradition of

[11] *Ibid.*, p. 233.

[12] Proceedings of the Council of the Royal Asiatic Society, 20 June 1881. Also 4 July 1881.

[13] Canon, Garland, *Oriental Jones*. A biography of Sir William Jones (1746-1794). (New Delhi, 1964), p. 126; also pp. 130ff.

state patronage to Indian learning. A Sanskrit college—The Jonathan Duncan Sanskrit College in Bengal—was set up together with schools for Arabic and Persian studies and till about 1834, funds were made available for the "revival" of Sanskrit learning.[14]

European interest in Pali was not only of more recent origin, but had been confined to a group of scholars. In 1837 George Turnour, a British civil servant in Sri Lanka, translated into English the *Mahavamsa*—an ancient historical epic in Pali verse. Turnour had translated thirty-eight chapters of the epic which chronicled the island's history from about the fifth century B.C. to the fourth century A.D. Although Turnour had opened new vistas for European scholarship—his work helped in attempts made to decipher the Asokan inscriptions—as far as the continuation of Pali studies was concerned, Turnour's lead had not been followed. In 1858 Victor Fausboll, a noted European Palist, translated the *Dhammapada,* a collection of stanzas in Pali which pithily summed up the essence of Buddhist teaching. The *Dhammapada* was by far the best known part of the Khuddaka Nikaya in the *Sutta Pitaka,* the second main division of the *Tripitaka.* The frontiers of European knowledge of Pali was further extended by Robert Childers. He had been a civil servant in Sri Lanka before Rhys Davids, and had energetically studied Pali. Childers had the distinction of preparing the first Pali text to be published in England. The work was the *Khuddaka patha*—literally the "text of small passages" in the *Sutta Pitaka*—and appeared in the *Journal of the Royal Asiatic Society* in 1869 with an English translation and numerous scholarly notes. Moreover, Childers had taken upon himself the monumental task of compiling a Pali dictionary which he was able to publish in London in 1875, shortly before his premature death. The next point of advancement was achieved in 1880 when V. Fausboll published in the Sacred Books of the East series, the *Sutta Nipata*—a collection of discourses within the category of the *Sutta Pitaka.*

The milestones on the road of European scholarship were few and far between. "When we call to the mind," mused Rhys Davids, "the passionate patience with which well known and less important studies are pursued among us, it is a matter for wonder that a nearly unworked mine, where the nuggets of gold can still be gathered on the surface, should have thus far remained neglected." But scholars

[14]Spear, Percival, *A History of India* Vol. 2 (London, 1965), p. 126.

in truth could not be blamed because it was the well worn studies which really afforded a means of livelihood. The founding of the Pali Text Society was therefore a happy inspiration. But how were the objects of the Society to be attained? Early in the day it became apparent that much would depend on the assistance the Society might receive from the Buddhist monks or—to use the proper term—*Bhikkhus*—in Sri Lanka. Rhys Davids was able to put to good use the friendly relations he had been able to maintain with the Buddhist clergy. The very nature of his official duties, as well as his interests as a scholar, had brought him into contact with many *Bhikkhus*.

He was very much *en rapport* with the priesthood, especially with its leading luminaries. He loved and respected the *Bhikkhus* and believed that intercourse with "the yellow robed and tonsured recluse" was a means of opening "a new world of thought." In a simple and technical sense, Rhys Davids knew the language and, as he himself modestly confessed, "something of Buddhist ideas." He could therefore dispense with interpreters and phrase books. Above all—speaking as a European—he believed that in establishing relations with *Bhikkus* one should rid one's mind of notions of superiority and regard the *Bhikkhu* as an equal. In a more mundane sense, in his day it was not uncommon for British civil servants in Sri Lanka to refer in overtones of contempt to the corruption and worldliness of Buddhist priests, especially in their management of the temporalities belonging to the Buddhist temples. As an administrator Rhys Davids was not unfamiliar with the problem. He thought, however, that on balance the *Bhikkhus* were preserving the old standards and the spirit of the order. For every Buddhist priest who was indolent, ignorant and self-righteous—"there were such men to be found in the ranks of the clergy of all religions"—there were scores of others who were disciplined and virtuous.[15]

His attitudes were coloured by Rhys Davids' close acquaintanceship with a Buddhist monk who was distinguished for his learning. It was from Yatramulle Unnanse, who lived in Bentota in the district of Matara in Sri Lanka, that Rhys Davids had learnt Pali. When Rhys Davids met Yatramulle Unnanse the monk, who had earlier taught Pali to Childers, was gravely ill with "a painful and incurable malady." There was, however, no lessening of his intellectual power. Childers had told Rhys Davids that Yatramulle Unnanse's learning

[15] *Hibbert Lectures, op. cit.*, pp. 185ff.

was "perfectly astonishing." Moreover, to both Childers and Rhys Davids Yatramulle Unnanse epitomized the very essence of the Buddhist ideal of mendicancy. The monk rarely left his temple and avoided publicity. His personality, too, left an indelible impression. "There was," recalled Rhys Davids years later in England, "a strange light in his sunken eyes . . . there was an indescribable attraction about him, a simplicity and high mindedness that filled me with reverence." Childers had told Rhys Davids that Yatramulle Unnanse had made an equally overpowering impression on him. Rhys Davids thought it probable that in the long history of Buddhism there would have been monks of Yatramulle's calibre who had influenced "those who had eyes to see and ears to hear." An enlightened priesthood, he added, had been the principal means by which Buddhism had held sway over the mass of the people in many Asian countries.

However, in spite of the goodwill there were formidable obstacles to overcome. Some *Bhikkhus* in Sri Lanka plainly saw that the work of the Pali Text Society would amount to a virtual re-writing of the Buddhist *Piṭakas* or scriptures. On the abstract question of writing down the scriptures orthodox thinking was fundamentally influenced by the larger Indian tradition. From time immemorial the *Vedas* as well as the commentaries concerning the *Vedas* had been preserved not in writing but had been handed down orally. Printing was regarded as a less satisfactory mode of perpetuating the tradition. The argument was that although all the printed copies of the *Vedas* might be destroyed, the *Vedas* would still survive in the memory of the priests whose business it was to safegured the tradition and hand it down. In Sri Lanka too—in spite of a broadly more liberal and accommodating religious outlook—the oral tradition had not passed into oblivion but was very much alive. On more than one occasion Rhys Davids had tried to persuade Yatramulle Unnanse about the usefulness of printing the *Piṭakas*. But all to no avail. Yatramulle Unnanse had declared that if the *Piṭakas* were to be written they would be better preserved on palm leaves than on flimsy printed paper.[16]

Other *Bhikkhus* in Sri Lanka were, however, more flexible. In 1882, when the Pali Text Society was struggling to survive, over seventy well known monks had written to Rhys Davids and expressed their appreciation of its objects. They had also subscribed in advance

[16] *Ibid.*

the costs of printing some of the texts. As Rhys Davids pointed out, it was no small thing that an established clergy should so forthrightly support the publication of the sacred books of its religion by scholars of an alien faith in an alien tongue.[17]

The difficulties which William Jones had to contend with about a hundred years before—Rhys Davids made no explicit reference to William Jones—illustrated the point. For a long time William Jones simply could not find a pundit to teach hims Sanskrit. It was considered sacrilegious by many Brāhmaṇas that profane Christian eyes should even see the sacred books. By dint of perseverance, the great scholar had overcome the problem. In Rhys Davids' own time it was a moot point whether such attitudes had altogether disappeared in India.

The response of the monks in Sri Lanka together with the possibility of more support induced the Committee of Management of the Pali Text Society to make a significant change. At first it had been the intention of the Society to publish Jain and Sanskrit Buddhist texts in addition to the Pali texts, as it was thought that the former texts could throw light on those religious developments out of which the Pali texts came into being. It was now resolved to devote the energies and funds of the Society for some years at any rate, to take in hand the Pali texts which were preserved in the "bright and beautiful" island of Sri Lanka. Rhys Davids hoped that subscribers to the Pali Text Society in Europe and in the U.S.A. would approve the change.[18]

Many of the Pali texts which the Society published were in fact obtained from Sri Lanka as manuscripts. Monks like the scholar monk Waskaduwe Subhuti, and Wimalesena Unnanse of Ambagahapitiya Vihare, in Galle, had readily provided the manuscripts and helped also to increase the number of subscribers in Sri Lanka.[19] Meanwhile, Mudaliyar E.R. Goonerate, himself a native of Galle, rendered Yeoman service to the Pali Text Society till his death in 1914. He used to collect ancient manuscripts from various temples throughout the Island, often copying them himself.[20]

The young Society developed from strenght to strength. In 1900 Caroline Rhys Davids, who had increasingly begun to take into her own capable hands the work of the Pali Text Society, in a letter which

[17] *Journal of the Pali Text Society* 1882, p. 2.
[18] *Indian Antiquary* Vol. I., 1872,pp. 162ff.
[19] *Ibid;* also J.P.T.S. 1884, p. XIV.
[20] *Journal of the Maha Boddhi Society*, September, 1914.

she wrote to Anagarika Dharmapala—the leading Sinhalese nationalist of the time—listed forty separate texts which the Society had published. A few more major texts remained to be published. "As you see," she declared, "land is really in sight of the little vessel." She added that the phase of "struggling on with dwindling finances" was over. By 1912 the financial position of the Pali Text Society had improved to such an extent—because of increases in the European category of subscribers—that the Society was able to buy the manuscripts it wanted and pay for work done by scholars who translated them. Translations had hitherto been done generously without remuneration.

With just pride Rhys Davids recalled how it had all begun. He had been warned that the Pali text project was "doomed to failure" and that "no one cared enough for Pali."[21] When he was sorely tempted to abandon the idea, the King of Siam—who had already been a benefactor to Max Müller—gave Rhys Davids the money for the first volume.[22] Friends had subscribed to bring out the second. From then onwards, the "little vessel" had begun to build up its own momentum.

III

The Pali Text Society work blended harmoniously with Rhys Davids' activities in the Royal Asiatic Society, of which he became a distinguished office bearer.

In 1885 W.S.W. Vaux, who had served the R.A.S. as its secretary for ten years, died. The Council of the R.A.S., which was its governing body, set about selecting a new secretary. The stipulation made in the advertisement which was published in the *Times* and in *Trubner's Journal* that a knowledge of oriental subjects, though not indispensable, was desirable, encouraged Rhys Davids to apply for the post.[23] Eighty-three applications were received. Rhys Davids was one of six from whom the council decided to make its final selection. Stanley Lane Poole, S. Beal and C.E. Wilson—themselves specialists in oriental studies—were the other contenders.[24] Rhys Davids, with notable

[21] *Ibid.*

[22] *Ibid.*

[23] Proceedings of the Council of the Royal Asiatic Society (Special Meeting) 26 June 1885.

[24] Proceedings of the Council of the R.A.S. Meeting of Sub-Committee appointed to deal with selection of new secretary, 31 October 1885.

publications in his name, seemed to have the edge over his rivals. Events, however, took an unexpected turn. At a special meeting, the council decided that the post should be offered to Sir Frederick Goldsmidt although he was not one of the applicants. The brief minutes of the proceedings do not shed any light on the point. We are, however, told that the choice was unanimous and that it had been made after considerable discussion. The minutes record further that Goldsmidt was "by far the fittest person for the office."[25]

Fate, however, decreed yet another change. In April 1887, Goldsmidt announced that he was resigning from the post of Secretary in spite of efforts which the Council made to dissuade him. The Council, avoiding the tedious formalities which had preceded Goldsmidt's appointment, selected Rhys Davids for the post without hesitation.

If the secretaryship of the R.A.S. gave added lustre to its incumbent, it also carried with it considerable responsibilities. Their nature was not fully indicated in the advertisement which, with almost a suggestion of quaint humour, merely declared that the secretary must "read with a distinct voice the manuscript papers that are selected for reading at the meetings and conduct the correspondence and keep the accounts with a clear hand. Business habits, regularity of attendance and precision are necessary."[26]

The unpublished papers of the R.A.S., however, show that the stewardships of successive secretaries were judged on more significant criteria. Thus although there was a Treasurer, it was the Secretary's business not only to keep the accounts but to manage the finances of the Society. As Secretary Rhys Davids was a member of a small committee which was specially set up to reorganise the business side of the Society's affairs.[27] The printing and publication of the R.A.S. Journal was by far the weightier burden of a secretary's duties. In this respect Rhys Davids' experience counted in two ways. He had personal contact with many orientalists who could be relied on to write articles and learned disquisitions to the Journal. Moreover with a background in publications he had acquired a certain expertise in the technical aspects of printing and publishing. As early as in 1888, Sir Thomas Wade, who was the president of the

[25] Special Meeting of the Council of the R.A.S., 2 November 1885.

[26] Proceedings of the Council of the R.A.S., 18 April 1887; Proceedings of the Council of the R.A.S., 1 July 1885; Proceedings of the Council of the R.A.S., 18 November 1889.

[27] Minutes of Meeting of the Council of the R.A.S., 1891-1905, 21 October 1891.

R.A.S., commenting on the skill with which Rhys Davids had reorganised the publication of the Journal, also expressed gratitude for the "large saving" which the R.A.S. had thereby been able to achieve.[28]

Rather more typical of the accolades which were periodically showered on him by his colleagues in the R.A.S. were the remarks which Sir William Hunter made in 1893: ". . . It has never been our privilege to listen to a more satisfactory Report . . . not only is our financial position sounder but there is a real life going on in our society which as a member of many years standing I do not remember to have observed before . . ."[29]

The secretary of the R.A.S. was also its Librarian. The duties involved were clearly much less onerous. During his tenure of office Rhys Davids completed a catalogue of the Society's books. The Catalogue was printed.[30] He was the moving spirit in a small committee which was appointed to catalogue the Sanskrit Mss. belonging to the R.A.S. He moreover persuaded the R.A.S. to buy a collection of sacred Jain books which were being sold in Bombay.[31] Rhys Davids also got the R.A.S. to interest itself in a number of oriental manuscripts which had been used by William Jones but whose existence was "nearly unknown to the orientalists."[32]

Not only as secretary but because of his total commitment to oriental studies, Rhys Davids was thoroughly identified with various causes which the R.A.S. espoused to further Asian studies and culture. During his time the main energies of the R.A.S. were taken up with the object of making more ample provision for oriental studies—see next chapter—in Britain. It was a cause dear to Rhys Davids' heart.

Meanwhile, the happy accident that the Secretary of the R.A.S. and the President of the Pali Text Society were the same person augured well for the infant organisation Rhys Davids had created. With benign paternalism the R.A.S. decided that the Pali Text Society, though not directly connected with the R.A.S., was nonetheless to some extent under its aegis.[33] Consequently the R.A.S. readily accepted Rhys Davids' proposal that the publications of the Pali Text Society should be permitted to use on the title pages the imprimatur

[28] Meeting of the R.A.S., 16 April 1888; *J.R.A.S.* Vol. XX, part III, July 1888.

[29] Anniversary Meeting of the R.A.S., 9 May 1893; *J.R.A.S.*, July 1893.

[30] Proceedings of the Council of the R.A.S., 17 November 1890.

[31] Minutes of Meeting of the Council of the R.A.S., 1891-1905, 13 December 1892.

[32] Proceedings of the Council of the R.A.S., 17 February 1890.

[33] Report of the Annual Meeting of the R.A.S., 14 May 1901; *J.R.A.S.* 1901, p. 632.

of the R.A.S. with a view, no doubt, of giving the Pali Text Society a better chance of selling its publications on the market.[34] The R.A.S. also decided to make an annual grant of ten guinneas to the Pali Text Society to help the publication of a new Pali dictionary which Rhys Davids had planned and which was to replace Robert Childer' pioneering work.[35] From a financial point of view, the gains were small. But to an unknown and struggling society, every penny counted.

IV

Indeed neither learned societies, much less individual scholars, could ignore the more pedestrian aspects of academic work. After all, what did scholarship amount to in terms of economic gains? If the Earl of Northbrook, who was a President of the R.A.S., was to be believed, scholarship and money matters were conventionally thought to be incompatible. Nonetheless, at the annual meeting of the R.A.S. in 1893, he wryly remarked that he had "never come across better men of business than the great scholars who are members of the Royal Asiatic Society or a better man of business than our secretary."[36] Rhys Davids—to whom, of course, Northbrook referred—considered the question to be one of recurring personal relevance. The meagre autobiographical details we have make no mention of incomes which Rhys Davids enjoyed from strictly private sources like land or bequests. There probably were none.

In the circumstances the R.A.S. secretaryship alone ensured a steady income. In Rhys Davids' time the Secretary of the R.A.S. was given an annual salary of £200 with facilities to live in the premises if he so desired. In view of residence £50 was paid, together with a further allowance of £60 for a housekeeper. Sometimes small sundry allowances were paid to meet the costs of clerical assistance and the services of an errand boy.[37] By way of further perquisites the R.A.S. also paid the income tax of its Secretary.[38]

[34] Minutes of Meeting of the Council of the R.A.S., 1891-1905, 13 December 1898.

[35] Minutes of Meeting of the Council of the R.A.S. 14 March 1905.

[36] Anniversary Meeting of the R.A.S., 9 May 1893; *J.R.A.S*,. July 1893.

[37] Special Meeting of the Council of the R.A.S., 2 November 1885; Proceedings of the Council of the R.A.S., 1 July 1885.

[38] Minutes of Meetings of the Council of the R.A.S., 1891-1905, 13 April 1897.

For some time Rhys Davids was content. However, in order to improve his economic position—in other respects his relations with the R.A.S. were on a satisfactory footing and working conditions there were pleasant—Rhys Davids decided to apply for the post of Librarian of the India Office when a vacancy occurred in 1892. He urged the Council of the R.A.S. to help him by passing "such a resolution as he could send to the India Office in support of his candidature."[39] The R.A.S. generously referred to the services which Rhys Davids had rendered since he became its Secretary. Special reference was made to his work for the Journal and—significantly—to the "business qualities of a high order" which Rhys Davids had shown.[40]

At the last moment, however, Rhys Davids seems to have changed his mind and decided to stay on with the R.A.S.—the evidence throwing little light on the point. The R.A.S. decided to increase Rhys Davids' salary by an additional £50. However, the Council made it clear that the enhancement was strictly personal to Rhys Davids. After he stepped down the salary of the Secretary would remain at the £200 level.

The long delayed wrench came in 1905 when Rhys Davids resigned the R.A.S. secretaryship to accept the post of Professor of Comparative Religion in Manchester. He did not hesitate. In London his income had been derived from three sources. His books on Buddhism sold well. In a sense it paid to write on Buddhism in Victorian England. "When I returned to England," Rhys Davids recalled, "I knew very little about the subject (Buddhism) but I found that I knew more than most people and publishers and editors asked me to write books and articles about it."[41] The S.P.C.K. book on Buddhism in particular enjoyed immense popularity. There was secondly his income from the R.A.S. Finally, there were his earnings—if it could be described as source of income at all—from University College London where Rhys Davids was Professor in Pali. Remuneration was, however, by fees rather than by means of a fixed salary. As shown in the next chapter, there were in England, in contrast to some of the European countries, very few professorships specifically to do with oriental or Asian studies and on account of which the incumbents were remunerated by endowments—as in Oxford or in Cambridge—or by means of a fixed salary. The Chair of Comparative Religion in

[39] Minutes of Meetings of the Council of the R.A.S., 1891-1905, 17 May 1892.
[40] *Ibid.*
[41] *Minutes of Meetings of the Council of the R.A.S., 1891-1905, 8 March 1898.*

Manchester University came within the privileged category. London—in spite of being the metropolis—could not offer comparable opportunities. As Lord Reay who was President of the R.A.S. at the time pointed out, it did not reflect well on the state of oriental learning in England that "a man of Professor Rhys Davids' reputation should be unable to remain in the metropolis as would be the case were he at Paris, Vienna or Berlin," He would not have felt obliged to accept an appointment at another University. "We may well envy," he added, "the young University of Manehester the privilege of having such an eminent orientalist on its teaching staff."[42] Echoing the sentiments Vincent Smith declared that the University of Manchester deserved to have Rhys Davids because it had the progressive outlook of a "young" and "scientific" institution.[43]

But Manchester did not necessarily imply a diminution in academic prestige. Rhys Davids was the first distinguished incumbent of the Chair of Comparative Religion in Manchester University. The post was the only one of its kind in Britain or, as Rhys Davids proudly observed, "the only one in existence in the whole world."[44] Time showed how the bold initiative taken by Manchester had paid rich dividends.

Manchester was the point of arrival in another sense too—the novel experience of receiving reasonably ample monetary rewards for academic work. He had always believed that this should be so. In truth, however, scholars were shabbily treated. They were as a rule poor in purse and subtly despised by society on that account. On many occasions Rhys Davids expressed himself with great bitterness on the subject. He believed that those who were involved in academic work provided society with a service or facility which society needed, just as it would use this or that commodity. Ordinarily services and commodities were paid for but not academic work. No one, he said, would go to a tailor and say "you are well known in the town for the skill and accuracy of your work. Make me therefore a coat or suit for no money. . . . It is not yet considered a disgrace to say to a scholar . . . 'write me an article (or a book) for nothing.' Why this difference? Is it

[42] Rhys Davids in interview with the *Morning Post*, quoted in *Journal of the Maha Bodhi Society*, Vol. XXII, June 1914, no. 6.

[43] *J.R.A.S.* (Great Britian and Ireland) 1906, p.520.

[44] Anniversary Meeting of the R.A.S., 16 May 1905; *J.R.A.S.* 1905, p. 597.

entirely a question of economics?" He thought not. The answer was a certain attitude in society which Rhys Davids stigmatised as "social pride." It was exemplified in the pharisaical attitudes of the successful men of the world who had amassed wealth and position. "When one marks the careless air of self-complacency one is inclined to think that *Manna* (pride) no less than *Moha* (ignorance) may also enter into the argument."[45]

The bitterness was mildly underlined by functional expressions of hope. "In any case the age of barbarism, the age which values wealth and birth above knowledge and insight cannot last forever. That too is *Annicam* (impermanence) . . ."[46]

It was at best a forlorn hope.

[45] Interview with the *Morning Post, J.R.A.S., op. cit.*

[46] *Journal of the Pali Text Society, Circa* 1885.

ORIENTALISM AND THE PROBLEMS THEREOF

The theme of scholarship and impecuniousness had wider connotations.

Whether oriental studies would inspire lasting interests in the West was uncertain. Like many of his contemporaries Rhys Davids, too, perceived that although Britain had wide connections with the East to an extent her neighbours could scarcely match, the study of the languages and religions of the East had evoked little enthusiasm.

The mainstream of scholarship in Britain and elsewhere in Europe was clearly flowing along an already well defined, if somewhat ancient, course. The classical heritage was its predominant feature. European culture, with which the classical tradition was closely intertwined, was regarded, in the words of Rhys Davids, as "the only progressive culture in the world." India and the East in general counted for little. Western classical scholars, the high priests of European culture, were loath to admit that classical thought as well as classical institutions may well have been influenced by the East "however grudgingly that privilege was conceded to Egypt." In a word, Europe was the measure of all things.[1]

No doubt greater familiarity with "the personalities of oriental peoples" would help to eradicate prejudices to which scholar and Philistine had alike succumbed. Rhys Davids' sojourn in Sri Lanka had been the means of his own enlightenment. But how few had hao similar opportunities? After is return to England Rhys Davids determined to devote his energies and meagre resources to educate his countrymen towards an understanding of the East.

The means which he could resort to were varied. He appealed to history—a powerful antidote to Europocentrism. Rhys Davids, who made constant reference to history in his writings, declared that he was first a historian, and in an entirely subordinate sense, a Palist and orientalist. The study of Buddhism and the Pali texts, though they loomed large as ends in themeselves were, to his way of thinking, a

[1] Rhys Davids, T.W., *Buddhism its History and Literature*, American lectures on the History of Religions (New York, 1896), p. 218.

means to a well defined end—the entirely praiseworthy exercise of understanding alien civilizations and cultures.

The study of history had undergone significant changes which had immensely enhanced its usefulness as an enlightening medium. History, observed Rhys Davids, had dramatically extended its frontiers because of the use of coins, developments in archeology, and the intensive use of literary records. "When we were boys," Rhys Davids recalled, "history meant the study of a century or two of Greece and Rome oblivious of the centuries that lay behind. Then with a jump we come to the Reformation and the French Revolution and an epitome of the battles and politics of our native country was held to complete the picture. The disjoined fragments of the history of Greece and Rome were called 'Ancient'." There had been a shift in emphasis too. In the old fashioned history stress had been laid on mere episodes, personal adventures and dynastic intrigues. The evolution of social institutions and the growth of human ideas had been ignored. "There was no trace of what for want of a better word we must call WELTGESCHICTE. Each event recorded was regarded as isolated, unaccounted either as cause or effect with what followed or with what had gone before."[2]

The most significant development was, however, the comparative approach to history. The phrase "comparative study of history" which recurs so much in Rhys Davids' writings was full of meaning. Social institutions, religious beliefs, philosophical ideas and even "scientific attainments" were best studied on a comparative basis rather than simply in terms of religions and countries. The idea of the essential unity of the human experience would serve to displace the parochialism which had hitherto led scholars to attach an exaggerated importance to particular regions like Europe. Scholars were compelled to think in terms of a broader canvas and to realise that there were similarities and even startling parallels between various segments in the canvas. What was the ultimate result? there would be a better understanding and a greater tolerance of other cultures and histories which had hitherto been ignored on the ground of their "alienness."[3]

[2] Horrowitz, A.E., *A Short History of Indian Literature*. See introduction by Rhys Davids. (London, 1907).
[3] Ibid.

History could be a corrective in other ways, too. Rhys Davids believed that much of the prejudice against Eastern studies was derived from European notions of racial superiority. Writing as one who was happily free from its influences, Rhys Davids reflected on the "physical repulsion" which the so-called "advanced races" in Europe felt towards the "savage races." The factor of colour had been formidable. There was also a sense of alienness arising from dissimilarities of custom and culture. History, however, showed that the great races of the world had some kind of common origin. Rhys Davids subscribed—somewhat uncritically one feels—to the view which was very much in vogue at the time, that there had been originally a single Aryan race with a common home, possibly in Central Asia. The Aryans, however, had scattered hither and thither in subsequent migration. In the Hibbert Lectures in 1881—in which he put together for the first time many of the ideas which came to be associated with him—Rhys Davids referred to the Seven Great Aryan Races. The Hindus, on whom Europeans poured so much scorn, were part of a confraternity which included the Teutons, Celts, the Greeks and the Romans.

To Rhys Davids it was the common Aryanism which mattered above all else. It was a chastening thought that the ancient literature of India was the work of men who were "intellectually akin to ourselves." What use was there, he asked, in attempting to study the evolution of ideas and institutions of the Aryan nations of Europe without parallel studies concerning "the Aryans in India"?[4]

Europocentrism had, of course, its political overtones. Actual contact with Asia and the East and the establishment of varying degrees of political ascendancy was widely regarded both as a reflex of the supremacy of Europeans in purely political and military sense, as well as a vindication of the superiority of Western civilizations.

A notable feature in the writings of Rhys Davids, on the other hand, was their apolitical character, especially with regard to Europe and the White Man's burden—matters on which some of his contemporaries were wont to enthuse over, although they were writing on strictly non-political subjects. Indeed, one does not encounter in Rhys Davids the conventional references to "British rule", "our Empire," although over and over again he refers to an "ourselves" and "they" in matters of religion, to "our Bible" and "our religion." Instead

[4] *Ibid.*

Instead it would seem that Rhys Davids was rather fond of poking fun at the symbols and trappings of imperial splendour and did so with impish irreverence. "The Sinhalese," he wrote, "have an epithet which they apply in good humoured sarcasm to Europeans and which means fellows with hats, hatfellows (*Toppikarayo*). These fellows with the hats and eighty ton guns and other signs of artistic and spiritual eminence are sometimes gifted with a sublime and admirable self-complacency . . ." More trenchantly, in a letter to the *Spectator* which he wrote sometime in 1889 in defence of Buddhism, which had been unfairly criticised by a correspondent, Rhys Davids remarked ". . . no doubt the European with his railways and his tall hats and his hundred ton guns and his exhibitions . . . and many other signs of his artistic and spiritual supremacy will continue to look down with contempt on the wisdom of the East. The gospel of getting on (in this world and the next) will suit him better for sometime to come . . ."[5]

Politics was a practical question. There were not only the Indians of ancient India whom Rhys Davids wrote but there were the Indians of his own day. British attitudes to Indians were derived from diverse sources. There were the experiences of the administrators in India. The mood of disenchantment and suspicion in the mind of officialdom which followed the Mutiny had been strengthened with the disturbing evidence of Indian nationalist fervour. There was clearly the feeling that the educated Indian was hard to please, over-ambitious, and above all, undependable. To some extent, too, prevailing attitudes were moulded by the plethora of writings on India varying from travel books to rudimentary anthropological studies—neither contributing much to bridge the growing alienation between Englishman and Indian—as well as by the great classics on India. In the last category, Macaulay's writings on India held pride of place. His unflattering picture of the Hindu became almost a stereotype or symbol of what the run of the mill Englishman thought the Indian was, or could be expected to be—a curious amalgam of passivity, defiance and instability of temperament. At a less elevated level, to the man in the street, the Indian student whom he was getting accustomed to seeing, even in Rhys Davids' time, was part of the exoticism, the curiosa of Empire.

But Rhys Davids would admonish his countrymen that the Indians were the descendants of the Aryans. They, too, had their

[5] Rhys Davids' letter to the *Spectator* (n.d.) quoted in the *Buddhist* 1889, Vol. I, no. 37

hours of political glory. It would seem that in his time the Indians were being badgered with both ends of the political stick. On the one hand, they were being blamed for premature political and nationalist stances—witness the behaviour of Indian students in London—and on the other hand, they were being taxed with "the absence of political movements and ardent patriotism." The dependence on a vegetarian diet, the proneness of Indians to be overwhelmed by the forces of nature, the influence of physical geography—in Rhys Davids' picturesque phrase "the depressing majesty of great mountains"—and above all the harmful effects of an enervating climate, were possible reasons for the presumed supineness of Indians. Rhys Davids thought the explanations too facile. Climate least of all was relevant. Many Europeans who had lived in the East had, like himself, found that "a great amount of energy and work both physical and intellectual was not only possible but habitual." Indian backwardness, political or otherwise, could, he believed, be better explained in terms of economic conditions and the nature of social institutions.[6]

Politics had a subtler dimension, too. History had shown how kingdoms big and small, nay even splendid empires, had passed into oblivion. Many had been almost entirely forgotten. In a sense that evidently meant much to Rhys Davids, their ephemeral character recalled to mind the Buddhist idea of *Annicca*—the impermanence of all things. In the East, where one almost intuitively grasped the idea, history was full of examples of the transient nature of political power. *Buddhist India,* which Rhys Davids wrote for the Story of Nations series in 1903, was in a sense a reflex of his treatment of history. The chapters dealing with Candragupta, Asoka, and Kaniṣka, in particular, exemplified the melancholy moral. Rhys Davids, who confessed that he was inspired by Gibbon, added that the rise and fall of Buddhist India was as "instructive" as that of Rome.[7]

Rhys Davids was clearly well suited for the great task he had set himself. He would educate his countrymen. However, in his efforts to combat Europocentrism he clearly veered towards the opposite extreme. He was hardly dispassionate in appraising the prospects of oriental studies. Renaissance Europe had been enriched by the rediscovery of Greek and Latin. Rhys Davids would have his readers conjure glowing visions of the devoted labours of the "little band" of scholars who made the West aware of the immense importance of the

[6]Rhys Davids, T.W., *Buddhist India,* Story of Nations Series (London, 1903), p. 31.
[7] *Ibid.*

Greek Mss. He believed that oriental studies would exert a comparable influence. The philosophies of the East and mostly Buddhism would exercise "a marked influence in shaping European thought." Evoking an equally lyrical analogy, he wrote that the discovery of oriental language and religion was no less significant than the great industrial and technological changes which transformed Europe: "... crank of machinery . . . the whizz of the oncoming motor need not deaden our perception to other sounds. . . . in silence unobserved by the daily press a revolution was being wrought. . . ." All this was in a sense a revealing reflex of how Rhys Davids evaluated his own work. He liked to think of himself as one of a microscopic minority of orientalists who unearthed the "palm leaf Mss" which threw light on "intellectual efforts that have moved the world."[8]

And yet for all the idealism there was the saving grace of earthiness too. Among orientalists of his time, probably Rhys Davids alone faced up to the question of the relevance of Eastern studies and Western industrial society with its emphasis on the individual economic ethic. "What can be," he asked, "the real value of literatures"—and one may add religions, since in many ways the two were so closely intertwined—"that have contributed little or nothing to the intellectual equipment of the races that rule the world with so much practical success." What indeed? There were the ideological affinities between the rise of individual entripreneurical capitalism in the West and aspects of Christian teachings. By contrast the great religious systems of the East—especially Buddhism—laid stress on otherworldliness and held the accumulation of worldly wealth and the individual's effort in this direction as being contemptible of, in the Buddhist way of relating aims to ends, as a disorientation.[9]

II

The difficulties of publishing books on oriental subjects, the problems which voluntary academic organisations like the Royal Asiatic Society had to encounter in increasing their membership, and the condition of oriental studies in England in general, showed the bread and butter nature of the question.

[8] Rhys Davids, *Buddhism its History and Literature*, *op. cit.*, p. 80; Horrowitz, Introduction, *op. cit.*; speech by Rhys Davids on occasion of presentation of testimonial to him by the Royal Asiatic Society, *J.R.A.S.* 1906, p. 522.

[9] Horrowitz, *op. cit.*

To the superficial observer in Rhys Davids' time it may have seemed that oriental studies were amply provided for in Britain. In University College and King's College, London, Sanskrit, Pali and a number of Modern Indian Languages like Bengali, Hindi and Marathi were taught.

In Oxford, where the celebrated Max Muller held the chair in Comparative Philology, there were professorships in Sanskrit, Chinese, and in Arabic. There were also "teacherships"—a humbler stratum in the hierarchy usually occupied by specialist native teachers—which dealt with subjects which were popular with candidates for the Indian Civil Service. In Cambridge there were professorships in Sanskrit and Arabic as well as University teacherships in Modern Indian Languages. Further north there was in Edinburgh a Chair in Sanskrit. In the University of Dublin, too, there were chairs in Sanskrit, Arabic, and Persian.[10]

By 1904, when Rhys Davids was invited to address the British Academy on the subject of oriental studies, the picture had not significantly altered, although chairs in Egyptology—which had become dramatically popular in many universities—had been set up in London, Oxford, and in Liverpool. Moreover, the basis on which University teachers in oriental subjects were remunerated revealed the darker and even less pleasing side of the picture. In University College, London, where Rhys Davids was the Professor in Pali, professors as well as teachers were paid fees rather than fixed salaries. A similar practice prevailed in King's College, the professor in Chinese alone being paid out of an endowment. Because subjects like Sanskrit and Pali were not notably popular with university students, teachers of oriental languages were placed in a frankly unenviable position. Rhys Davids, who was well aware of their predicament, commented angrily on "the amazing absurdity of men appointed as professors and yet compelled by the arrangements made to spend the best hours of the day not in the work of their chairs, but in earning their living as clerks and secretaries in Libraries and Journals."[11]

In Oxford, where as in Cambridge endowments were the order of the day, remuneration was admittedly more satisfactory. The profes-

[10] Statement of the Royal Asiatic Society on Oriental Learning in Britain, *J.R.A.S.*, Vol. XXX, part II, April 1887.

[11] T.W. Rhys Davids, *Oriental Studies in England and Abroad*, paper read at the British Academy on 24 February 1904 and subsequently published. London, 1904.

sor of Chinese received an annual salary of £3000 and the Boden Professor in Sanskrit was paid £1000. The Lord Almoners Professor in Arabic, on the other hand, received a lowly stipend of £50, although his salary was supplemented by fees. Teacherships carried an annual salary of £200 and were in turn enhanced by fees.[12]

On the whole it was evident that in Britain full professorships were few and far between. The majority were titular or honorary positions. By contrast a number of European countries, notably Germany, were better served. A survey made by R.A.S. towards the end of the last century showed that there were in Germany 51 fully paid professors. There were also numerous *Privatdocents,* a genre described as graduates who were in training for professorships. They were remunerated by means of fees and occasionally a nominal salary was added. The number of poorly paid titular professors of the sort that existed in England was by contrast few. Oriental subjects were in addition taught in the Oriental Seminary in Britain which was part of the university there. The Oriental Seminary received an annual grant of about £8000 from the state and had the resources to maintain a Library and publish its own journal. An institution of similar stature was the Ecole Speciale des Langues Oriental Vivantes, in Paris. It enjoyed facilities comparable to the Berlin Seminary and received in turn a state grant of about £7000. The R.A.S. survey also revealed that in the University of St. Petersburg in Russia, there were as many as twelve teachers who had full professional status apart from a number of Assistant Professors and privatdocents. There were also in St. Petersburg an independent faculty of oriental studies—one of four major faculties to which the University was divided.[13]

The contrast was outstanding. Rhys Davids surmised that possibly the love of oriental studies which one encountered in continental countries simply did not exist in England. The English faith in the ability to "muddle through somehow" too had been a factor in encouraging apathy. Moreover, there was in England the belief that in education, character and moral training were more important than competence in specialised and rather narrow skills. Were a man—educated in the ideal English sense—put in charge of a district, or were he to hold a consular post, he would soon pick up "any further

[12] *Ibid;* also *J.R.A.S.*, Vol.XXX, *op. Cit.*
[13] *Ibid.*

knowledge that may be necessary for useful and practical work." So the theory ran. Presumably officials in the Foreign, Indian and in the Colonial services, as well as leading merchants with interests in the East, had done well by just such qualities. Rhys Davids believed that since pragmatism had paid off so well the Establishment or the powers that be attached little value to the formal acquisition of oriental subjects.[14]

But what crucially weighed in the scales was that oriental studies were not a marketable commodity. Orientalists were loud in their lament that young men—particularly in the universities—when faced with the choice of a career looked askance at the world of orientalism however efficiently it had cast its magic spell over scholar and dilettante alike. What in reality were the prospects of the bright young men? In universities the openings were too few and were inadequately remunerated. The authorities presumably did not see why existing facilities should be enlarged if oriental subjects were poorly patronised. Vincent Smith, a pioneer British historian on India who shared Rhys Davids' earnest concern for the cause, pointed out that the problem was not that there were too few people to teach oriental subjects but that there were too few students. Moreover, in the allocation of clearly limited resources between contending disciplines, the claims of oriental subjects were often ignored. Science was becoming increasingly popular. It had dramatically challenged the paramountcy which classics had long enjoyed in universities. Rhys Davids, with his wonted eloquence, compared science to a handsome young eagle which swept down majestically every now and then and "carried off the spoils." It was all rather sad that as a result, the study of Eastern languages, religious and social institutions should have suffered. The system of endowments in Oxbridge—where of course the national standards were set—really helped the older subjects like Classics, Theology and Mathematics. The government, too, relied on endowments and did not think it necessary to make independent provision for university education.[15]

[14] *Ibid.*

[15] Rhys Davids' testimonial speech to Royal Asiatic Society, *J.R.A.S.* 1906, *op. cits.* Report on the Anniversary Meeting of The Royal Asiatic Society, *J.R.A.S. 1901, pp. 635ff; Rhys Davids, Oriental Studies in England and Abroad, op. cit.;* Statement of the R.A.S. on Oriental Learning in Britain, *op. cit.*

Apart from the universities there were a few rather specialised institutions like the British Museum which had openings for orientalists. They were, however, few in number. The opportunities in the Foreign Office and in the Indian service were obviously greater. In the Indian service there were about a hundred posts with monthly salaries ranging from Rs. 250 to Rs. 2450, for which a knowledge of oriental languages was necessary. Professorships in leading government sponsored educational institutions, as well as posts in the Indian education service, like directorships and inspectorships, were reasonably attractive if one was of course willing to live a few years in the East.[16]

Theoretically it was possible to stimulate the demand for oriental studies. Like a number of his contemporaries in the R.A.S., Rhys Davids believed that the government—which controlled employment in many spheres—could insist that a knowledge of oriental subjects was necessary for employment in certain areas. The India Office, the Foreign Office and the Colonial Office were spheres in which the rule could be more amply and rigidly enforced. The R.A.S. urged the India Office to make Pali an optional subject for candidates who would serve in Burma. It also declared that the government should restore Sanskrit as a compulsory subject for the final examination in the Indian Civil Service. Some members of the R.A.S. felt that the government should make ultimately a wide range of oriental subjects compulsory for those who were selected to serve His .Majesty's Government in the East.[17]

Assuming that the strategy was successful, it was by no means certain that existing facilities could match an increased demand for oriental subjects. Britain did not possess an oriental institution or school exclusively devoted to the speciality and which was well provided with funds and other facilities. Some imaginative spirits, however, visualised the sort of institution which Britain should ultimately have. Vincent Smith declared that if universities in Britain with a bias for "the classical tradition" were unsatisfactory, efforts should be made to revive the old East India Company's college at Haileybury but "on a magnified scale." It would be possible to provide courses in many of the colloquial Eastern languages as well

[16] Rhys Davids, *Oriental Studies. op. cit.,*

[17] Anniversary Meeting of the R.A.S., *J.R.A.S.* 1900, p. 605; Minutes of Meeting of Council of the R.A.S. (1891-1905), 9 November 1897; Anniversary Meeting of the R.A.S., *J.R.A.S.* 1906, pp. 763ff

as to teach the history, manners and customs of the people in the East. On the other hand, to Rhys Davids—a steadfast admirer of continental examples—the ideal was the Seminary in Berlin. Classical languages like Pali and Sanskrit were taught in the Seminary and provision had also been made for Chinese, Japanese, Arabic and a number of African languages like Swahili and Hausa. The teaching was in the hands of German professors who were assisted by a number of native teachers. The Seminary had not neglected "practical" aspects. There were courses in the products of tropical countries, tropical health, colonial law and a professorship in "the political economy and finance of German colonies."[18]

In a sense all this was not mere futile speculation. In the 1890s it became evident that the government intended to set up a proper teaching university in London. The R.A.S., which had actively supported the idea—Rhys Davids was a member of a deputation which had urged the government to do so—was determined that an oriental school should be established as part of the new university. Rhys Davids was also a member of a sort of action committee which was formed in this connection. The R.A.S. formally adopted a resolution urging the government to set up a "faculty of oriental languages and literature" as part of the University of London.[19]

Meanwhile various Boards of Studies and the University Senate had been set up. But by 1900 it was still uncertain whether there would be a separate faculty or school of oriental studies. To bring stronger pressure on the University Board and Senate the R.A.S. joined forces with the Central Asian Society, which had agitated independently for an oriental school. A joint committee of the two societies was formed. Rhys Davids took part in its deliberations too. The joint committee called upon the government to set up an oriental school as part of London University or as part of one of the older universities. Until the step was taken the government was urged to give financial assistance to maintain existing facilities for teaching oriental subjects and in general recognise oriental degrees in recruit-

[18] Speech by Vincent Smith at Anniversary Meeting of the Royal Asiatic Society, 14 April 1902, *J.R.A.S.*, 1902, pp. 714ff. Also Rhys Davids, *Oriental Studies*, *op. Cit.*

[19] Minutes of Meetings of the Council of the Royal Asiatic Society, (1891-1905 Vol.), 8 November 1898; Minutes of Meetings of the Council of the Royal Asiatic Society (1891-1905 Vol.), 5 April 1898.

ment to government departments.[20]

In many ways the agitation for the establishment of a faculty of oriental studies reflected concern over wider problems. In India, observers noted the widening gulf between officials and the more articulate elements in Indian society in a context of growing political consciousness. Some members of the R.A.S. felt that officials who were better trained should be sent out to India. The trouble was that the energies of prospective officials had been solely expended in mechanically "mucking up" a few Indian languages for purposes of examination. A genuine knowledge of India's past and her ancient literature would bring about a sense of real sympathy towards Indians.

Some orientalists also contended that the study of Eastern languages, history and social institutions would mean that Britain would have at its disposal knowledge which could be politically useful. In other words an oriental school could serve either as a useful auxiliary to existing intelligence departments or become an intelligence department in its own right. It was said—in consonance no doubt with the national mood of self-chastisement brought about by the growing strength of Germany—that in this very respect both Germany and France had the edge over Britain. The grave pronouncements of Lord Reay, who was the president of the R.A.S., in particular reflected prevailing anxieties. England would soon discover, he declared, that her rivals had overtaken her because ". . . they have forestalled us in training the men who defy our competition . . . then comes the cry 'what has the Intelligence Department been about?' I hope it will never be our fate in the East to be thus outmatched . . . the ignorance of the language and customs of a certain tribe might give rise to friction and difficulties." Lord Reay was sure that an oriental school for which the R.A.S. was so persistently agitating would effectively serve as "the Intelligence Department of your Eastern Empire." Referring specifically to developments in the Far East following the rise of Japan, Lord Reay also declared that Britain should be represented in the area "by those who have been able to avail themselves here of complete equipment for their duties."[21]

[20] *J.R.A.S.* 1905, p. 600; Minutes of Meetings of the Council of the Royal Asiatic Society (1891-1905 Vol.), 19 July 1904; Minutes of Proceedings of the Council of the R.A.S. (1905-1922 Vol.), 9 July 1906; Minutes of Meetings of the Council of the R.A.S. (1891-1905 Vol.), 10 May 1904.

[21] Anniversary Meeting of the Royal Asiatic Society, 8 May 1900, *J.R.A.S.* 1900, pp. 605ff; Anniversary Meeting of the R.A.S., 10 May 1904, *J.R.A.S.*, p. 507.

In spite of himself Rhys Davids, too, began to speak in the military idiom. In comparing the number of professors in oriental subjects in Germany and in Britain he remarked "we cannot gain much comfort in the face of the overwhelming foreign supremacy in battleships and cruisers by comparing the figures as to minor crafts." Just as Britain would, in making her naval estimates, consider the extent of the naval strength and activities of foreign powers, it was essential that she should "make an Intelligence Department in oriental matters at least as strong as that of any two of the other great powers." Echoing Lord Reay, Rhys Davids added that Britain "ran great risk" by the neglect of "this branch of the Intelligence Department."[22]

The cause of the oriental school had its ups and downs. The Statutory Committee charged with the task of forming the new university in London rejected the R.A.S. proposal that a faculty of oriental languages, history and archaeology should be set up. More effectively, the R.A.S. appealed to the newly constituted university Senate.[23] Consequently, in 1901 a Board of Oriental Studies was established. It had its meetings in the rooms of the R.A.S. By 1904, as a result of the recommendations made by the Board, it became possible for students to offer oriental subjects for the B.A. degree. Provision was at the same time made for an honours course for those who wanted more specialised knowledge. The R.A.S. however, was not content with the gains that had undoubtedly been made. It kept on the vigour of its agitation for an independent faculty of oriental school. In 1908 a committee of which Lord Reay was himself the Chairman unequivocally urged the creation of such an institution as an integral part of London University. The government accepted the proposal.[24]

The R.A.S. had at last won its battle. And one may add that Rhys Davids had won his battle too. The two were no doubt closely linked. At least in a largely symbolic form society had recognised—albeit belatedly—the importance of oriental studies. The recognition in turn implied an awareness of the pioneering role of men like Rhys Davids, their sacrifices and passionate devotion to the cause.

[22] Rhys Davids, *Oriental Studies*, *op. cit.*

[23] *J.R.A.S.* 1900, p. 588; also p. 604. Minutes of Meetings of the Council of the R.A.S., (1899-1905 Vol.), 13 November 1900.

[24] Anniversary Meeting of the R.A.S., *J.R.A.S.* 1901, p. 625; Anniversary Meeting of the R.A.S., *J.R.A.S.* 1904, p. 506.

The euphoria in Rhys Davids' mind at any rate evaporated ere long. By 1913 he was expressing misgivings about the new school of oriental studies, especially on two counts. The sceptre of lack of funds had always haunted the progress of oriental studies in Britain. During the dark days when the R.A.S. was agitating for the establishment of an oriental school, one of its members had suggested with bizarre earnestness that the government in India should suspend railway construction for a single year and instead devote the money—a sum of £ 10,000 was mentioned—for the advancement of oriental studies in Britain. With greater restraint, but with his customary forthrightness, Rhys Davids denounced the "incredible meanness" of the British government which was evidently showing great reluctance to give the necessary financial support to the School of Oriental Studies. Instead, the government was making it plain that private charity and benefactions must help the institution.[25]

Rhys Davids had misgivings, too, about the policies of the School of Oriental Studies. He complained that there was too much emphasis on contemporary languages and the neglect of the study of the classical languages like Sanskrit and Pali. Little attention was being given to the study of history, too: "... it seems to me to be the aim," he said, "to turn out students with just sufficient knowledge of the languages of the East to fit them to become dragomans while the ancient language and literature will be neglected. . . ." He had expressed the distinction admirably. Rhys Davids was not unmindful of the Germans who, it seemed, had somehow held a balance between pragmatic needs and the loftier ideal of making oriental studies the means of achieving a real understanding of alien people and their cultures.[26]

[25] Anniversary Meeting of the R.A.S., *J.R.A.S.* 1904, p. 502; Rhys Davids in interview with the *Morning Post Journal of the Mahe Bodhi Society*, no. 6, June 1914.
[26] *Ibid.*

Part IV
On Buddhism and Buddhists

12

QUESTIONS OF FAITH:
Beyond Man-made Identities

OVER a hundred years have passed since Max Muller wrote his preface to the *Upanishads,* the first volume in the series of the Sacred Books of the East. Neither the specific context in which he wrote nor changing perspectives in the study of religion has made his observation obsolete.

Superficially it might seem that Max Muller was wholly concerned with the problems of translating the religious texts of Hinduism, Buddhism and Zoroastrianism. The difficulties were clearly numerous and formidable and led him to declare in despair that it was best to read the originals.

In a deeper sense, Max Muller's preface had everything to do with understanding other religions. He wrote in an intellectual climate in which there was widespread unfamiliarity with Eastern religions, a cultural reluctance to understand them, and a penchant for using the Christian norm as a yardstick to measure non-Christian faiths. Indeed Max Muller had encountered many who contended that the sacred texts were unworthy of the scholar's interest because there was much in them that was absurd, improbable, and whimsical or that the texts were plainly offensive to Western ideas of morality and religion.[1]

But to Max Muller and his colleagues in the great project of the Sacred Books of the East—among whom Rhys Davids played a key role—there was also in the religious texts a great deal that was morally worthy and inspiring. The study of religions other than one's own had to be done sans private prejudices and inherited beliefs, and in a spirit of genuine sympathy. "The religions of antiquity," admonished the great scholar, "must always be approached in a loving spirit and the dry and cold blooded scholar is likely to do here as much mischief as

1. Muller, F. Max, *The Upanishads,* Vol. I. The Sacred Books of the East, translated by various oriental scholars, Oxford, 1879.

the enthusiastic sciolist." Nor should one disregard the texts on the grounds that some parts of the texts were repugnant to personal tastes. It was the whole text, warts and all, that gave a clear picture of Eastern religious thought. A true lover, declared Max Muller, using an analogy which did not quite accord with scholarly gravitas, did not ignore faults and failings of the object of his love.[2]

The context in which Max Muller worked has dramatically changed. His enlightened *Vade Mecum* would today seem somewhat superfluous. Cultural relativity has replaced the old provincial ego-centrism. Cultures are no longer today swept under the carpet because they are "strange" or "curious" however exotic they might appear to be. They are dissected, analysed and studied in detail and judged from within. Moreover, the world has also culturally diminished in size. There has been a reaching out to reduce the isolation of diverse cultural entities. Above all, the reality of a religiously plural world has been accepted.

Nonetheless, it is by no means certain that the problems of understanding other men's faiths has been altogether overcome. The spate of books on the Great Religions of the World, on Living Faiths—the typical titles of religious anthologies—would suggest that there is no such problem. Their objects are threefold. The first is to discover the outward facts concerning any given faith; the next to understand their religious meaning; and the third and final task to draw generalizations. In addition, the popular religious anthologies share a curious defensiveness. The authors, not insensitive to their private religious allegiances, protest that they have been objective in their study of other religions. Some, however, truly confess that no real objectivity is possible and that all that one can do with regard to "other religions" was to describe rather than evaluate them. The latter are probably right. Built-in prejudices cannot be wished away or exorcised in the name of intellectual objectivity. A writer subscribing to theistic beliefs would not be ideally suited to write about a religious philosophy which spared no pains to repudiate theism. By the same

[2] *Ibid.*

token, a Buddhist would fail to really understand Christianity. Much of its inner meaning, subtlety and mysticism would elude him.[3]

A Hindu or a Buddhist confronted with religious anthologies may well ask the question, "Is this a fair representation of my faith?" A Buddhist would contend that whereas it was possible to gain mere knowledge about Buddhism from books—granted that such books were reasonably accurate and did not deliberately falsify—the knowledge would not measure up to the understanding of a committed Buddhist. The experiences of mindfulness and the insights thereof can be understood only by those who have undertaken rigours of meditation. To take other examples, what would *Dāna* and *Sīla* mean to the non-believing Buddhist? A Hindu could say with as much conviction that one did not become a Hindu, but was born a Hindu. Religion, to the committed believer, was a personal experience which went over and beyond mere intellectual understanding.

But notwithstanding the disjunction between the believer and the non-believing interpreter, the task of understanding other men's faiths could not be approached in a spirit of hopelessness much less abandoned. When Max Muller wrote, it was about a moral imperative to understand. His solution was unconventional as it was bold. To understand Hinduism, Buddhism or Jainism, Max Muller grandly declared, one should become a Hindu, a Buddhist, or a Jain, as the case may be, "at least for the time being."[4]

Theoretically there was much in common between Hinduism and Christianity. It was not impossible for a European Christian, be he a scholar or otherwise, to become a Hindu as Max Muller suggested. In spite of appearances, there was in religions like Hinduism clear evidence of what Max Muller called the "divine afflatus." The idea constantly recurs. Early in the nineteenth century, the Bengali scholar reformer, Ram Mohun Roy, juxtaposed the two faiths remarking on much that was common between them. He drew attention to the monotheism of the *Vedānta* and the *Upanishads*. One hundred years after Ram Mohun Roy wrote *The Idolatrous System of the Hindus*, which

[3] Hume, Robert E., *The World's Living Religions*, with special reference to their sacred scriptures and in comparison with Christianity, New York, 1959.

Jurfi, Edward J., *The Great Religions of the Modern World*, Princeton, New Jersey, 1946.

Gaer, Joseph, *What the Great Religions Believe*, New York, 1963.

Smith, Wilfred Cantwell, *The Faith of Other Men*, New York, 1963.

Muller, Max, *op. cit.*

marked a turning point in the Christian-Hindu confrontation, J.N. Farquhar, in the course of investigating the relationship between the two religions argued that Christianity, in the person of Christ, fulfilled the highest aspirations of the Hindu ideals.[5]

Buddhism, however, was a different kettle of fish. Christianity and Buddhism were totally divergent faiths. Ethically there seemed to be common ground, but the ethics sprang from widely dissimilar assumptions. Small wonder that Christian Protestant missionaries in South Asia should have hurled their bitterest shafts at Buddhism rather than Hinduism, although the latter—no doubt on account of political reasons connected with the British presence in India, especially in the time of the East India Company—loomed larger in the picture. The moral was plain. Buddhism, the personification of atheism, was deadlier than Hinduism.[6]

And yet Rhys Davids identified himself with Buddhism over and beyond the position which Max Muller had urged. In modern terminology, Rhys Davids would be described as a liberal. He stood for intellectual liberty and tolerance and was attracted so intensely to Buddhism because Buddhism—Rhys Davids would italicize Early Buddhism—exemplified these very virtues. Moreover, Rhys Davids did not belong to the Established Church. A long Nonconformist tradition had made the Rhys Davids family familiar with persecution and the heavy hand of civil and religious disabilities. His father, a Congregationalist clergyman, had been well known for his writings on Nonconformism. In Wales,where the Rhys Davids family hailed from, there was a strong Congregationalist religious tradition which expressed mistrust of established religion, upholding instead a liberal spirit both on questions of belief and Church organisation. The background influenced Rhys Davids' view of religion. In the Empire the great non-Christian faiths were left out in the cold *vis-a-vis* Christianity, in a relationship similar to that of the Nonconformists and the Established Church in the mother country. Buddhism was the

[5] Farquhar, J.N., *The Crown of Hinduism*, Oxford, 1913. See chapters X and XI.

[6] I have discussed this aspect in great detail in my thesis "The Policies of the Government of Ceylon Concerning Education and Religion, 1865-1885," D. Phil. Thesis, Oxford. 1966. There are a number of general books on the subject:

Kaye, J.W. *Christianity in India*, London, 1859.

Tennent, Sir James Emerson, *Christianity in Ceylon*, London, 1850.

De Silva, K.M., *Social Policy and Missionary Organizations in Ceylon, 1840-1855*, London, 1965

underdog. Underlying Rhys Davids' attitudes to Buddhism was the subtle identity between Nonconformism in the English context and Buddhism. It was his task to set the record straight, to articulate the Cause of Buddhism as a worthy religion, just as his father had so devotedly served Nonconformism.[7]

II

But what was Buddhism? There was no easy answer. Then as now the question was viewed from divergent standpoints.

In Rhys Davids' writings the historian's approach was plainly evident. Siddhārtha Gautama, the Śākyan prince who was born six centuries before Christ, in Kapilavastu, a kingdom situated in North Eastern India at the foothills of the Himalayas, was a human personality who lived and died as such. He was not, as orthodox Buddhists believed, a supra-human being who in countless previous existences or births had developed the *paramis* (perfections of Virtue) for Buddhahood. The story of the Buddha, beginning with the scene in the Tusita heavens in which the gods implore the Buddha-to-be to go down to the world of mortals to preach the *Dharma*, his miraculous birth in the womb of Mahāmāyā, the queen of King Śuddhodana, the ruler of Kapilavastu, and the episodes connected with the youth, manhood, and death of the Buddha, were manifestations of the excess piety of his followers. A key element in the mythologising process was the Cakravartı notion of a mighty monarch whose power transcended the confines of his own state and who was at the same time the personification of righteousness. The idea of a Cakravartı had come into vogue with the gradual disappearance of the old patrician and aristocratic republics which had existed in Buddha's time, their place being taken by aggressive monarchies. The Kingdom of Kapilavastu was small, but the modest kingdom was metamorphosed to a powerful state and its ruler Śuddhodana became a mighty monarch. The transformation gave added point and no small colour to the Abhinishkrama Naya or the Great Renunciation of the Buddha. It was the power, the princely comforts untold and the pleasures of a mighty kingdom that Siddhartha Gautama had renounced for the sake of suffering humanity, not the negligible appendages of a

[7] See chapter 1 in part one of the book.

lowly state. Apart from the Cakravartī notion, Buddhism had also assimilated the Hindu ideal of a perfectly wise being who had attained a condition of wisdom in succesive births by ritual and sacrifice.[8]

What had Rhys Davids achieved? A notable feature in nineteenth century writings on Buddhism was the lack of Rhys Davids' discrimination between the probable and the improbable in the biography of the Buddha. There was either a total rejection of Buddhism—the baby, as it were, being thrown away with the bath water—or an eccentric preoccupation with the purely biographical aspect. In his *Manual of Buddhism,* which was regarded as the most authoritative work on Buddhism, Spence Hardy, the Wesleyan missionary in Ceylon (see chapter 1) had devoted as many as seven chapters to a detailed exposition of the legendary elements in the life of the Buddha which Rhys Davids, in his own treatise on Buddhism, deftly dealt with in a few lucid paragraphs. The result was that in Spence Hardy's work (a typical example) the metaphysical and ethical aspects of Buddhism the more worthwhile field of inquiry—had received inadequate attention.[9]

To Rhys Davids, once the identity of the Buddha was established the historian's next task was to assess his contribution to religious thought. At the time of the Buddha, India was in a condition of religious ferment. Men speculated on the very questions which became the concern of Buddhism. The Buddhist tradition refers to no less than sixty-two schools or sects which were particularly preoccupied with the hareafter and the nature of the soul. In his own attempts to put forward a new answer to the age old question of *Vimukti* or spiritual liberation, the Buddha had necessarily to build on foundations that already existed. Buddhism was therefore no novel theology but very much part of the larger Indian religious tradition. The idea that salvation depended on the choice of a right ideal, the emphasis on self culture and ethical training, the belief that goodness was a function of intelligence, the grand theory of Karma and the doctrine of *Anicca* were not unknown when Buddhism arose. Buddhism was therefore a re-statement, a change in emphasis and the priorities of

[8] Rhys Davids. T.W., *Early Buddhism*, London, 1908, pp. 26ff.
Rhys Davids, T.W., *Lectures on the Origin and Growth of Religion as Illustrated by Some Points in the History of Indian Buddhism, New York, 1881.*
Rhys Davids, T.W., Buddhism, Its History and Literature, India, 1896, pp. 90ff.

[9] Hardy, Robert Spence, *A Manual of Buddhism,* London, 1853. See chapters IX and X.

existing beliefs. The founder of Buddhism, declared Rhys Davids, had poured the old wine of Indian religious thought into new bottles.

There was, however, much that was distinctive. The existing schools of religious speculation in India were in one way or another strongly identified with Brahmanic beliefs concerning a deity or extra-cosmic being which Buddhism repudiated. The gods of popular belief were the *devas* of the *Brahmaloka*. They were, however, themselves in need of salvation and were subject to the *saṃsaric* cycle of birth and death. It was futile, therefore, to propitiate them by means of rituals and sacrifices, much less look to the gods for salvation. The virtuous man, the one who knew the *Dharma* and lived accordingly, was on a par with the gods.

The departure from orthodox religious tradition was particularly striking with regard to the doctrine of *Anatta*. The Buddha repudiated the notion, which was widely held, that there was in human beings an entity called the soul which survived death. Various theories concerning the soul had dominated Indian religious thinking. Some believed (Sassatavāda) that souls were eternal. Others (Ekacca Sassatika) declared that some souls were eternal—like the souls of the gods but that other souls were not. A third belief (Uddhama Aghatanika) was that human souls would survive death and exist in a dormant form. The followers of another school (Ucchedavada) believed that there was a soul but that it would cease to exist either at the point of death or in some future existence (Dittha-Dharma-Nibbana-Vada). Yet another belief was that there was a soul and that on account of its existence men could achieve bliss in their own lifetime by states of mental development or *jhanas*. Human beings, according to the Buddha, were in reality made up of aggregates or *skandhas*, or assemblages of various properties. There were five such groups, each group dividing itself into numerous sub-groupings. At death the aggregates—the total physical, psychological and mental attributes of a human being—perished.[10] The soul was not enumerated as part of the *skandhas*.

Because he saw the origin of Buddhism in terms of historical continuity Rhys Davids was not concerned with a question which curiously preoccupied some nineteenth-century Protestant missionaries in their studies of Buddhism. How did the Buddha acquire knowledge of the philosophical system which came to be known as

[10] Rhys Davids, *Buddhism, Its History and Literature*, *op. cit.*, pp. 156ff.

Buddhism? Did he do so by intuition, self-enlightenment, reasoning, or was the knowledge inspirational? Missionaries like Spence Hardy and Gogerly were plainly irked by the Buddhist view that Siddhārtha Gautama attained enlightenment by his own efforts or that he was "self-taught."[11] Buddhists believed that there were several Buddhas who had preceded Gautama Buddha, each of whom had taught the *Dharma* for the benefit of mankind. Successive Buddhas arose because the knowledge of the previously known *Dharma* at each stage had disappeared altogether. When the *Dharma* disappeared the cosmic order, the *sakwalas* or world systems also disappeared or were destroyed. Subsequently, after an inconceivably long period of time—and time in the Buddhist version of the apocalypse was computed on a mind boggling scale—the cosmic order rejuvenates, mankind comes into existence, and everything, as it were, starts afresh. A Buddha is born again to teach the *Dharma* to suffering mankind. But the new Buddha has himself to acquire the knowledge of the *Dharma* by self-enlightenment as his predecessors had done. In the *Angatha Vamsa* (the Chronicle of Future Events) the Buddha himself discusses the stages of the apocalypse and the disappearance of the *Dharma* when Sariputta, his senior disciple, asks him;

> The Hero that shall follow you
> as Buddha, of what sort is he?
> The account in full I fain would learn
> Declare to me, thou Seeing One.[12]

Nor did Rhys Davids attach much importance to Buddhist cosmogony which obsessed many Western writers. The veracity or otherwise of Buddhist ideas on the subject had led to acrimonious debate. Typically Rhys Davids believed that the study of religion should not concern itself with the parochialism of establishing that any one religion—usually Christianity—was superior to another. To Rhys Davids Buddhist cosmological notions were irrelevant because he had a clear grasp of what was centrally important in Buddhism. In Buddhism, in the final analysis, there was a key or paramount problem. What sort of life was worth having? And how might man emancipate himself from a perpetual condition of sorrow which existence in this birth, and in successive births, made him heir to? The

[11] Hardy, *A Manual of Buddhism, op. cit.* p. 389. Also Hardy, *Eastern Monachism*, London, 1850, pp. 346ff, p. 387.

[12] Hardy, *Manual, op. cit.* See chapters I and IV; Warren, Henry Clarke, *Buddhism in Translation*, New York, 1963, pp. 481ff.

problem fascinated Rhys Davids intellectually. All other questions which men were wont to ask, or speculate upon, out of a legitimate sense of human curiosity—as, for example, on cosmogony—were irrelevant and futile. They were questions which the Buddha discouraged not so much because their consideration was beyond human comprehension but because they were eccentric to the central concerns of Buddhism.[13]

Writers like Spence Hardy, however, saw the matter in a different light. Buddhist ideas concerning cosmogony were to be highlighted as part of a simple and effective strategy designed to show the absurdity of Buddhism, especially as the ideas seemed to be derived from the Buddha's own opinion of the cosmic order.

In the Buddhist tradition there were innumerable world systems, each having its own sun, moon, continents and oceans, as well as its hells and heavens. These were the *sakwalas*. The outer peripheries of the *sakwala* of which earth was a part was formed by an immense rocky circle at the center of which was the great mountain Maha Meru. The mountain was surrounded by seven rocky circles. Between these circles and the outer rocky periphery were the four continents of which *Jambudvipa* (the Indian continent) was distinguished as the land fit for a Buddha to be born in. The *sakwalas* were divided into various *lokas* or worlds. There were the *satwa lokas* (worlds of sentient beings), the *awakasa lokas* (worlds of space) and the *sanskara lokas* (the material or purely physical worlds). Or again the *sakwalas* were divided into worlds without form, worlds with form but with no sensual enjoyment, or worlds with form and sensual enjoyment. The diverse worlds and the entire cosmic system was, however, susceptible to disintegration and renovation—a cyclical process which took place during an incalculably long period of time.[14]

Rhys Davids contended that Buddhist notions of cosmogony had a subtler meaning. Buddhism was emphasising the immensity of time and space and the utter insignificance of man in relation to a cosmic vastness. The cosmos was in a state of flux. Buddhist cosmogony emphasised the futility of belief in the transmigration of souls and the hopelessness, too, of looking for salvation to another world, "a world beyond." Worlds there might be, the Buddhist would say, in the vast cosmos. But what relevance had they to man struggling with the

[13] Rhys Davids, *Early Buddhism, op. cit.*, pp. 69ff; also pp. 82ff.
[14] Hardy, *Manual op. cit.*, see chapter I

burden of existence? Let a man bestir himself to the task of his own salvation and do so earnestly here and how rather than look to a hypothetical hereafter.[15]

III

However, understanding the religions of Asia was not altogether a matter of coming to grips with recondite metaphysics and whimsical cosmogony. In the West religious systems were judged in close relationship to Christianity. And their value was seen, in the final analysis, in essentially ethical terms. The attitude provided the European colonization of Asia with an inner meaning and with more than a surface veneer of morality. The Western presence in Asia was seen not as a prosaic exercise in economic penetration but rather as a civilising process—to make Asian societies responsive to Christian morality and ethics.

Traditional Asian societies were found to be wanting. Deficiencies of character, absence of integrity, lack of moral courage, indecisiveness, apathy and indolence—the all too familiar socio-biological stereotypes which described the Indian in nineteenth-century literature—were seen as consequences of religious systems which had failed, or rather could not by definition, provide a true supportive basis for creating a better type of human being, much less a better social order.

Buddhism, however, did not seem to fit the general theory. Its distinctive feature was an elaborate system of ethics. It forbade the taking of life, theft, lying, abuse, slander, malice, convetousness, pride and a variety of forms of conduct and behavior designed to make man morally whole. On the positive side, Buddhism inculcated the virtues of kindness, charity, good will, and tolerance. In the *Sigala Vada Sutta*—which the Buddha preached to Sigala, a Brahmana—he laid down the morality which should govern an individual's relationships with those with whom he ordinarily came into contact, as well as with society. In short, the true Buddhist was the personification of the perfectly virtuous man.[16]

[15] Rhys Davids, *Early Buddhism, op. cit.*, pp. 82ff.

[16] Rhys Davids, *Buddhism, Being a Sketch of the Life and Teachings of Gautama, the Buddha*, London, 1894, chapter V.

The morality of Buddhism posed a very real problem to Christian missionaries in Ceylon It was possible to argue with Buddhist—the dialogue was going on all the time, its apogee occurring in the mid-nineteenth century when formal public debates were held between Buddhists and Christians—about fallacies in Buddhist ontology, metaphysics or cosmogony. But not about morality and ethics. A Buddhist's rejoinder was that whatever the apparent deficiencies might be, nonetheless his religion was not only morally good but superior to Christianity. Whereas Christ had urged the need for love between man and espoused the brotherhood of man, the Buddha's love had embraced all living things without distinction. The Buddhists certainly saw no moral gain in becoming Christians.

The notion of superiority conditioned the general response to Christianity. The missionaries would not have been surprised had there been an open hostility to Christianity or a combative reaction. The Buddhists, however, did not oppose missionary activities, not even the establishment of missionary schools in their villages. They expressed opposition to Christian schools—the main method of proselytization—whenever the missionaries disregarded caste in the conduct of their schools. An opposition to Christianity and missionary effort as a matter of principle was a comparatively late development and occurred towards the end of the nineteenth century with the birth of a self-conscious Buddhist revivalist movement. In general. with patronising tolerance—which the missionaries found distasteful—the Buddhists admired Christianity and the personality of Jesus Christ who was regarded as a "good man." Some Buddhists were willing to show reverence to Christ—to the extent of attending church to please a particularly persistent and "good" missionary clergyman—but remained devout Buddhists. One may therefore understand the recurring complaint in nineteenth-century missionary documents about "nominal" converts and "lapses into heathenism" of those who had embraced Christianity in apparent good faith. To sum up, the Buddhist response to missionary evangelism was a mood of indifference. The exasperation of the missionaries was aptly expressed by Spence Hardy who remarked that whereas a battering ram might well be effective in bringing down a citadel, it was of little use against a too yielding rampart of earth.[17]

[17] Wickremeratne, ". . . Education and Religion," unpublished Oxford Thesis, *op. cit.*; Hardy, *Eastern Monachism*, *op. cit.*, p. 430.

The missionary counter-strategy took two forms. Some missionaries contended that however lofty Buddhist ethics were, there was a very obvious gap between practice and precept. The Buddhist was "sinful" in his everyday conduct, not in a Christian sense but in that he broke the very canons enjoined by his faith. Buddhist moral precepts were universally honoured in the breach. The ethics were in effect a broken reed and had no impact on society. Consequently the Buddhist in Ceylon too manifested those very moral deficiencies which were common to traditional Asian societies.

Some of the more able missionaries, however, attacked the ethics of Buddhism on theoretical grounds. Buddhist ethics had no binding force. Would that binding force be *karma*—the fear of retribution for bad or evil acts? Daniel Gogerly, the doyen of Wesleyan missionaries in Ceylon, for example, reasoned that although according to *karmic* theory every good or bad action committed brings corresponding "fruits" or consequences in this life or in some futures birth, it was possible for a Buddhist, by religious observances and worship, to "put off" paying the price for his deeds—". . . however flagitious may be the conduct of a man," he wrote, "he is instructed that if, with faith in the doctrines of the Buddha, taking refuge in him, his doctrines, and his priesthood, he makes oblations and worships the image and the priest, he will be saved from the consequences of his crimes for one or more births." Gogerly went on to argue that the ordinary Buddhist therefore did not feel a natural sense of awe against doing crimes, much less feel that bad acts were morally reprehensible. He concluded, "The moral precepts of Buddha, therefore, are rendered inefficacious not only by the general depravity of mankind, but by those doctrines which remove to an incalculably distant period, the dread of punishment for crimes committed."[18]

Spence Hardy went a stage further. According to Buddhism there was a moral law—the law of *karma*—which governed the entire universe. The law worked, however, on its own accord. There was, he pointed out, no moral law giver like a divine and intelligent deity to give the moral law its necessary sanction and preside over its workings. *Karma* was a principle. But more than a mere principle was needed to govern men. Christian principles of conduct and morality, the Christian struggle against evil, had the backing of divine authority.

[18] Bishop, Arthur Stanley, ed., *Ceylon Buddhism Being the Collected Writings of Daniel John Gogerly*, London, 1908, pp. 6ff.

Moreover, if a Buddhist abstained from crime or an act of evil he did not do so because of the idea of exceeding sinfulness but because a bad action or *Karma* would cause him some personal misfortune. To the Buddhist there was no "moral pollution" in sin *per se*. The idea that good and bad or unfortunate consequences were necessarily connected with *karma* or action made the Buddhist selfish. He looked upon his actions not in terms of how they might affect society's well-being but rather in terms of a personal *karmic* tally or account. He was in truth not unlike—the specific comparison made by Spence Hardy—a Chinese merchant who was obsessed with balancing the credit and debit side of the ledger.[19]

Characteristically, Rhys Davids kept aloof from the great debate. Instead he often expressed his conviction that the nobility and beauty of Buddhism were really derived from its ethics. Rhys Davids constantly stressed that in actual fact there was no significant divergence between practice and Buddhist precept. Buddhist countries like Ceylon had been spared those crimes and vices and moral malaise which had been the bane of economically more developed societies. Evidence of an increase in crime or in drunkenness, for example, was a consequence of the white man's economic penetration. History too Showed that in general Buddhist communities had lived by the faith. "How happy would have been," he mused, "the village or the clan on the banks of the Ganges where the people were full of the kindly spirit of fellow feeling, the noble spirit of Justice which breathes through these naive and simple sayings." The question really was whether Buddhist morality was practicable in modern society. Rhys Davids was sceptical. Modern economic society, with its emphasis on individualism was, he believed, inimical to Buddhism.

Possibly the most telling point that Rhys Davids made was that in Buddhism morality was not an excrescence but was significantly related to larger metaphysical concerns. The final goal in Buddhism was salvation or escape from an endless round of birth, suffering and death. All Buddhism, it was said, had the flavour of salvation or *vimukti* just as the water of the oceans had the flavour of salt. The Buddhist seeking salvation had necessarily to walk along the path of emancipation—the Noble Eightfold Path—which the Buddha had pointed out. Not everyone, however, could enter the Path. He would enter the Path who had the necessary insight, grasped the real nature

[19] Hardy, *Manual, op. cit.*, p. 399; also pp. 506ff

of things, who had the strength of will, and who was—a significant prerequisite—morally purified. The morality which touched the life of the ordinary layman was the *Adi Brahmacariya,* so called to distinguish it from the *Marga Brahmacariya,* or the higher morality of the Noble Eightfold Path. The *Adi Brahmacariya,* or lower morality, made men noble, purified their character, and prepared them for the Path. The higher moral standards or perfect righteousness which one would associate with a person who was experiencing the spiritualism of the Path—a perfectability in speech, conduct, aims, etc.—was the *Marga Brahmacariya.*[20]

There was in Buddhism a close relationship between the seemingly disparate elements of morality, knowledge or wisdom, and salvation. The wise man in the Buddhist sense was a virtuous man. He had necessarily to be so. He was moral because he saw the point of morality. He did not lie or steal or commit murder because of the futility of doing so in terms of Buddhist goals.

IV

In a rather more personal sense, two facets of Buddhism—*karma* and *'annica*—interested Rhys Davids immensely. *Karma,* like the Inidan words *chela* and *Mahatma,* had come into popular usage in the late nineteenth century in England as well as in the U.S.A., partly as a result of the work of the orientalists and—more significantly—because of Theosophy and its splendidly charismatic leaders. It was fashionable to use the terms lightheartedly too. A typical British cartoon of the period, for example, portrayed a foppish young man asking a woman—evidently as the opening gambit in a conversation—"How is your *karma?*"[21]

There was, however, no suggestion of levity in Rhys Davids' use of the word which occurs at two levels in his writings. In describing Buddhism he naturally discussed *Karma* at length because *karma* was an integral part of Buddhist doctrines. *Karma,* rather than the soul, survived death and linked one life and the next. *Karma* was also moral law. It held that there was a correlation between what a man did and the results of his actions—good or bad consequences arising from actions which were morally right or wrong. Each man—to use an

[20] Rhys Davids, *Life and Teachings of the Buddha, op. cit.,* p. 148.

[21] Williams, Gertrude Marvin, *The Passionate Pilgrim. A Life of Annie Besant,* New York, 1931, pp.198ff.

illuminating Christian idiom—reaped what he sowed. Above all *karma* presumed to explain the differences in the condition of men, particularly in terms of wealth, poverty and suffering. A Buddhist would stoically suffer the "slings and arrows of outrageous fortune" in the absolute conviction that he and he alone was responsible for his tribulations because of what he had done in past births.

However, Rhys Davids clearly wavered in his view of the *karmic* theory. He was unwilling to accept that *karma* was in reality the link between one life and another. He saw no "proof" of the existence of *karma* other than the widely held presumption of a connection, and declared that *karma* was "an imagined cause beyond the reality of reason." Curiously the view was, however, tempered by the reflection that after all there was an element of truth in the *karmic* idea. The nagging doubt persists in his writings. He quotes the German philosopher Friedrich Wilhelm Schelling, who had remarked that in every man there was a certain feeling that he had been what he was, from all eternity. He was also fond of quoting the lines

Our deeds follow us from afar
And what we have been makes us what we are

and declared that therein was in intuitive understanding of the meaning of *karma*. Neither sentiment, however, strictly accorded with the "proof" Rhys Davids was looking for.[22]

Rhys Davids also referred to *karma* parenthetically—albeit no less significantly. The recurring use of the word *karma* in this sense and the contexts of usage point to the strong possibility of some sort of personal belief. Whenever he was under great stress, he referred to *karma* as if *karma* was a means of reconciling himself to the situation. Rhys Davids often felt that he was ill-used, that he did not receive just recompense—especially economic rewards—for his labour, and above all, that he had to struggle hard for whatever he got in life. He was also extraordinarily sensitive to blame and censure. On such occasions—very much as an orthodox Buddhist would if he did not see a discernible and immediate cause to account for some misfortune—Rhys Davids gave vent to feelings of suprise, indignation and startled disbelief. The reactions found poignant expression during the events that preceded his dismissal in Ceylon. At no point in the painful official investigations did Rhys Davids feel that he was guilty. Ineptitude? Yes. Morally culpable? No. He passed through the crisis in a

[22] Rhys Davids, *Early Buddhism, op. cit.* pp. 75ff.

mood of perpetual perplexity and asked himself why fate had decreed that he should be the principal actor in the drama.[23]

Annica—the Buddhist notion that all things were in a state of flux, of continuous change and impermanence—had too a subtle personal relevance. If *annica* were true, there was the pleasing prospect that the philistines of the world, the smug, self-complacent professional people who cared so little for scholarship, would disappear, together with the social order with which they were identified. But surely scholarship was of a different order? Must the scholar's work—and his own—perish? Did scholarship not have an enduring quality because the work of the scholar—usually accomplished at great cost and hardhsip to himself—contributed to the good of society? Curiously, the possibility that the individual scholar's efforts would in the course of time be negelected and be forgotten filled him with sadness.

V

Karma and *annica* were part of a deeper intellectual identification with Buddhism. In 1879 Rhys Davids spoke to the Sunday Lecture Society in London on the improbable subject "Is Life Worth Having?" In the *Dharmachakra Sutta* or the discourse or *sutta* on the Foundation of the Kingdom of Righteousness (the first sermon preached by the Buddha after Enlightenment), Rhys Davids declared that there was an answer which Europeans should seriously consider. The sermon had, however, to be cast in the modern idiom because many of the underlying assumptions were totally foregin to Western thinking.[24]

The Buddhist notion of suffering was a crucial example. A man born into the economic and cultural ethos of underdevelopment—in India or in Ceylon, for example—would not find it difficult to grasp the idea that life, or the business of living, was sorrowful. The stark realities of coming to terms with hopeless poverty, disease, and a complexity of disabilities, have given a bizarre validity to the notion. The Westerner, on the other hand, the product of historically different economic conditions, would protest. He would deny that the mass

[23] C.O. 54 No. 238 Sir William Gregory to Lord Kimberley, 14 November 1872. C.O. 54 No. 259 Gregory to Kimberley, 27 November 1872. *Report of the Pali Text Society*, 1891-1893, pp. IXff; *Journal of the Royal Asiatic Society*, 1906, pp. 520ff.

[24] Rhys Davids, *Is Life Worth Having?* And *Eternal Hope: An Answer From Buddha's First Sermon to Some Questions of Today*, London, 1880

of humanity was born into a condition of suffering from which it was really powerless to escape. The history of centuries of economic development in the West suggested altogether a different moral—a continuing progression from successful forms of production to even more effective and sophisticated levels of economic activity. Life—and surely both protagonists were thinking primarily of life in economic terms—may certainly be "an ever striving," a struggle. But the ratio of economic endeavor to economic achievement clearly proved that the striving brought ample economic rewards. To Rhys Davids' own Victorian contemporaries with their self-assuredness and faith in industrial capitalism, the Buddhist notion of suffering and perpetual striving was hard to grasp. At a strictly philosophical level the Westerner would also contend that birth, death and the implied traumas were everyday occurrences, so banal and commonplace as to be unworthy of the emphasis which Buddhists were wont to place on them. Were he a Christian, the Westerner would echo the poet's words and wonder whether death was after all a dreadful calamity. The grave was denied its sting and death was merely a passing through to a condition of unalloyed joy and peace.

Significantly, Rhys Davids told his audience in the course of the Sunday Lecture that he did not really expect them to readily accept a theory which was so "new" and "strange." The theory of suffering had been elaborated on in great detail by the Buddha. It was a deeply perceptive exposition of the basic human malaise and was called the First Noble Truth. Rhys Davids categorically declared that he personally believed that there was a great amount of truth in the Buddhist theory of suffering.[25]

Suffering insofar as it was not related to feelings for others, like a fathers's grief over the death of a son, or—to take a diametrically opposite example—the stress caused by having to put up with an unpleasant social relationship, was in essence the product of desire or craving. It was possible that individual desires were centered on praiseworthy objects like a breadwinner's struggle to come to terms with rising prices so that he continues to provide adequately for his family. More generally, however, human desires and cravings (***tanha,*** in Buddhist terminology, meaning tenacious, grasping, continuing desire) were directed towards the satisfaction of whims and fancies and superficial pleasures. Buddhism, however, ignored the distinction. It was not so much a question of legitimising desire in terms of subjective value judgements but rather the realization that all desires, be they just or otherwise, engendered equally a condition of stress and were potential sources of sorrow. Desire satisfaction was elusive because the objects of desire were illusory and had no real existence, because of obstacles which the individual was powerless to circumvent or because of the intervention of totally unforeseen circumstances in a given situation. Ironically, were desires—especially of a purely individualist or selfish nature—fulfilled, their very fulfilment engendered an opposite condition of dissatisfaction, a condition of *ennui* and disenchantment. Desire and dissatisfaction were in the final analysis a reflex of the state of the individual's mind. In Buddhism, there was no real dissociation between the psychology of desire or *dukkha*, to use the proper Pali term, and economic matters. The two blended. The validity of the Buddha's thesis on suffering did not therefore stand or fall merely on how good or bad economic conditions were.

If desire was the cause of suffering, desire in turn was engendered by individuality or by what Buddhists conventionally called egoism. Every man was striving to give expression to his individuality. It governed all his actions. Individuality was really an illusion. Rhys Davids graphically explained the Buddhist view, resorting to typical Buddhist imagery. Let us suppose, he said, that a man was looking at a swiftly flowing river from the vantage point of a bridge. He sees the river throwing up bubbles, especially where the waters swirl furiously around the buttresses and supports of the bridge. It would seem that the bubbles, as they are thrown up into the air, are independent of the river. But soon they disappear to become part of the river. Or, to take another example— a favourite with Rhys Davids—a watchman looking down on the plains below him from a tower sees a man driving a chariot. The man drives with such force that at certain moments the horse and chariot leap into the air and seem to be no part of the earth. The charioteer shares the illusion. But ere long the chariot falls back to the earth of which it had all the time been a part. Notwithstanding the attractive analogies, however, the Buddhist position was hard to grasp. Individuality was the basic motivating force in human activity. It was certainly the basis of the tremendous material progress which Western society had achieved.

26 *Ibid.*

The Buddhist analysis of the human malaise was not without its purpose. In the Dharmacakra Sutta and elsewhere the Buddha had preached the Noble Eightfold Path which led to *Vimukti* or ultimate emancipation. It was the famous Middle Path of Buddhism, so called because it avoided the practices of asceticism and self-mortification which had become part of Indian religious life, as well as the purposeless sensualism indulged in by those who saw life purely in materialistic terms. The Eightfold Path was, however, proverbially difficult. It called for an excellence or perfection with regard to aims, views, endeavour, speech and conduct as well as an excellence in mental tranquility and equipoise. Moreover, in striving to attain such excellences it was necessary to contend with obstacles, the fetters which impeded progress along the Path. The Lions of the Path, like the Delusion of self, Doubt, Ill Will, Pride and Self-Righteousness, were formidable. The Delusion of Self was the hardest foe to combat. "So long as a man is wholly occupied with himself," wrote Rhys Davids, "chasing after every bauble that he vainly thinks will satisfy the cravings of his heart, there is no Noble Path for him. Only when his eyes have been opened to the fact that he is but a tiny part of a measureless whole, only when he has realised how impermanent a thing is his temporary individuality, has he even entered upon the narrow path."[27]

At the end of the Path was the attainment of the perfect state of mind called *arhatship* or the state of being an *arhat*. To Rhys Davids the terms *arhatship* and *nirvāṇa* were synonymous. Few aspects of Buddhism had been so widely misunderstood, especially by Westerners. Literally the word *nirvāna* means "going out" or "dying out" as in the case of a flame going out or dying out. The image of the flame was particularly apt as the condition of mental perfection was represented in Buddhism as a dying out in the mind of the three fires of Self, ill will or hatred, and ignorance. This was clearly the original meaning of the word as found in the Pali texts.[28]

Confusion as to the precise meaning of the word *nirvāṇa* had subsequently come about in two ways. Hindu scholars and theologians had "adopted" the word. They thought that the Buddhist *nirvāna* was on a par with the Hindu ideal of *ānanda*, or bliss. In more modern times the missionaries working in Buddhist lands like Ceylon had added to the confusion. As Rhys Davids explained, ". . . the

[27] *Ibid.*

[28] *The Buddhist Review*, 1909, pp. 198ff.

missionaries, being told that Nirvāṇa was the ultimate ideal of the Buddhists thought, very naturally, in accordance with their own beliefs, that such an ideal must be sought for after death. Themselves giving up the world as hopeless, they could not understand the optimism of the Buddhists . . ." Both the missionaries as well as the Hindus assumed that everyone, including the Buddhists, believed in the existence of a soul and that if Buddhism talked of *anattā* (the idea of no soul) they meant that the soul was "annihilated" after death. With such preconceived ideas it was difficult to understand the Buddhist position that the ideal of Perfection or Nirvāṇa could be perfected here on earth. "That the highest aim of men," Rhys Davids declared, "could be considered to consist only of an inward subjective change, during this life, was an idea so strange that it was beyond the grasp of those who were accustomed to think the highest happiness could only be attained in heaven, when all the *outward* conditions of men's existence would be changed."[29]

VI

Rhys Davids' long involvement with Buddhism is best understood at two levels of responsiveness. We find him in the role of a professional *guru* explaining Buddhism, aware both of the demands of the publishers, and the need in his writings and lectures to make himself understood by those to whom Buddhist ideas were far removed from familiar modes of religious thinking. Rhys Davids also responded to Buddhism at a level of personal assimilation. In his writings the two streams of responsiveness cannot always be conveniently disengaged.[30]

The Buddhist Path with its emphasis on introspection was a useful means of attaining mental equipoise. Rhys Davids called the process "self-culture." The Noble Eightfold Path was difficult. But even the first cautious steps were not without immediately felt rewards. Here was a therapy for living and meeting life's daunting stresses. Self-culture was a means of understanding oneself and the true nature of one's ego or individuality.

Rhys Davids also constantly referred to the "manly" character of Buddhism. He emphasised that Buddhism was not a pessimistic

[29] *Ibid.* Rhys Davids, *Is Life Worth Having?*, *op. cit.*
[30] *Ibid.*

creed, as was widely believed. The true Buddhist was an optimist. Having grasped the problem of living in all its stark realities, he did not give way to despair but "manfully" came to terms with life and the business of living. Life, if properly understood, was a search for salvation. There was in Buddhism no real dichotomy between a so-called secular life and religious living. But how was salvation to be achieved? Salvation did not depend on rites, rituals or on the propitiation of gods. That was the recourse of the weak. The essential prerequisites were the perceptivity which enabled one to see the true nature of things and the strength of will and determination to apply the remedies of the Path to attain salvation. The vision of the Buddhist manfully taking up "arms against a sea of troubles"—the precise imagery which Rhys Davids used—was in a sense a reflex of his own life. How well he remembered the tribulations he had suffered in a long chequered life. Like Tennyson's Ulysses, he could truly say that he had drunk life to the lees. And yet when all seemed lost he had manfully come to terms with himself and harsh circumstance to turn an overwhelming personal defeat to an enduring triumph.[31]

VII

Was Rhys Davids a Buddhist? When he visited the U.S.A. in 1894 to deliver a number of lectures on Buddhism at the invitation of the American Philosophical Society, a reporter from the *New York Sun* asked him whether he was a Buddhist. Rhys Davids' reply was significant.

> "I am a student for the sake of the knowledge of my fellow men. A man who tells the world something that it never knew before accomplishes more than any man who succeeds in making millions of dollars. Such knowledge too is the one thing that never dies."
>
> "Are you a Christian?" asked the perplexed reporter.
>
> "All we Englishmen are born into the Established Church, are we not?" he replied.

The reporter commented on Rhys Davids' noncommittal responses.[32]

[31] *Ibid.*

[32] Quoted in *Journal of the Maha Bodhi Society*, Vol. IV, no. 1, May, 1895.

In Rhys Davids' time there were a number of people in England who were Buddhists but who did not care to call themselves such. Rhys Davids himself did not like to be described as a Buddhist in a narrowly sectarian sense. For much as he loved Sinhalese Buddhists, he also felt that they had betrayed Buddhism. Their idolatry had led them to regard the Buddha as an all-powerful being—a God—just as other men had deified the progenitors of their faiths. Moreover, the Sri Lankan Buddhists believed in a veritable plethora of gods—the *deviyo* of the Sinhalese—and expended their best energies in acts of ritual and propitiation in seeking the intercession of the gods in putting to right their disordered worldly concerns. All too easily the Buddhists had forgotten the spirit of the *Dharma* and were unwilling to manfully walk the Path.

Rhys Davids declared that he would not have devoted a lifetime to its study had he not thought that Buddhism had something to offer to modern society. In November 1907, Rhys Davids and a number of others who shared his views met in a house in Harley Street, London, and formed the Buddhist Society of Great Britain and Ireland. A Committee was immediately elected and given the task of drawing up the constitution of the new society. At the inaugural meeting of the society, Rhys Davids, who was elected its President, declared that the importance of Buddhism lay in its ability to give "profound solutions" to the questions of the "why and the wherefore of things." He added that Buddhism—reiterating a favourite theme—was certain to be a significant catalyst in bringing about ideological changes in Europe, analogous to the revival of classical learning in the Middle Ages. The "new gospel" of the age was Buddhism.[33]

Consequently the primary object of the Buddhist Society of Great Britain was to propagate Buddhism. It was felt that Westerners who were "Aryans" by descent would respond to Buddhism because "its teachings were Aryan."[34] The Buddhist Society, however, did not have the funds to propagandise widely. Its meetings were confined to London and to the main towns. Rhys Davids himself lectured extensively in Liverpool. Some members of the Buddhist Society felt that it should reach out to the rural areas too, where presumably there was greater potentiality for the spread of Buddhism. In the large towns the Buddhist Society—without quite intending to make such a

[33] Rhys Davids, *Buddhism, op. cit.*, p. 7. *The Buddhist Review*, Vol. I., no. 1, January 1909.

[34] *The Buddhist Review*, Vol. XI, 1921, Notes and News.

distinction—was addressing itself to the patrician elements rather than to the working class.[35] A closely allied object of the Society was the promotion of the study of Pali.

Other hopeful objects which the Buddhist Society contemplated in its early years were the formation of a lay brotherhood "to follow the teachings and imitate the life of the Buddha," the establishment of a Buddhist order of monks in Britain, and the setting up of a Renunciation Fund, so that individual members would give up some object which belonged to them "as a means of practising Buddhism." The infant society, however, failed to make any headway with regard to these particular objects.[36]

The Buddhist Society was also concerned with questions of contemporary social relevance. It opposed capital punishment because Buddhism was against the taking of life. It took a stand too against the slaughter of animals. In championing the rights of women—an issue which was very much in the public eye in England at the time—the Buddhist Society pointed out the irrelevance of sex distinctions in Buddhism. Women in Buddhist countries, it was said, had a better place in society than their sisters who lived in the more advanced countries in the West. Above all, the British Buddhists opposed the War. Before its actual outbreak in 1914, they pressed for arbitration, pointing out that all forms of belligerency and militarism—and not the German brand alone—were deplorable.[37]

Meanwhile, in spite of the emphasis on Buddhism the British Buddhist Society was not concerned with the personal religion of its individual members. The rules and principles of the Buddhist Society did not make necessary a specific avowal of Buddhism. Many of the original members of the Buddhist Society, or "promoters," as they were called, like Lord Mexborough, Professor Edmund Mills, Edward Greenly, and Francis John Payne, were in fact Buddhists. Lord Mexborough (John Horace Saville, fifth earl of Mexborough) was till his death in 1916 a Vice President of the Buddhist Society. His adoption of Buddhism—as the London *Times* recalled in an

[35] *The Buddhist Review*, Vol. IX, 1917, Notes and News.
The Buddhist Review, Vol, II, no. 1, 1910, Notes and News.

[36] *The Buddhist Review*, Vol. I, no 1 1909.

[37] *The Buddhist Review*, Vol I no. 1, 1909.
The Buddhist Review, Vol. VI.
The Buddhist Review, Vol. III, no. 3, 191.
The Buddhist Review, Vol. IX, no. 2, 1917.

obituary—had aroused much public interest. Professor Edmund Mills, who was the President of the Council of the Buddhist Society, often spoke with great enthusiasm and feeling about Buddhism. Greenly and Payne made no secret of their profession of Buddhism. Payne declared that he did not see why the entire population of England, "our sorrowing land," should not accept "the Good Law."[38] Their profession of Buddhism gave substance to a curious belief prevalent at the time that British Buddhists had in their former lives been Buddhists too.[39]

In Rhys Davids significantly one does not encounter the breast beating profession of Buddhism. Religion was a matter of personal taste. He would no doubt have agreed with Howell Smith, the editor of the *Buddhist Review,* the official organ of the British Buddhist Society. "We must," Smith cautioned, "make a distinction between Buddhism as a philosophy and as a cult." He added that as a cult Buddhism had manifested all the follies and failings of other cults.[40]

Rhys Davids' friends in Sri Lanka were, however, less subtle. Had not the Buddha attached the greatest importance to the propagation of the *Dharma?* They recalled the Buddha's words. "He who helps the spread of the Dharma will shine like a full moon in the sky of my religion." Sri Lankan Buddhists saw Thomas William Rhys Davids in the edifying glow of a *Dharmaduta,* or propagator of the *Dharma.*[41]

Curiously, they were not far off the mark. Rhys Davids' enigmatic reply to the reporter of the *New York Sun* was really pregnant with Buddhist meaning. He, Rhys Davids, had made known to humanity knowledge that was previously unknown. His work, like the truth of the *Dharma,* would survive when all else, including himself, had perished.

[38] *The Buddhist Review,* Vol. I, no. 1.1909.
The Buddhist Review, Vol. VIII, no. 3. 1916.
The Buddhist Review, Vol. XI, 1921.

[39] *The Buddhist Review,* Vol. I, no. 3, 1909.

[40] *The Buddhist Review,* Vol. VIII, no. 3, 1916.

[41] *Journal of the Maha Bodhi Society,* Vol. IX, no. 11, 1901.
Journal of the Maha Bodhi Society, no. 1, 1892.
Journal of the Maha Bodhi Society, Vol. IX, no. 12, 1901.

RUPAM JIRATI NAMA GOTTAM NA JIRATI

Mortals, so ran famous Pali lines, must decay and pass away. The good they do in life, the fair names and just reputations they acquire, would alone survive.

To Thomas William Rhys Davids in the evening of his life slowly the realization dawned, bringing with it peace and serenity that in truth there was no oblivion or obscurity to dread. The doer of deed—a pitiful ephemeral creature of the shifting *sankharas*—perished. But the deeds survived.

13

SRI LANKAN BUDDHISTS

The interest in Eastern religions—a noteworthy feature in nineteenth century European scholarship—sometimes brought about an alliance between scholar and religious activist. If one took pride in the grand impartiality with which he surveyed the panorama of religion, the other was consumed by those passions which religious causes and the sectarian spirit have been known to inspire.

Rhys Davids was a scholar. He devoted himself to the task of making his countrymen aware of Buddhism both as a religion in the conventional sense and as a great civilizing force which had influenced the lives of thousands in other parts of the world. To Rhys Davids as well as to his European readers it was essentially an intellectual exercise in which neither party had a direct stake as partisans. In Sri Lanka however, Rhys Davids' writings were read, marked, and inwardly digested in a more tense and militant context.

II

During the nineteenth century, as in other Buddhist countries which had been subject to colonial rule, in Sri Lanka too Buddhism had to respond to new challenges, and come to terms with a state of affairs which was in many ways dissimilar to the congenial context in which the religion had long flourished under indigenous rulers. Many Buddhists reflected on a prospect that was full of anxiety and foreboding. Under successive dynasties of Sinhalese kings Buddhism had enjoyed the protection of the state and the privileges of an established religon. The more articulate Buddhists complained that the British government was not only indifferent but at times hostile to Buddhism notwithstanding guarantees given at the beginning of the century when the British had established their control over the island. The idyllic and exaggerated overtones often implied in the contrast were plain.

But if in matters of state the Buddhists had to put up with an order of things which they had neither the power nor, often, the will to change, they were much less reconciled to the activities of the Christian missionaries. Early in the nineteenth century the major missionary organisations in England—the Baptists, the Wesleyans and the Church Missionary Society—had established themselves in Ceylon, with considerable government backing. The number of converts they made was not significant. The situation however was beginning to change, or so it seemed to Buddhists. They were perturbed by reports of conversions to Christianity evidently made not only in populous urban areas but in remote villages in the interior long considered the bulwarks of Buddhism. Many Buddhists realized with uneasiness that they could no longer complacently assume that the spread of Christianity was a mere reflex of anglicisation. Moreover they deeply resented the attacks which missionary organisations made on Buddhism in an unceasing flow of tracts, newspapers, and on public platforms.[1]

If the majority of Buddhists felt helpless, an articulate minority—English educated and wealthier than the rest—were determined to counter the missionary challenge. Their leader was Anagarika Dharmapala. Born into a wealthy and influential Buddhist family, many avenues of advancement were open to him. Instead early in life Dharmapala chose to devote himself to the cause of Buddhism. He become a *Brahmachariya,* a celibate seeker of the truth who abjured wealth and family ties. With passionate ardour and more than a fair share of a reformer's legitimate intolerance and impatience, Dharmapala tried to fill Buddhists in Sri Lanka with a sense of shame at the condition of Buddhism. He travelled widely especially in India where his activities in the cause of Buddhism enhanced his charismatic image. Dharmapala epitomized the archetypal Buddhist ideal (unknown in colonial Ceylon)—a self-sacrificing world renouncer and a seeker after truth.[2]

Over and above Dharmapala's efforts, Buddhists in Sri Lanka received a considerable psychological boost from the activities of the theosophists who extolled Buddhism and as in India deflated to a

[1] De Silva, K.M., *Social Policy and Missionary Organisation in Ceylon* 1849-1855 (London, 1965); "Religion, Nationalism and Social Change in Ceylon, 1880-1885," *Journal of the Royal Asiatic Society* (G.B.), no. 2, 1969.

[2] Wickremeratne, L.A., "Annie Besant Theosophism and Buddhist Nationalism in Sri Lanks," *Ceylon Journal of Historical and Social Studies,* New Series, Vol. VI, no. 1.

large extent the smug complacence of the missionaries. The co-founders of the Theosophical Society, Colonel H.S. Olcott, a New York lawyer and journalist, and Madame Blavatsky, a Russian emigre to the United States who had attracted considerable public attention on account of her controversial writing on the esoteric dimensions in religion, visited Sri Lanka for the first time in April 1880. Olcott who had previously been in touch with a number of leading Buddhists was aware of the condition of Buddhism in the island. They were welcomed with extravagant warmth and friendliness by Sinhalese Buddhists. By their actions—Olcott and Madame Blavatsky dramatically embraced Buddhism amidst immense fanfare and publicity—and pronouncements, the visit of the theosophical leaders raised the spirits of the demoralized Sri Lankan Buddhists. Olcott who visited Sri Lanka subsequently on no less than sixteen occasions till his death in 1907, did so to implement a carefully thought out program for the rejuvenation of Sri Lankan Buddhism. He helped the Buddhists in Sri Lanka to organise themselves into a self-conscious movement, and brought pressure on them to unite. Olcott took in hand the complex problems of the relations of the Buddhists with the government in Sri Lanka, and obtained from the state important concessions concerning the rights of Buddhists. The establishment of Buddhist system of schools as a counterpoise to missionary education, and the commencement of the first vernacular national newspapers were other notable achievements of the Theosophical Society on behalf of Buddhism in Ceylon.[3]

There was a more signficant dimension in the Buddhist confrontation with the Christian missionaries. Many missionaries is Sri Lanka had criticized both Buddhism and Buddhists on the ground that there was notable gap between Buddhist practice and precept. They contended that the Buddhists lacked a moral sense because Buddhism—denying as it did the idea of a meaningful relationship between god and man—was basically spiritually deficient. Ethics which Buddhism boasted alone could not make men moral. Other missionaries—scholars like Daniel Gogerly, Spence Hardy, and Reginald Coplestone—had carefully studied Buddhism. They attacked Buddhism on theoretical grounds particularly the key Bud-

[3] *Journal of The Royal Asiatic Society* (G.B.), *op. cit.*

dhist doctrines concerning the origin of things, *Anatta* and *Nirvana*, which the Buddhists had thought were unassailable.[4]

The Buddhists countered missionary arguments. Sometime after they began their activities in Sri Lanka, the various missionary societies had set about producing a plethora of tracts attacking Buddhism. Rather belatedly the Buddhists responded with their own stream of propaganda produced in modest makeshift printing establishments. By the beginning of the 1860's there were also often confrontations between Buddhist leaders and Christian missionaries. Some of the confrontations took the form of well publicized debates or *vadayas* in which the relative merits of Buddhism and Christianity were cantankerously argued. The debates epitomized a new spirit of Buddhist resistance—the Buddhists were regarded usually as a passive and docile lot—to the spread of Christian influence. The Buddhists realized, however, that whatever they said in defense of Buddhism could carry greater weight if their arguments were backed by authorities who had no part in a sectarian quarrel but whose intellectual credentials the Christian missionaries would be compelled to accept. Contemporary European scholarship in religion—impartial and conscientious —as exemplified in the work of Max Muller and Rhys Davids met the need. To the Buddhists in Sri Lanka Rhys Davids, who was the leading European authority on Buddhism, was a great source of intellectual strength.

III

In many ways Rhys Davids had endeared himself to the Buddhists in Sri Lanka. In a spirit of gratitude Dharmapala often referred to the work of the Pali Text Society. It seemed to Buddhists that Rhys Davids had removed two obstacles which had stood in the way of a wider knowledge of Buddhism. Although Buddhists like Dharma-

[4]Hardy, Spence H., *Eastern Monarchism* (London, 1850); *A Manual of Buddhism* (London, 1853). Spence Hardy relied heavily on the writings of the Rev. J. Gogerly, who had been the General Superintendent of the Wesleyan Mission in South Ceylon. Unlike Spence Hardy, who used exclusively later Sinhalese works for his studies on Buddhism, Gogerly mastered Pali. His writings on Buddhism were published in the *Ceylon Friend*, a Wesleyan journal and to some extent in the *Journal of the Royal Asiatic Society* (Ceylon Branch). Much later (Gogerly wrote in the 1830s), Gogerly's Ceylon writings were published in their entirety. See, Bishop, Arthur Stanley, *Gogerly Daniel John. Ceylon Buddhism; being the collected writings of Daniel John Gogerly* (Colombo, 1908).

pala were familiar with Buddhism as it was elucidated in the Pali canon, they had not thought it worth-while to make Buddhist scriptures accessible to those who were unfamiliar with Pali and the Buddhist ethos. Their occasional references to the Pali Canon—in contentious rebuttal of this or that Christian claim—had savoured too much of the partisan spirit to carry conviction. On the other hand, Europeans who were interested in Buddhism, but who as a rule did not know Pali, and therefore had no access to the Buddhist scriptures—were compelled instead to depend on sources like the writings of Christian missionaries which orthodox Buddhists repudiated. To Buddhists in particular it now became a comparatively easy task to elucidate Buddhism, resorting to sources that were at last known to all and which were regarded as the ultimate in textual authority.[5]

There was much in Rhys Davids' writings that flattered Buddhism. Expressions of admiration for the lofty morality and philosophical insights in Buddhism occur frequently. The sociological overtones were as plain. The damage which colonial rule in Asia had wrought was more real than the so-called economic exploitation. It was cultural and psychological. Asians were weighed down by a sense of inferiority. Theories of race, technology, military inferiority, and a sense of mystique assiduously cultivated by the rulers had all played their part. The literature of the Victorian age—so eagerly and masochistically devoured by anglicised Asians—fuelled the sense of inferiority. The missionaries too had got into the act to point out to Indians and Sri Lankans that after all there surely was a palpable connection between Christianity and the superiority of Western civilization. Rhys Davids in common with other European scholars who studied Asian societies however changed the rules of the game. They firmly and unequivocally rejected industry and technology as criteria of judgment. Over and over again Rhys Davids makes the point. Instead they extolled the non-utilitarian and non-modern aspects in Asian cultures and societies, to point out that these very qualities had given Asian societies a strong sense of continuity and equilibrium.

Rhys Davids had had much to say also on Buddhism as it actually existed. In Sri Lanka the *Sanga*—the Buddhist priesthood whose

[5]*Journal of the Maha Bodhi Society*, Vol. V, nos. 1-4 (May 1896); *JMBS*, no. 1 (May 1892); *JMBS*, Vol. X, nos. 8-9 (December 1901); *JMBS*, Vol. IV, no. 5 (September 1898); *The Buddhist Review*, Vol. V, no. 2 (April 1913).

business it was to keep alive the knowledge of the *Dhamma*—had often been criticized by missionaries on the grounds of their inutility and worldliness. According to Rhys Davids, however, the monks were living abstemious and simple lives, being in general content with the food and raiment provided by the laity. In a more positive sense, the *Sanga* had maintained a tradition of literary activity preserving on the one hand the sacred scriputres and on the other hand acting as the moral preceptors and educators of the people notwithstanding numerous obstacles. The result was, in the words of Rhys Davids, that the average intelligence of the Sinhalese was very high and "...they alone of the Aryan tribes in India have succeeded in preserving for us a literature over two thousand years and containing materials of the religious history of India and Ceylon."

Within their order, the priests also maintained a noteworthy tradition of liberalism which Rhys Davids called "the spirit of freedom." There were, he pointed out, numerous rules binding on the *Sanga*. The rules were concerned with discipline and right conduct, the *Vinaya*, of the monks rather than with matters of individual belief. As far as beliefs were concerned, no member of the order—in spite of its hierarchical structure—had any power over any other. "Of all religious orders...in the history of religion, the Buddhist was the one in which there was the greatest freedom, the greatest variety of thought."[6]

But what of Buddhism as it had affected the mass of the people? That surely was the acid test. Rhys Davids believed that the ideals of "humanity, toleration and self-training" which Buddhism stressed had influenced public conduct in Buddhist countries. There was, for example, the comparative absence of crime. "Crimes of jealousy there may be," he conceded, "but such a thing as highway robbery is unkown." There was little evidence too of other social vices like drunkenness and prostitution which Rhys Davids pointedly said were "never known among the Buddhists is Ceylon...until Christianity was introduced." The negligible effect which caste had on everyday life in Buddhist lands—if one took India as the norm—was also to be attributed to the benevolent influence of Buddhism. Moreover, the condition of women in Buddhist countries compared favourably with that of their counterparts in India. Buddhism had favoured the

[6]*Encyclopaedia of Religion and Ethics,* Vol. XI, p. 307; Vol. III, p. 331.

idea of monogamy. It discouraged early marriages and in general frowned on sexual promiscuity. Buddhism had thus helped to raise the status of women in a traditional male dominated society.[7]

In other ways too Buddhist norms impinged on society and social behaviour. The Buddhist was taught that in living it was the attainment of higher goals—a disciplined and conscious refinement of the mind—that was worth striving for. A Buddhist was also ideally speaking filled with a sense of the transitoriness of material achievement. Consequently, there was in him less of the acquisitive, combative, economic spirit. To Rhys Davids it seemed that the contentment and simple living which he had seen in Buddhist countries was partly derived from their attitudes and partly they were a reflex of the unsophisticated nature of the prevailing agrarian economies.

IV

However, to Dharmapala the relevance of Rhys Davids' view on Buddhism was made evident in the equally important context of the Indian scene.

By the 1890's Dharmapala had become increasingly absorbed in his Indian plans. His objects were twofold. The first involved Buddhagaya where the Buddha had attained enlightenment and was therefore an object of inense veneration and piety to Buddhists the world over. Dharmapala first visited Buddhagaya in 1891 and was overwhelmed with emotion. In the initial act of worship he confessed he was moved by a strong impulse to stay on in order to take care of the place. It was manifestly in a state of dilapidation and neglect being indifferently looked after by the incumbent (the Mahant) of the Hindu temple which had sprung up in the immediate vicinity and was by contrast in a flourishing condition. Dharmapala resolved to obtain from the British government in India, the custodianship of Buddhagaya into Buddhist hands but was chagrined to discover that the Buddhist temple and its revenues legally belonged to the Mahant. The latter pugnaciously resisted Dharmapala. A long and bitter legal battle ensued exasperating as it was futile. It attracted considerable attention in India and elsewhere and established for all time Dharmapala's stature as a hero in the eyes of his Sri Lankan countrymen. His

[7] *Ibid.*, Vol. III, p. 490: *JMBS*, Vol. XXII, no. 6 (June 1914).

second object was to revive Buddhism in India not really to convert four million Hindus to Buddhism as much as to bring about a change in the innately negative attitudes of Hindus towards Buddhism. Typically Dharmapala did not think that either object was extravagant.[8]

Conservative Hindus looked askance at Buddhism. They believed that Buddhism, by its atheism, its unconventional view of the soul, and by its clear repudiation of caste, had been antagonistic to Hinduism. Within the tradition of Indian religious developments—with its distinct Hindu overtones—Buddhism was an excrescence which Hinduism had failed to absorb. The missionary work of Dharmapala in India—especially the question of Buddhagaya, which had become a much publicised *cause celebre*—seemed to presage a "Buddhist revival" in India. A Hindu newspaper, *Hope*, compared the Buddhist movement to a small cloud no bigger than a man's hand in the troubled horizon of Hinduism. The *Light of the East* called attention to the "increasing influence of Buddhism in India." Meanwhile, the support theosophists gave Buddhism—especially in Olcott's time when there seemed to be a close identity of interests between Buddhism and theosophy—gave additional cause for Hindu anxieties.[9]

But Annie Besant, when she became President of the Theosophical Society after Olcott's death at Adyar in 1907, was determined to restore the balance in favour of Indian Hinduism. She was aware that if theosophy was to make more effective headway in India, the goodwill of the Hindus was clearly a *sine qua non.* On and off she had herself been censured for supporting Buddhism. The *Hope* warned Annie Besant that "no Hindu will side her if she continues to work for Hinduism with the aid of her Buddhist leaders." The matter had so far been judged largely on appearances. Whereas Olcott had visited Sri Lanka frequently—thereby unwittingly giving colour to the belief that there was a special connection between Buddhism and theosophy—Annie Besant stayed away. Moreover, she did nothing to alleviate the estrangement that had crept into her relations with Buddhist leaders in Sri Lanka, especially with Dharmapala. Instead, her unsolicited pronouncements on Buddhism filled Buddhists with consternation and uneasiness. In sum, Annie Besant contended that "Southern Buddhists"—that is to say the Theravada Buddhists in Sri Lanka—

[8] *Ceylon Journal of Historical and Social Studies, op. cit.*
[9] *Ibid.*

had "misunderstood" and "perverted" the teachings of Gautama Buddha. Above all, she did not think that Buddhism was uniquely great religion in many ways superior to Hinduism. Annie Besant often declared that Gautama Buddha was merely the Ninth avatar of Brahmanism and that Buddhists had no place in India but in lands "other than the land of Aryavarta." As for India, it had to "keep unshaken its faith in the gods."[10]

Dharmapala appealed to more moderate Hindu opinion. He reasoned that there was little difference between Hinduism and Buddhism. Dharmapala made a convenient distinction between Hinduism of a pristine order which had had affinities to Buddhism, and Brahamanism. Ritual and ceremony had been made ends in themselves by Brahmanism to the neglect of the more important ends of morality and spiritual discipline. The Brahmins, who were the guardians of the Hindu faith, had opposed Buddhism because it had posed a clear threat to their privileges. Nor was Buddhism atheistic. Many Buddhists worshipped Hindu deities. Historically also—Dharmapala made much of the point—there had been great friendliness between the religions, although occasionally Buddhism had been persecuted by zealous Hindu reformers. If Buddhism had declined in India and it had finally disappeared, it was because it had been subjected to ferocious persecution by the Muslim invaders.[11]

Dharmapala, as well as the pro-Buddhist Hindus, found ample inspiration in the writing of Rhys Davids, who had drawn attention to the basic Indian character of Buddhism as well as of its founder. Before Buddhism arose, there had been in India a well established tradition of religious thinking. Rhys Davids explained that there was a wide variety of beliefs, theories, and speculations, which later became the concern of Buddhism. The new creed of Buddhism had therefore had to take cognisance of an existing religious structure now accepting, now modifying, and at other times rejecting, facets of the structure.

The line of reasoning had its merits. Many reform conscious Hindus, notably the followers of the Brahma Samaj and the Arya Samaj, had themselves drawn a distinction between Hinduism in its pristine undiluted form and modern Hinduism. The corollary when related to the Buddhist context which Dharmapala often used was

[10] *Ibid.*
[11] *Ibid.*

that ideologically original Hinduism was really close to Buddhism. Dharmapala's insistence that Buddhists and Hindus after all worshipped the same gods therefore carried conviction especially as he took care to play down a vital difference: that to Buddhists the gods of Hinduism, (Vishnu and Brahma not excepted) were a genre of comparative unimportance. Hierarchically they were inferior to the Buddha and were themselves widely presumed to be aspirants to Buddhahood. The heavy emphasis on the Muslim invaders rather neatly helped in getting over the awkward question of the probable complicity of Hinduism in the demise of Buddhism in India. Dharmapala in short tried heroically to exorcise Hindu feelings of historical guilt at the condition of Buddhism in India.

A significant segment in Hindu thinking was not slow to respond. Surendranath Bannerjee who virtually led the Indian national movement during this period declared that Buddhism could well be a means of realising India's political and spiritual rejuvenation. Romesh Chunder Dutt took time off from the self-imposed burdens of articulating India's economic grievances to give lyrical expression to his deep admiration for Buddhism. In his *Lays of Ancient India* the moving inspiration was Buddhism. Elsewhere Dutt enthused on "the beauty of the Buddha's pure and saintly life and of his noble precepts and maxims." Swami Vivekananda declared that Buddhism and Hinduism should draw closer in a mutually vitalising relationship. Addressing Dharmapala and the Buddhists he was moved to say "we cannot live without you nor you without us." The *Indian Mirror* in the hands of Norendra Nath Sen became virtually a Buddhist propagandist organ as was Jadu Nath Mozumdar's *Hindu Patrika*. Charu Chara Bose another well-known figure of the period made the first translation of the *Dhammapada* into Bengali. There were others too including South Indians like Biligiri Iyengar and Lakshmi Narasu.[12]

The paeans of praise had subtler pragmatic overtones. There was a strong feeling among pro-Buddhist Hindus that Buddhism with its emphasis on self-reliance, sacrifice and endurance could be a source of inspiration to Indian nationalism. Pro-Buddhist Hindus also believed that some at any rate of the problems which faced Indians could be best explained in terms of Buddhism. The idea of *Karma* for

[12] *Journal of the Maha Bodhi Society*, Vol. XI, no. 2, June 1902.
Vol. IV, no. 2, June 1905.
Vol. No. 1, May 1892.

example was given a clearly extended and contemporaneously relevant meaning. Just as the wellbeing of individuals was governed by their *karma* or actions, "national karma" too was determined by the activities of the mass of people in a country. In India misguided Hindus had subjected Buddhism to harassment and persecution. "We banished Buddhism from the land. We converted Buddhist temples and Hindu temples...ingratitude could not further go." Consequently Indians in modern times had to reap what their forbears had sown. "Retribution for those sins overtook us only too soon." Witness the political condition of India. How often and how easily she had been subjugated and taken advantage of economically? In *The Decline and Fall of Hinduism*, S.C. Mukerjee, a Bengali barrister, argued that with the decline of Buddhism the degeneration of the Hindus had begun. What precisely the connection was between the two Mukerjee left unexplained. He was content to describe the Buddhist period as the "Golden Age" in Indian history implying no doubt that the periods which followed were necessarily periods of comparative decadence. The result however was clear. The Indians either because of retributive justice or on account of their spiritual decadence had become an easy prey to foreign invaders beginning with the invasions of the Muslims. By contrast, reasoned Norendra Nath Sen, who best typified the mood of Hindu repentance, neighbouring Buddhist lands unburdened by national *karma* of the magnitude which Indians were called upon to bear—were "better off by far in all respects than India". But if modern Indians repented and made amends "...we may re-embark on a career of national greatness and prosperity."[13]

In much the same vein it was said that famine which was so commonplace in India was related to public morality. The expulsion of Buddhism at the hands of the Hindus had ushered in a long period of "unrighteousness". At such times famine and kindred calamities occurred. Men it would seem forfeited the good will of the gods who in turn "ceased to send down rain". In the *Indian Mirror* Norendra Nath Sen explained that although the idea was not unknown to the Hindus, it more explicitly figured in Buddhist scriptures. In particular he drew attention to the ***Bhamma Vagga*** of the ***Anguttara Nikaya***

[13] *The Buddhist Review*, Vol. XI, 1921.
JMBS, Vol. XI, no. 2, June 1902.

which described how the Buddha in answer to a question put to him by a group of Brahmins had made the point at some length.[14]

Placed in the broad historical perspective, Buddhism was really part and parcel of the existing Indian religious tradition in which the Hindu strands predominated. "There was not much in the metaphysics and psychology of Gautama." Rhys Davids concluded, "which cannot be found in one or other of the orthodox systems and a great deal of his morality could be matched from earlier or later Hindu works." Elsewhere, Rhys Davids had also declared that Buddha's role had been to ennoble, enlarge, and systematize as well as carry to a logical conclusion "that which had already been well said by others."[15]

If he had overstated the similarities, as it might have seemed to partisan Buddhists like Dharmapala, Rhys Davids restored the balance. The essential differences—so much valued by the identity conscious orthodox Buddhist—were made explicit in the Hibbert Lectures and in the course of his tour of the U.S.A. in 1901. The truly distinctive feature in Buddhism was that it turned away from the great theories of the soul which had so strikingly dominated Indian religious thinking. In the time of the Buddha there had been religious teachers who had preached that the soul was annihilated on or after death. There were others who had said that the soul continued as it was an indestructible entity. In a more specific sense there was the universal Hindu belief—often expressed with lyrical grace and majesty in the *Upanishads*—that the individual soul or self (ātman) would finally become united with the Absolute (Brahman), reachieving its original purity and becoming forever free (Moksha) from the limitations and entanglements of *saṃsāric* existence. This was the ideal of salvation, the ultimate beatitude to which a Hindu aspired.

To the Buddhist, on the other hand, salvation depended on a clear perception of the real nature of men and things. The Buddhist strove to attain a state of perfection as his final goal which Rhys Davids described with admirable felicity as "the dying out in the heart of the three fell fires of lust, ill will and delusion." It was on account of these evils—clearly elucidated in the Buddhist scriputres—that man suffered an apparently endless cycle of births, the force of their mis-

[14] *JMBS*, Vol. IX, nos. 2 and 3, June-July 1900.
[15] *North American Review* (15 October 1900).

guided actions (karma), rather than the soul, providing the connecting links. Clearly the Buddhist view implied a complete rejection of the soul theories on which the existing religious tradition was largely built. "...for the first time in the history of the world" declared Rhys Davids, "Buddhism had proclaimed a salvation which each man could attain for himself and by himself...without any the least reference to God or to gods either great or small."[16]

In other ways, too, the departure from the existing religious practices was striking. Buddhism turned away from the appeal to a myriad of gods who were themselves not above the laws of the *Dharma*, from ritual and ceremony, and above all from the path of penance and self-mortification by which man sought to manifest his spiritual worthiness. Inspired by the Pali canon which referred to asceticism, Rhys Davids portrayed the futility of the ascetic's endeavour—in the Buddhist view—albeit conveying something of the awe which the ascetic nonetheless commanded.

On a somewhat more pragmatic plane, Rhys Davids' interpretation of the Buddhist view of caste was of obvious relevance to both moderate Hindus as well as to the Buddhists. The latter were perturbed by assertions which Annie Besant often made—with characteristic *panache* and insensitivity—that the Buddha had condoned caste. According to her, the Buddha had conceivably condemned its cruder manifestations but had certainly accepted the assumptions underlying caste. Annie Besant claimed that the Buddha had been born into a high caste family, had himself followed caste observances, and had consorted most with people who belonged to the higher castes.[17]

To Rhys Davids on the other hand caste was strictly not a part of Buddhist doctrine. It was a facet of contemporary Indian social life outside Buddhist doctrine. If salvation was open to all and sundry, provided one had the perception to see the path and the great strength of will to progress along the path, it followed that caste, social position, and other distinctions to which man attached so much importance ceased to have meaning. Indeed, in Buddha's own time there had been many men of low caste who had joined the order just as many Brahamins had done so. While on the one hand there had

[16] Rhys Davids, T.W., *Is Life Worth Having and One Eternal Hope: An Answer From Buddha's First Sermon* (London, 1880).

[17] *North American Review. op. cit.*

been no institutional barriers to the Brahamins doing so, it was also true that they did not embrace Buddhism in so great number as to deprive Hinduism of its high caste following. However, because ideas about caste existed so widely the question naturally called for comment from the Buddha on several occasions. There were certain well known instances—to which the Buddhist scriptures drew particular attention—which showed how unequivocally the Buddha had condemned caste.

One could not, however, go so far as to say—as many Buddhists and Indians evidently did—that the Buddha had "abolished" caste: a view which clearly exaggerated the influence which Buddhism had had in India and which invested Buddhism with a degree of secular power which in any event it did not possess and towards which it was at most times indifferent. Rhys Davids contended that ideas concerning caste as they existed in modern India were unknown in Buddha's time. It was questionable whether the Brahmin caste had succeeded in establishing their claim to superiority. One could much less speak of a caste system in India six centuries before Christ. What system there was, had certainly lacked the rigidity and immutability which was associated with the modern caste system in India. It was hardly credible that there was in Buddha's time or soon afterwards, a clash of almost titanic proportions between Buddhism and the caste zealotry of Hinduism. Summing up, Rhys Davids observed that the Buddha had adopted "the only course open to any man of sense." On the one hand, he endeavoured to influence public opinion on caste by "a constant inculcation of reasonable views." On the other hand, within his own order over which alone he had "ignored completely and absolutely all advantages or disadvantages arising from birth occupation or social status and swept away all barriers and disabilities..."[18]

To the Buddhists in particular it seemed that Rhys Davids had explained the vexed question concerning caste with pleasing equipoise.

His views on the decline of Buddhism in India were equally acceptable, especially to Dharmapala. To both the culpability of Muslim iconoclasticism was plain. Rhys Davids declared that the Muslims had "ruthlessly destroyed" Buddhism. Many worthy monks as well as valuable Buddhist books perished in the holocaust. Rhys

[18] *Ibid.*

Davids added that the destruction had been wrought "without any military necessity that is now perceptible."

But what of Hinduism and the Hindus? In spite of Dharmapala, many Buddhists in Sri Lanka thought as a matter of course that the gentle creed of the Buddha with its pacific overtones had been the victim of Hindu persecution. Rhys Davids, who rejected the view, pointed out that there had been in ancient India a worthy tradition of religious toleration. In Buddha's own time and during centuries which followed the two religions had, it seemed, co-existed. Moreover, just as there were apsects in Buddhist teachings which were clearly opposed to Hinduism—and were recognized as such—there were the counterbalancing similarities not only in Hinduism but to the older religious tradition. Small wonder that there should be in Rhys Davids' own time many Hindus, no doubt of the more modern and liberal genre, who regarded the Buddha as a saintly Indian religious teacher who had emerged evidently to "purge" Hinduism of its shortcomings. In the words of Rhys Davids, it was the very "Indian-ness" as it were of the founder of the Buddhist faith that appealed to the Hindus. In a famous passage, which Norendra Nath Sen was fond of quoting, Rhys Davids had described the Buddha as one who had been born a Hindu and had died a Hindu. Indeed, the Buddha was the greatest of all Hindus.[19]

But what then had led to the fall of Buddhism in India? Going beyond the rather banal limits of Dharmapala's analysis, Rhys Davids drew attention to the convenient anonymity of certain impersonal "historical" factors. In this sense, mused Rhys Davids, the fall of Buddhism was not surprising. A religion which taught that salvation could be achieved by one's own efforts—without what the Buddha called "sham supports"—and which brought the very gods within the ambit of the *Dharma,* or the Law, had little chance of surviving in a society in which the very atmosphere was impregnated with beliefs which supported the very opposite of the Buddhist view. Moreover, in Rhys Davids' words, Buddhism had "aimed its keenest shafts against just those forms of belief in the supernatural that appeal most strongly alike to the hopes and fears of the people." There was also no gainsaying that Buddhism "in pouring new wine into old bottles" had retained ". . . too much of the ancient phraseology for lasting success .

[19] *Ibid.*

. ." Above all had fought "too many vested interests" at one and the same time, thereby weakening the chances of its survival.[20]

More controversially, Rhys Davids argued that the Conversion of Emperor Aśoka to Buddhism—the grand apogee in the history of early Buddhism—had in the long run exerted a rather harmful effect on Buddhism. Aśoka had not only embraced Buddhism but, as the "first real overlord of India," had made Buddhism the state religion of his empire. To Rhys Davids the event marked the beginning of the end. "The adhesion of large numbers" he explained of "nominal converts produced weakness rather than strength." The day of compromise had come. Every relaxation of the old thoroughgoing position was heartily welcomed and widely supported by converts only half converted. The margin of difference between Buddhists and their more formidable opponents gradually faded, almost entirely away."[21]

The implications were plain. State patronage of Buddhism had not been an unmixed blessing. However, notwithstanding their deep regard for Rhys Davids' views and the total acceptance of his *bona fides*, Dharmapala and his Buddhist contemporaries in Sri Lanka continued to visualize the restoration in modern Sri Lanka of an ideological Buddhist state in which the rulers (as in the days of Asoka) would be totally identified with Buddhism.

V

The role of being the *Kalyani Mithraya* or the special friend of Sri Lankan Buddhists found expression in yet another sphere. Here Rhys Davids was something more than a passive and somewhat aloof observer of distant events. Instead he virtually presided over the demolition of the once cherished connection between Theosophy and Ceylon Buddhism.

Buddhist attitudes to Theosophy were characterized by elements of ambivalence. Buddhists in Sri Lanka were grateful to the Theosophists particularly for the immnese work Olcott had done on their behalf. It was, however, just as true that many Buddhists looked upon the Theosophists with frank mistrust. They felt that Theosophists

[20] *Ibid.*

[21] *Ibid.*

were making use of Buddhism for their own ends. The promotion of Hinduism at the expense of Buddhism was a reproach that was constantly levelled at the Theosophists. There was also the feeling that, although leading Theosophists like Olcott, Madame Blavatsky, C.W. Leadbeater, and Charles Powell, had all embraced Buddhism in Sri Lanka—amidst much publicity and fanfare—they had not been genuine. Powell, who was the leading resident Theosophist in Sri Lanka at the turn of the century reported that it was being often said that the Theosophists were not "true Buddhists" and that they lacked "the necessary faith." To add insult to injury, as it were, the irrepressible Annie Besant declared that Madame Blavatsky had confessed to her that her conversion to Buddhism was dictated by considerations of expedience. Annie Besant made clear that Buddhism certainly was not her perosnal creed.[22]

At first however great harmony and friendship prevailed. Pragmatism and elements of self-interest played their own part in keeping mutual relations on even keel. In the early years of the Theosophical Society it was in Sri Lanka that the new movement scored its notable triumphs. Its achievements in reviving Buddhism the most blatantly partisan Christian missionary—could scarcely gainsay. In short, the Sri Lankan connection gave the Theosophical movement—harassed by unremitting criticism and ridicule in Europe—credibility which it so badly needed. On the side of the Sri Lankan Buddhists Theosophy was clearly the sure fire means of achieving their revivalist aspirations. Here was no oriental subtlety but simple common sense. There was besides the broad synchronocity between Theosophical beliefs and those of the Buddhists in Sri Lanka. Of particular topical importance—in view of the ongoing conflicts with the missionaries—was the categorical repudiation by Theosophists of the idea of an anthropomorphic god in the conventional Christian sense and their open and enthusiastic acceptance of *Karma* and reincarnation. For the first time an identifiable group of Westerners had it seemed accepted centrally important Buddhist ideas, and were willing to be martyred by the great mass of their conservative and intolerant Victorian contemporaries for doing so.

[22] Besant, Annie, *The Birth of New India*, Adyar, 1917). See "The Work of The Theosophical Society in India."

The mutually pleasing *modus vivendi* might have survived indefinitely but for attempts made by some of the early Theosophical leaders to re-state Buddhism. They were convinced that many Westerners had misunderstood the teachings of the Buddha. There were the vital issues of *Anatta* and *Nirvāṇa*. Man did not possess a soul—an indestructible entity that survived death. *Nirvāna*—in Victorian times often translated simply as annihilation or extinction—was the *summum bonum* of Buddhism. It was the goal towards which the diligent Buddhist struggled in successive lives. In sum the Buddhist position amounted to this: the world was not a fit place to live in. It was full of suffering and profoundly vexing uncertainties. Individual suffering did not end with death. Reborn by the sheer force of his desires an individual continued to suffer life after life. The process was interminable. It could only be arrested by walking the path to complete spiritual perfection (which ensured the extinction of desire) and which led to the attainment of *Nirvāṇa*.

Many Westerners conditioned by years of familiarity with diametrically different ideologies and assumptions, were convinced in turn that the Buddhist view was pessimistic and negative. What was the point of intense spiritual endeavor if everything was to end in a state of nothingness? Was this the precious goal to which for a millenia and more successive generations of Buddhists aspired with such ecstacy and truly exemplary piety? "A pessimism so thoroughgoing and deadly" remarked a Christian journal of the time "could hardly it would seem take a very general possession of any race in whom the vital forces were strong." A more polemical Christian source, chagrined at the growing sympathy towards Buddhism in some Western quarters, exclaimed, "No god! no revelation! no soul! and we are told that Buddhism is the Light of Asia."[23]

Pioneer Theosophists who often wrote on the theme of the Western understanding of Buddhism—notably Madame Blavatsky and A.P. Sinnett—claimed that responsibility for the widespread misunderstanding of Buddhism could be fairly and squarely laid at the door of European oriental scholars. The process had begun with Brian Hodgson and Spence Hardy whose works had made a fairly wide spectrum of Westerners first aware of Buddhism. In their own time Max Muller and Rhy Davids were specially signalled for attack.

[23] *The Theosophist*, Vol. VIII, no. 92, May 1887.

Sinnett contended that Rhys Davids, whose works were the most widely read, provided the main basis for misunderstanding. The Buddhist writings of Rhys Davids were ambivalent. His own interpretation of Buddhism on the one hand refurbished the popular image of negativism in Buddhism. And yet, on the other hand, the very text he was, as a Pali scholar, presenting to the public, flatly contradicted his premises. At many points the texts showed how often the Buddha was talking about a continuity after death, to other scenarios of post-mortem death, to next worlds and heavens, and how often he the Buddha was hinting that there was an esoteric meaning to all his preachings.

The Theosophists contended that the orientalists had been overly textualist in their study of Eastern religions. They relied solely on the texts they were translating. Consequently religion especially in the hands of Rhys Davids had become essentially an exercise in philology. Rhys Davids' interpretations of Buddhism were based on the central assumption that everything the Buddha preached was to be found within the parameters of the Pali texts. Could religion be understood on the basis of texts alone? The texts—however authentic—were at best a fragmentary revelation. It was indeed a moot point whether the texts were the last word on any given facet in Buddhism. A given premise or assumption otherwise wholly consistent with the spirit of the particular religion and its over-all doctrinal positions, would have to be discarded merely because the premise was not explicitly stated in the text. Moreover Eastern religious writings were susceptible to what Sinnett described as "paradoxical methods of expression." Was it not safe to sometimes trust broad conclusions rather than narrow textual interpretations?

Many Theosophists insisted too that there was a distinction between the exoteric and esoteric tradition in religion. It was a favorite theme with Sinnett. He declared that in reading Eastern religious material one had to be on the lookout for hidden meanings that revolutionized the literal sense of the words employed. As in other religions there was in Buddhist teachings too "an esoteric teaching of vital import." A misplaced contempt for "spiritualism" as well as an exaggerated faith in science had made men blind to esoteric knowledge. Carrying the thesis a stage further Sinnett maintained that the Buddha had preached one sort of Buddhism to the mass of the people and another to the monks and that the latter had never been made public.[24]

Annie Besant explained the view of the Theosophists in a significantly Indian context. She was skeptical about the claims made by orthodox Buddhists that the Buddha had revealed all ". . . without keeping anything back." If this were true, was it not folly she asked? "As a dry matter of fact," she observed, "you cannot give a person that which he cannot take, which he is unable to understand or to assimilate . . . that which is truth for the uneducated ploughman is not truth for the educated philosopher." There was in religion a proper distinction between ethical religion which was—at it ought to be—within the grasp of all, and the philosophical religion which was "the priceless treasure of the few." In India, for example, there were the *Purāṇas* full of stories of great moral beauty and heroic virtue which were clearly intended to influence the common people. On the other hand, there were the *Upanishads* with their philosphical subtleties which were clearly not intended for common consumption.

Insofar as specific doctrine was concerned, the Theosophists also maintained that the Buddhist had misunderstood the teachings of the Buddha, especially with regard to the soul and in their view of *Nirvāṇa.* Far from teaching *Anatta,* or the theory of the absence of a soul, the Buddha too had followed Hinduism and accepted the soul as an indestructible entity, which after death was absorbed into a supreme ego or self which the Hindus called Brahman. The Theosophists equated this condition with *Nirvāṇa* or *Nibbana* and declared that it was "a mark of sectarianism to say that *Nibbana* is not Brahman."[25]

At death the total aggregation of *Khandhas* which made up a particular individual perished. The soul too perished. But only in a relative and qualified sense. The inner essence of the soul (in contrast to the variable and transitory outer form) survived. It was really the force of continuing consciousness and manifested itself in successive births or incarnations. *Nirvāṇa* or ultimate spiritual perfection was the absorption of the inner essence in the supreme consciousness. This

[24] *The Theosophist,* Vol. VIII, no. 91, April 1887.

[25] *The Birth of New India, op. cit.*

See also *Buddhism: An Illustrated Quarterly Review,* 1903-1905, (Rangoon, 1905), p. 320 ff.

view of the doctrine of *Anatta* brought Buddhism closer to Theosophical ideas. It also invested Buddhism with a purposiveness and rationality which its Western critics long claimed it lacked. Theosophists with their bold and somewhat innovative exegetical approach could claim that they had successfully resolved "the European problem" in Buddhism. Sri Lankan Buddhists however did not see the matter in this light. They were outraged.

Many Buddhists in Sri Lanka were determined that the Theosophists should not go unchallenged. Dharmapala no doubt voiced universal fears when he said that the Theosophists were misleading thousands about Buddhism, especially with regard to the question of the soul. The Theosophists were relying too greatly on the alleged differences between the so-called Southern and Northern schools in Buddhism. In truth, textual and other evidence showed that the doctrine of *Anatta* was as much part of Northern Buddhism as it was of the Southern school. Both schools had accepted as common ground the central Buddhist concepts of *Anicca* (impermanence), *Dukka* (sorrow), and *Anatta* (soullessness). It was therefore unnecessary for Theosophists to refer—as they often did in their writings and speeches—to "the Southern doctrine of the impermanence of the soul."[26]

The Buddhists also poured scorn on the theories of "esoteric" Buddhism. The Buddha's teachings were remarkably explicit. After enlightenment the Buddha had for several long years preached the *Dharma*, holding nothing back so that the widest spectrum of humanity could benefit. Moreover, since by definition esoteric Buddhism could only be known to a few—and those to all intents and purposes were Theosophists like Annie Besant—Buddhists in Sri Lanka feared that the Theosophists were using esotericism as a pretext or smokescreen to pass off numerous claims, assertions, and generalisations as genuine Buddhist teachings. There was also the possibility that Buddhism at the hands of the Theosophists might come to be regarded as part of the Theosophist fantasies on account of which the Theosophists as a class had come to in far no small ridicule in the West as well as in India. The sectarian flavor of the Sri Lankan Buddhist protest was considerably mitigated because of the involvement of Rhys Davids in the controversy. Dharmapala and

[26] *Ibid.*

Rhys Davids kept up quite a correspondence. It is possible that Dharmapala urged Rhys Davids to denounce the Theosophists.[27]

Rhys Davids, a keen observer of the struggle, had his own reasons for viewing the Theosophists with stern disfavour. In his writings Rhys Davids often explained that Buddhism had in the course of its long history spread to many lands and that in each it had acquired rather distinctive characteristics. There were in truth not only two Buddhisms—the commonly made distinction between Northern and Southern Buddhism—but many Buddhisms.

To this extent, Rhys Davids' views were obviously in harmony with those of the Thosophists who drew the inference that, therefore, it was not possible for one brand of Buddhism to claim orthodoxy. But unlike the Theosophists, he attached very great value to the Pali canon which contained the scriptures of the Southern Buddhists. He also believed that in the Pali canon there was undeniably a comprehensive exposition of the Buddha's teachings and like the Buddhists he too felt that there was little reason to doubt its authenticity.

In a rather more practical sense, and one which had involved considerable personal sacrifice on his part, Rhys Davids' own life had been closely intertwined with the Pali scriptures. They linked what would otherwise seem to have been two entirely discontinuous phases of his life. The Theosophist attacks on Southern Buddhism seemed, although they were clearly never intended to be as such, to assail Rhys Davids' own position.

In some ways the fact explains the uncharacteristic virulence with which he denounced Theosophy on several occasions. He thought that serious students of history and religion should have nought to do with the "pretensions" of Theosophists. "The exponents of that creed" he declared, were "lamentably ignorant of the literatures of the East. They knew nothing of Pali....their ideas are based on the medieval alchemists which they mix up with a little misunderstood Indian thought."[28]

But in Rhys Davids' opinion the greatest harm the Theosophists had done was to Buddhism. They had succeeded in causing a wide-

[27] *The Buddhist Review*, Vol. XI, 1921.
JMBS, Vol. X, no. 7, November 1901.
JMBS, Vol. XII, no. 6, October 1894.

[28] *JMBS*, Vol. XXII, no. 6 (June 1914).
The Buddhist Review, Vol. I, no. 1 (July 1909).

spread confusion between Buddhism that "sane system of philosophical ethics" and Theosophy, which was full of"...speculations of very doubtful validity, really in many instances the rebound of half trained intellects from a crass materialism, and mixed up with historical heresies of a most startling character." The great linchpin, as it were, which had served the Theosophists well in this context, and was what they themselves described as esoteric theosophy, had been confused with esoteric Buddhism. The two terms had been used interchangeably. The term Esoteric Buddhism had widespread usage. A book of this title by A.P. Sinnett had become a Theosophist classic. Rhys Davids had wondered why Sinnett had selected the title for his book, because the text had no relation to either Buddhism or to what the Theosophists described as esotericism.[29]

Rhys Davids had no doubt that the original Buddhist doctrine as revealed in the Pali Canon was "the very contrary of esoteric." The Buddha in his long career as a preacher had made it his custom to unfold his teachings fully and to "speak quite openly to everyone of the whole of the view of life which he had to propound." The Buddha himself had put the matter beyond doubt when he addressed his favourite disciple thus:

> I have preached the Truth without making any distinction between exoteric and esoteric Buddhism; for in respect of the Truth, Ananda, the *Tathagata* has no such thing as a closed fist of a teacher who keeps things back.

Moreover, in the Pali scriptures too, Buddhist doctrine had been set out, in the words of Rhys Davids, "with a lavish expression which seeks alone all to make the whole matter clear to everybody, but is even explained with a length of detail which those not interested in the system find tedious in the extreme."[30]

Rhys Davids explained how the Theosophists had been able to foist esoteric overtones on conventional Buddhism. It was well known that although the Buddha had preached the *Dhamma* fully and in considerable detail, he had at the same time ignored certain questions of an abstruse nature which had been put to him concerning, for example, such matters as whence a person came into this world and whither he would go. The much quoted discourse between

[29] Sinnett, A.P., *Esoteric Buddhism* (London, 1883).
[30] *JMBS*, Vol. XXII, no. 6 (June 1914).

the Buddha and Vacchagotta was a case in point. The Buddha thought such questions irrelevant to the central theme of Buddhism and the goals to which the Buddhist aspired. They were speculations which lured the unwary into profitless byways from the path to Enlightenment. However, the evident reticence of the Buddha had been interpreted in two ways. It was said, as a result, that the Buddha was an agnostic and in some quarters in the West Buddhism had been regarded as an agnostic creed. The Theosophists on the other hand insisted that the Buddha was aware of the answers but had revealed them only to his closest disciples.

Rhys Davids also pointed out that the Theosophists had drawn great inspiration from the Mahāyāna books on Buddhism—books which had been compiled "many centuries after the time of Gautama." The Mahāyānist writers, according to Rhys Davids, had wanted to attribute to the Buddha "opinions different from those which he actually promulgated and had therefore alleged that there was an esoteric teaching in Buddhism. It was the only way the writers of these books could at the same time call themselves Buddhist followers of the Gautama and yet put forth new ideas contrary to those of Gautama."

The esotericism and all the talk of mysteries unveiled which the Theosophists were attempting to popularize, were in reality Indian in origin and were quite accessible to anyone who knew India reasonably well. The esoteric knowledge could be had from Indian teachers provided they were willing to teach. "The study of self-induced trance," observed Rhys Davids, "was common to all the Indian school... all the talk of 'astral bodies' and the different kinds of soul put forward in esoteric Buddhism was part of the *yoga* philosophy of India which is perfectly accessible to all the world."

Rhys Davids, however, thought that to some extent the Theosophists were mending their ways. The tendency to confuse Theosophy with Buddhism had, he thought, become notably less. He liked to think that his own work might have had something to do with the change— "an unconscious tribute to the success of the efforts that have been made in the last few years to render the authorities of the real original Buddhism accessible to the Western World." Just as much as in the other directions his own work would have had "no little influence" over Easterners who would be inspired to view their own traditional faiths more critically.[31]

But this, if true at all, was only partly so. There was no doubt that whenever Sinhalese Buddhists attacked the Theosophists they in doing so triumphantly quoted Rhys Davids. But on the other hand it was equally true that more pugnacious spirits were not so overawed by scholarship. Annie Besant, for example, told her audiences in Sri Lanka in 1907 that she had challenged Rhys Davids to elucidate certain points in Buddhism—significantly related to the soul—and that she had found him wanting. In much the same way, the Theosophists were also fond of relating how Professor Max Muller had been worsted in a chance encounter with the formidable Madam Blavatsky. He had evidently been asked how—if there were no tradition of esotericism in Buddhism—he could account for the claims put forward by Blavatsky in her book the *Voice of the Silence.* The Theosophists claimed that the great scholar was "unable to answer this question when challenged to do so." Interestingly, the Buddhists, who evidently did not think the story apocryphal, wryly remarked that "the learned Doctor had some business more important to attend to than to answer irrelevant questions."[32]

To the Sinhalese Buddhists Rhys Davids' denunciations of Theosophy were an earnest both of his understanding of the *Dhamma* as well as of his great friendliness towards Southern Buddhism. Dharmapala in particular was quick to draw their attention to Rhys Davids' opinions. In 1914, Rhys Davids, who had just passed his seventy-first year, was interviewed by the *Morning Post* in Manchester, where he had been living since 1907. He spoke freely of his life and work and in doing so touched quite incidentally,albeit with feeling, on Theosophy. He referred to the "pretensions" of the Theosophists and added that they had tried to popularise the idea of esoteric teachings "...though there is no esoteric teaching whatever in Buddhism." Dharmapala reprinted the entire interview in the *Journal of the Maha Bodhi Society* under the significant but plainly misleading caption "Theosophy Criticised" notwithstanding the fact that Rhys Davids had also touched on many matters which had little or no relation to Theosophy.

[31] *Ibid.*

[32] *Buddhism,* official journal of the International Buddhist Society, (Rangoon, Circa 1902).

14

EPILOGUE: BUDDHISM AND THE WEST

I'm not half the man I used to be
There's a shadow hanging over me
...I long for yesterday...I believe in yesterday
Beatles' Song

The British empire is no more. The sons of England who bore the white man's burden on the plains of India with such panache and stoicism are no more. The issues that concerned Thomas William Rhys Davids in Nuwerakalawiya one hundred years ago too are no longer with us. In an obvious sense one may blandly conclude that all this is part of a predetermined order of things—the inexorable Buddhist law of *Anicca*—a view which Rhys Davids would have found much to his taste and thinking.

While such explanations have a legitimate function of their own, they are in a sense not particularly helpful, too facile and reductionist, as if they were exculpating the writer from the burden of further thought on the problem. The fact is that today both in India, in Sri Lanka and elsewhere in Southern Asia new generations of Asians have grown up and are rapidly displacing those who in their own life time had some semblance of intimacy, some notion or direct contact with the *Raj* that is no more. The question is, to these newer elements, the new generations, what would the issues concerning the *Raj* mean both in India and Sri Lanka. The answer must be surely that they are really a distant, unmeaning irrelevance. Indeed in a surge of post-independent, chauvinistic nationalism in India and Sri Lanka the last, lingering vestiges of the Raj were dramatically done away with the removal of statues of imperial figures and personalities and the renaming of streets. Only the graves of Englishmen bore mute testimony to the fact that the British once ruled India and Sri Lanka.

In another sense, however, the notion, the sense of the *Raj* is assiduously perpetuated. The flames of memory are fanned with a strange enduring passion and not without a little rancor. In academia, in universities, in classrooms, in textbooks, the *Raj* lives on. The dead issues of yesterday are made to come alive with a deceptive reality like the reality of figures on a screen. And the *Raj* is continually arraigned, judged, appraised and evaluated. In retrospect, what did British rule in Asia mean and amount to and secondly what is the place of people like Thomas William Rhys Davids in the continual resurrection of the drama of British rule?

Patterns of South Asian historiography even in its more recent configurations clearly show that the view of the role of the British *Raj* in Asia has not really moved beyond its almost venerable thematic groove—the grand theme of an exploitive *Raj*. There is of course a certain rationality in all this. To Third World countries in Asia desperately trying to break through a truly intimidating array of seemingly insurmountable problems the study of the *Raj* has been a mandatory bloodletting ritual which must be periodically resorted to. Its propagandist and political overtones are all too plain. Whether in the foreseeable future it would be possible to view British rule in terms of fresh insights and paradigms is a moot question.

Thomas William Rhys Davids provides a clue, at any rate the potentialities of a clue, to the newer understanding we are talking about. It would not of course be a total explanation or an understanding of the complex phenomenon of British rule in Asia. But it will provide, or rather it will illuminate, a single facet of truth in a prism of multifaceted realities or truths, concerning British rule in Asia. It is hard to see Rhys Davids as an exploitive British servant. Indeed it is possible to see him (as indeed it is possible to see other administrators or servants of the British *Raj* in South Asia) really as a mediating force between a congeries of diversities and divergences. These divergences were so profound and so deep that they transcended in reality the exigencies and the specificities of so-called British policies in Asia which have unfortunately loomed so large in the study of British rule and in the historiography of British rule in Asia.

What, indeed, were the divergences? In a word the real theme of British rule in Asia was the continuous interaction between two sorts of view, and ideologies between the rulers and the ruled. Two sorts of world views, philosophies, attitudes, ethics, values, value systems, religions, and so on. The secular in Asian societies was subtly amalgamated with the underlying metaphysical notions. This was especially true of Buddhist Sri Lanka. To stress the externalities of policies at the expense of the underlying theme is to lose sight of the wood for the sake of the trees. Consequently, an ordinary servant of the *Raj* had necessarily to mediate between the varying sorts of divergences and cope with the tensions thereof.

It is of course in his relationship to Buddhism that Rhys Davids is best remembered. Here too the changes time has wrought are evident and indeed are painfully so. In his day Rhys Davids dominated the European scene as a colossus, as the leading Western interpreter of Buddhism. Today he has, it would seem, fallen from grace. The paramountcy of the Pali canon as the source for the study of Buddhism has been challenged and Rhys Davids has been unceremoniously assigned to the dust heap of the so-called anglo-German school of Buddhism from where presumably his manes looks with envy on the newer schools of Buddhism. The truth is that like history every age writes its own Buddhism. In Rhys Davids' time the problems of Buddhist studies were not what they are today. The subtle shift of emphasis in the field of Buddhist studies has left him cut away from the mainstream of things like a vessel stranded by the receding tide. Nothing has been more significant than the recent and still continuing emphasis in Buddhist studies on anthropology and anthropologically based studies of Buddhism. Indeed a compiler of a standard and much consulted bibliography on Buddhism has noted almost in tones of approbation that the real turning point in Buddhist studies in recent times has been the shift from philology to anthropology. It is possible that the distinction has been overdone. Rhys Davids for his part was no mere Palist, no mere grammarian. His writings with their clear sociological overtones indeed vindicate him and give him more than a surface veneer of modernity and current appeal. Instead one may more legitimately question Rhys Davids' abilities as a prophet.

Thomas William Rhys Davids believed that Buddhism would spread rapidly in the West and that many Buddhist ideas would become part of Western thinking. Secondly, he was also convinced that Buddhism would be singularly relevant to the West in terms of the needs and problems confronting the West, a belief incidentally which has inspired many a Buddhist missionary exercise since then. However, things have not quite turned out that way. If Buddhist ideas rather than Buddhism have become part of the matrix of Western religious consciousness, their inspiration has been undeniably the Mahāyāna rather than the Hīnayāna or Theravāda tradition.

To traditional Theravada Buddhists the contrast between the Theravāda and Mahāyāna schools of Buddhism and the manner in which the contrast is usually accentuated in the West must seem overly artificial and possibly based on the misapprehension of the spirit of Theravāda Buddhism. And yet the contrast is rightly or wrongly often insisted on in the West. It is plain that Theravāda Buddhism is often the predictable casualty in the exercise. Thus, Theravāda Buddhism is too psychological weighed down or bogged down by ponderous burden of arid metaphysical thought. It postulates an order of things sans gods, a sense of purposiveness, continuity and hope. By contrast Mahāyāna Buddhism offers warmth and compassion with the Buddhas themselves closely and humanly identified with the concerns and suffering of mankind.

Tragically or otherwise to Thomas William Rhys Davids Buddhism was exclusively a Theravāda affair. He did not seriously address his mind to Mahāyāna Buddhism being content to take the rather facile view that Mahāyāna texts and sources being further removed in terms of time from the Pali canon surely could not be a true reflex of the Buddhist teachings. The omission is all the more curious as in Rhys Davids' own lifetime Western awareness of Mahāyāna was notably on the increase.

Nor have Rhys Davids' predictions concerning the relevance and applicability of Buddhism been realized. He saw the relevance of Buddhism in terms of broad issues such as war and peace, women's rights, social problems and even class tensions little anticipating that finally in the West the individual concerned would decide the matter for himself with little regard for idealized and neatly symmetrical systems. Thus, while it is true that increasing numbers of Americans have been within the last few decades attracted to Eastern religious ideas, they have not necessarily become Hindus or Buddhists. Instead they have been eclectic. Eclectism has been the order of the day: the selection of this or that Eastern idea, belief, ideology, practice or precept which would best suit specific problems and which they think would be best related to their individual problems. Thus where one would look for a well-ordered world of conventional, classifiable, religious beliefs and systems one sees instead a veritable pastiche of cults, groups, and organizations presided over by chocolate brown colored gurus or more recently by a new breed of professional white *sadhus.* The interests are numerous and varied:

basic astronomy, *pranayama,* breath control, meditation, kundalini yoga, yogaerobics, spiritual tarot, pre-natal yoga, neo-sannyasa, to pick up a few items at random, gives some inkling of the profusion and variety of the new spiritual world. Whether all this amounts to the essential spirituality the Orient is conventionally credited with, or whether, instead the foci of interest really show a self-seeking, pragmatic outlook, a desire to live well in a world, sans the distress and stresses of an ecologically doomed industrial society, is altogether another question.

* * * * * * * * * * * *

Asirimath Rhys Davids! And so one might say thereby hangs a tale. In its telling there was neither great profundity nor subtlety. Here was no pious moral, no dread warning, merely a sadness, a wistful longing for things long passed and dead.

GLOSSARY

Amunum (Amuna)-	A measure of grain. The measure varied in different parts of the island. Generally. an *Amuna* consisted of four *pelas*. *Amuna* could also mean a dam or bund.
Anatta (Anatma)-	The Buddhist doctrine that there is no soul or permanent self in an individual.
Anicca-	The Buddhist doctrine of the impermanence of all things.
Arachchi-	An officer over a village or a group of villages. In rank, below that of a *Korala*.
Asweddumise-	Process of converting land (usually previously uncultivated) into paddy field.
Atamasthane-	The eight sacred places of Buddhism in the city of Anuradhapura.
Bhikkhu-	A Buddhist monk or member of the order of the *Sanga*.
Chela-	A disciple. A term popularised by Theosophy.
Chena-	Corrupt usage of Sinhalese word *Hena*. High jungle ground cultivated at intervals. The jungle is cut down and burnt for manure. The land is then sown with hill paddy, fine grain, etc.
Coolie-	Term used to describe labourers who were brought from South India to work in European plantations in Sri Lanka.
Dagoba (Dageba)-	Large bell-shaped structure in which the relics of the Buddha or some Buddhist saint or eminent personality is enshrined.
Dana-	A Pali word which literally means 'giving.' The practice of giving or generosity is much emphasised in Buddhism as a means of counteracting desire and individualism and encouraging selflessness. It is usually spoken of in close conjunction with the other Buddhist virtues of *Sila*

	(morality) and *Bhavana* (meditation).
Dhammapada-	An immensely popular and well known anthology of Buddhist sayings in verse. A summary of the essence of Buddhist doctrine from the *Sutta Piṭaka* of the Pali canon.
Durava (Durawe)-	The toddy tapper caste. Referred to often in early British documents as *Chandus.*
Gamarala-	Village chief or Headman.
Gamsaba (Gamsabha)-	Traditional village councils which the British effectively revived.
Goigama (Goyigama)-	The farmer caste.
Horouwa-	Sluice in bund or tank from which water is let out in an irrigation tank, lake or reservoir.
Jhanas-	A mental state in Buddhism achieved through concentration and meditation.
Kachcheri-	District Administration Centre. Sometimes spelled *Cutcherry* in British documents, the term is Indian in origins.
Kangani-	An inferior officer; usually an overseer of *coolies* in public works or on a plantation.
Karma-	The universal law in Buddhism (and more generally in Indian religious thought) concerning the actions of individuals and the consequences (*vipāka*) of such actions. Every action brings with it good (*kusala*) or evil (*akusala*) consequences, which the doer reaps in his present existence or in a future birth.
Korala-	A revenue officer under a *Ratemahatmaya.*
Korale-	The unit of administration over which a *Korala*'s power extends.
Kulumkattis-	Tank menders.
Kurakkan-	A particularly popular (in British times) dry grain produced in *Chenas.*
Maha-	The cultivation season which extends from October to May.

Mahatmas-	In Theosophical usage, personalities of great moral elevation and intellectual attainment from whom Theosophical teachings have been derived.
Mahavamsa-	A Pali chronicle which gives the history of early Buddhism in India and its introduction to Sri Lanka and subsequent history. Written in the sixth century of the Christian era.
Manna-	Pride. One of the pitfalls against which the Buddhist in his search for enlightenment must struggle, and avoid.
Moha-	In Buddhism, illusion.
Mudaliyar-	A high ranking native official.
Nayake Unnanse-	A chief priest or monk in a Buddhist temple.
Nirvāna (Nibbana)-	The Summum Bonum or final goal in Buddhism.
Pangu (Panguwa)-	Share.
Pangukaraya-	Shareholder or tenant.
Pansala-	The residence of a Bhikkhu or Buddhist priest. Originally it meant the hut of an ascetic or monk, made of branches and leaves.
Paramis (Paramitas)-	In Buddhism, the qualities or virtues which lead to enlightenment; usually ten (*Dasa Paramitas*) such qualities are specified.
Pattuwa-	A division of country.
Pela-	A measure of grain equal to one and one half bushels.
Peon-	Minor office functionary, usually doing the work of a courier or footman. Word probably derived from Portuguese (peao) and Spanish words meaning "footman."
Piṭakas-	The collective sacred canonical writings of Buddhism.
Rajakariya-	Traditional service obligation.
Ratemahatmaya-	Chief revenue officer of a Kandyan district.

Ridis-	A Kandyan silver coin, roughly eight pence (circa 1870) in value.
Sanga-	The order of *Bhikkus* or monks.
Sila-	Morality. A virtue of the utmost importance in Buddhism.
Skandhas (Khandhas)-	In Buddhism, the components (or aggregates) of the human personality. Physical, sensation, perception, volition, and consciousness are the five major groups.
Talapat (Talapata)-	Leaf of the talipot tree often used *inter alia* to record an award or grant. When this was done on an *ola* leaf, the document was called a *tudapata.*
Talawa-	An open glade or meadow.
Tathāgata-	Term used to describe the Buddha and one which he used himself. Literal meaning, "he who has thus arrived."
Tavalam-	Oxen laden with merchandise.
Tulana-	A division of country or district. The term was peculiar to the Nuwerakalawiya district.
Tuttuwa-	The equivalent of a half penny in the nineteenth century. *Loku tuttuwa* or *maha tuttuwa* would be roughly four times its value.
Vedas-	The sacred religious texts of the Hindus.
Vidane-	An inferior officer. Usually an agent of a landholding proprietor.
Vihare-	The dwelling place or abode where monks reside monastery.
Vipassana-	In Buddhism the "inward vision" or transcendental insight by which the truths of existence (suffering, impermanence, etc.) are understood.
Yala-	The cultivation season from April to August.

Bibliography

Remarkably little had been written on Rhys Davids. There certainly are no biographies to go by. No friendly reassuring landmarks or milestones in a journey over forbidding *terra incognita.* I have had the feeling in compiling this bibliography that the oblivion which Rhys Davids feared so much triumphed completely.

Nearly all the material which was used in writing this book has consequently been derived from largely unused sources which come within the genre of primary material.

The material may be divided into convenient categories.

I Manuscript Sources

A. The Importance of the manuscript material which I collected in the Department of National Archives of the Government of Sri Lanka (at the time temporarily accommodated in Gangodawila, Nugegoda) cannot be overestimated. For the period roughly covered by this book (1865-1872) I focussed on the following "lots" or groupings of files: Letters from the Assistant Government Agent of Anuradhapura to the Governor's Agent of the Northern Provinces (Jaffna), Letters from the Government Agent of the Northern Province to the Assistant Government Agent of Anuradhapura, Letters from the Colonial Secretary in Colombo to the Government Agent of the Northern Province. Letters from the Government Agent of the Northern Province to the Colonial Secretary. Letters from the Assistant Government Agents of Mullaitivu, and Mannar to the Government Agent, Jaffna. Letters from the Government Agent, Jaffna to the Assistant Government Agents of Mullaitivu and Mannar. The Diaries of the Government Agent, Jaffna. The travelling diaries of the Government agent of the Northern Province, the diaries of the Assistant Government Agent in Anuradhapura. Miscellaneous files relating to the Assistant Government Agencies of Anuradhapura, Mullaitivu and Mannar. The files of the Government Agent of the Central Province (1864-1867). Files relating to the correspondence between the District Judge in Anuradhapura and the Colonial Secretary. Files dealing with the Police Magistracies of Avisawella, Pasyala and the colonial Secretary Correspondence between the Police Magistracy of

Dambulla and the Colonial Secretary. Correspondence between the Police Magistracy of Galle and the Colonial Secretary.

B. The Manuscript sources of the Royal Asiatic Society of Great Britain, Queen Anne's Street, London. These include the following:
 1) Bound manuscript volume of the Minutes of the Secretary of the R.A.S. (1840-1891)
 2) Bound Manuscript volume of the Minutes of the Secretary of the R.A.S. (1891-1905)
 3) Bound mauscript volume of the proceedings of the Council of the R.A.S. (1905-1922)

C. The Public Recoıd Office, London
C.O. 54 series for the years 1864-1872. This series contains the despatches sent by the Governors of Ceylon to the Colonial Office. It includes the minutes made by the Colonial Office officers and the drafts of replies.

II Printed Sources

A. Official. The Public Record Office, London
C.O. 57 series for the Sessional Papers, the Administration Reports and the Minutes of the Executive Council.

B. The Journal of the Maha Bodhi Society, 1890-1923 (published by the Maha Bodhi Society in Calcutta).

C. The Journal of the Pali Text Society, 1882-1923 (published in London by the Pali Text Society).

D. The Journal of the Royal Asiatic Society of Great Britain, 1880-1923.

III (A) Major Works of Rhys Davids

Buddhism: Being A Sketch of the Life and Teachings of Gautama the Buddha, London, 1877. (Society for Promoting Christian Knowledge) Subsequent editions, 1882, 1887, 1894, 1899, 1903.

Lectures on the Origin and Growth of Religion as Illustrated by Some Points in the History of Indian Buddhism (The Hibbert Lectures, 1881) New York, 1882.

Buddhism. Its History and Literature (American Lectures on the History of Religions) New York, 1896.

Buddhist India (Story of Nations Series) London, 1903.

Early Buddhism (Religions Ancient and Modern) London, 1908.

III (B) Other Works of Rhys Davids

On the Ancient Coins and Measures of Ceylon, *International Numismata Orientalia,* London, 1877.

Is Life Worth Having? and The Eternal Hope: An Answer from Buddha's First Sermon to Some Questions of To-day (Sunday Lecture Society) London, 1880.

Horrowitz, E. *A Short History of Indian Literature* (An Introduction by Rhys Davids) London, 1907.

IV (A) Pali Texts Translated by Rhys Davids for the Sacred Books of the East Series (ed. Max Muller)

The Buddhist Suttas, Vol. XI, Oxford, 1881.

*The Vinaya Texts,** Vol. XIII, Oxford, 1881.

The Vinaya Texts (Part II), Vol. XVII, Oxford, 1882.

The Vinaya Texts (Part III), Vol. XX, Oxford, 1885.

The Questions of King Milinda (Part I), Vol. XXXV, Oxford, 1890.

The Questions of King Milinda (Part II), Vol. XXXVI, Oxford, 1894.

IV (B) Pali Texts Edited by Rhys Davids for the Pali Text Society

Abhidhammattna Samgaha, London, 1884.

Datha Vamsa, London, 1884.

Digha Nikaya, Vol I., London, 1893.

Summangala Vilasini, Vol. I., London, 1886.

Yogavacara Manual, London, 1896.

V Articles Written by Rhys Davids

A. *Journal of the Royal Asiatic Society (Ceylon)*

"On Methods of Taking Impressions of Inscriptions"; "Inscription at Weligam Vihare"; "Dondra Inscription-I", Vol. V, no. 16, 1870-1871.

"On An Inscription at Dondra No. 2," Vol. V, no. 17, 1871-1872.

B. *Journal of the Royal Asiatic Society of Great Britain and Ireland*

"Three Inscriptions of Parakramabahu the Great," 1874-1875, pp.152-171.

"The Sahassa Malla Inscription," 1874-1875, pp. 367-372.

"Two Old Sinhalese Inscriptions. The Ruwanweli Inscription Found in 1874," 1874-1875, pp. 353-355, 360-364, 372-375.

"Sigiri the Lion Rock and the Thirty-Ninth Chapter of the Mahavamsa," 1875.

"Kalidasa in Ceylon 522 A.D.," 1888, pp. 148-149.

*The three parts of the *Vinaya* texts were translated in collaboration with Hermann Oldenberg.

"The Sects of the Buddhists," 1891, pp. 409-422.
"An Embassy to Egypt," 1891, p. 479.
"Water in Sinhalese," 1898, p. 198.
"Sanskrit in Ceylon," 1894, p. 555.

C. *Indian Antiquary*-1872
"The Cave of the Golden Rock, Dambulla," p. 139; "Yatramulle Unnanse," p. 162; "The Jayasiri Maha Bodhin Wahanse in Chancery," p. 196; "The Dondra Inscription," p. 329; "Obituary on Mr. W. Skeen," p. 163.
Indian Antiquary-1874
"Inscriptions at the Audience Hall of Parakramabahu, Pulastipura, Ceylon," p. 246.

D. *Proceedings of the British Academy*
Obituary of E.B. Cowell, Vol. I, 1904, pp. 302-306.
"Oriental Studies in England and Abroad," Vol. I, 1904, pp. 183-197.
"Cosmic Law in Ancient Thought," Vol. VIII, pp. 279-289.

E. *Encyclopaedia of Religion and Ethics* (ed. James Hastings) (Short contributions of Rhys Davids)

Vol. I : Abhayagiri, (19)*; Adams Peak (87); Adultery 126); Agama (165); Ahimsa (231); Anagata Vamsa (414); Ananda (419); Anguttara Nikaya (483); Anuradhapura (599); Apadana (603); Arhat (774)
Vol.II : Bhilsa (557); Buddhagosha (885)
Vol.III : Celibacy (271); Ceylon Buddhism (331); Charity (381); Chastity (490)
Vol. IV : Crimes and Punishment (260); Devadatta (675); Dharmapala (701); Discipline (714)
Vol V : Elder (252); Expiation and Atonement (640); Family (727)
Vol. VI . Hinayana (684); Hospitality (798)
Vol. VII : Hymns (3); Kandy (651); Law (827)
Vol. VIII: Mahında (631); Moggalleana (768)
Vol IX : Patimokkha(675)
Vol.X : Precepts (224)
Vol. XI : Sects (307)
Vol. XII : Tonsure (386); Wheel of Law (736); Wisdom Tree (747)

VI Selected Works

Bishop, Arthur Stanley (ed.). *Ceylon Buddhism being the Collected*

Writings of Daniel John Gogerly, London, 1908.

Canon, Garland. *Oriental Jones*. A biography of Sir William Jones (1746-1794). New Delhi, 1964.

Cockshut, A.O.J. *Anglican Attitudes. A Study of Victorian Religious Controversies*. London, 1959.

______. *The Unbelievers, English Agnostic Thought, 1840-1890*. London, 1964.

Copleston, R.S. *Buddhism Primitive and Present in Magadha and Ceylon*. London, 1862.

De Silva, K.M. *Social Policy and Missionary Organizations in Ceylon, 1840-1855*. London, 1965.

Farquhar, J.N. *The Crown of Hinduism*. Oxford, 1913.

Gaer, Joseph. *What the Great Religions Believe*. New York, 1963.

Hardy, R. Spence. *Eastern Monachism*. London, 1850.

______. *A Manual of Buddhism in Its Modern Development*. London, 1853.

Hume, Robert E. *The World's Living Religions* with special reference to their sacred scriptures and in comparison with Christianity. New York, 1959.

Jurfi Edward J. *The Great Religions of the ModernWorld*. Princeton, New Jersey, 1946.

O'Malley, L.S.S. *The Indian Civil Service, 1601-1930* (2nd ed.). London, 1965.

Smith, Welfred Cantwell. *The Faith of Other Men*. New York, 1963.

Spear, Percival, *A History of India*, Vol. 2. London, 1965.

Tennent, Sir James Emerson. *Christianity in Ceylon*. London, 1850.

______. *Ceylon: An Account of the Island, Physical, Historical, and Topographical*, 2 Vols. 4th ed. London, 1860.

Toussaint, J.R. *Annals of the Ceylon Civil Service*.

Warren, Henry Clarke. *Buddhism in Translation*. (Originally published by Harvard University Press, 1896.) New York, 1963.

INDEX

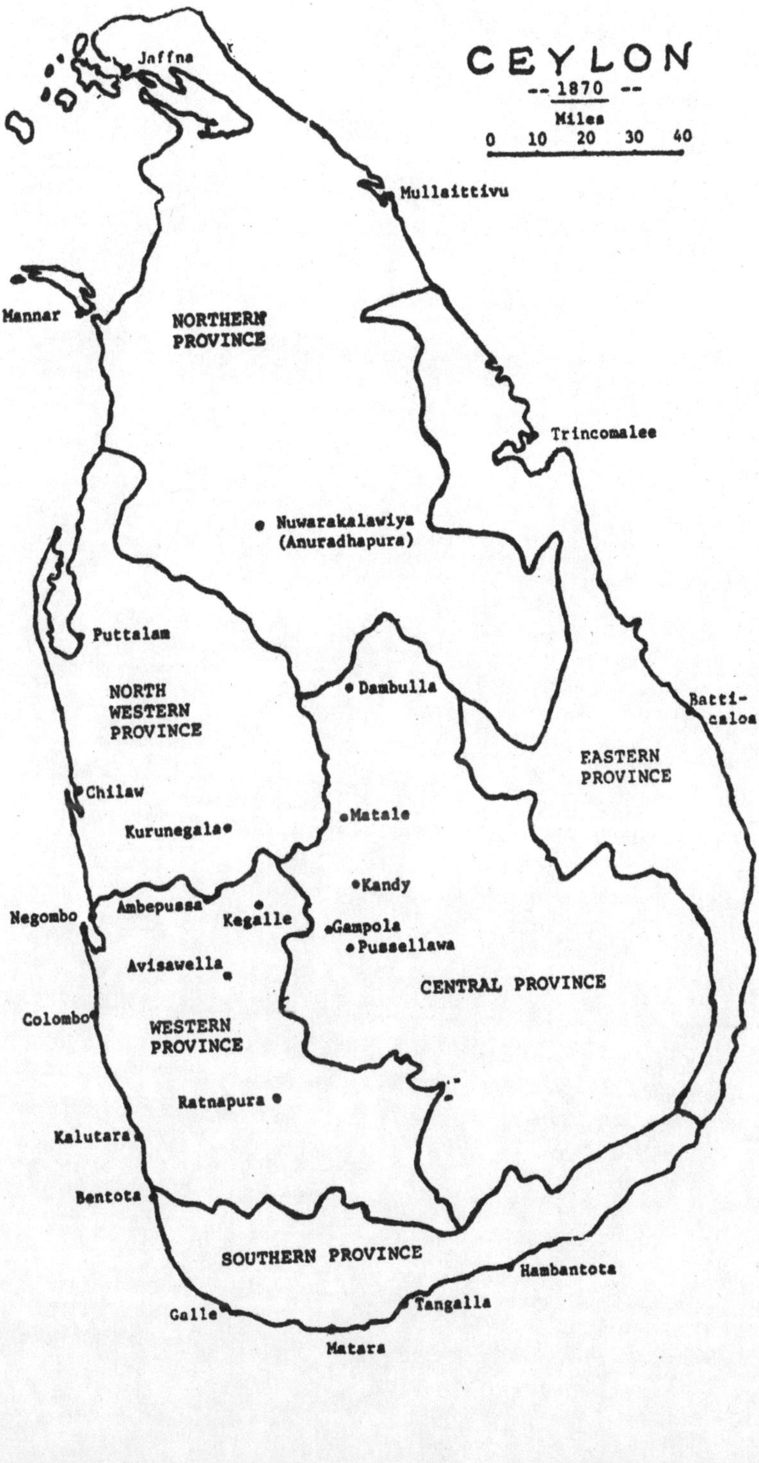

CEYLON
-- 1870 --
Miles
0 10 20 30 40
Jaffna
Mullaittivu
Mannar
NORTHERN PROVINCE
Trincomalee
Nuwarakalawiya
(Anuradhapura)
Puttalam
Dambulla
NORTH WESTERN PROVINCE
Batti-caloa
EASTERN PROVINCE
Chilaw
Matale
Kurunegala
Kandy
Ambepussa
Negombo
Kegalle
Gampola
Pussellawa
Avisawella
CENTRAL PROVINCE
Colombo
WESTERN PROVINCE
Ratnapura
Kalutara
Bentota
SOUTHERN PROVINCE
Hambantota
Tangalla
Galle
Matara